D1559263

you have a home computer with Internet access you may:
- request an item to be placed on hold.
- renew an item that is not overdue.
- view titles and due dates checked out on your card.
- view your own outstanding fines.

view your patron record from your home computer click on
atchogue-Medford Library's homepage: **www.pmlib.org**

# HELEN REDDY
# THE WOMAN I AM

# HELEN REDDY
# THE WOMAN I AM

## A MEMOIR

JEREMY P. TARCHER/PENGUIN

*a member of Penguin Group (USA) Inc.*

*New York*

JEREMY P. TARCHER/PENGUIN
Published by the Penguin Group
Penguin Group (USA) Inc., 375 Hudson Street, New York, New York 10014, USA ·
Penguin Group (Canada), 90 Eglinton Avenue East, Suite 700, Toronto, Ontario
M4P 2Y3, Canada (a division of Pearson Penguin Canada Inc.) · Penguin Books Ltd,
80 Strand, London WC2R 0RL, England · Penguin Ireland, 25 St Stephen's Green, Dublin
2, Ireland (a division of Penguin Books Ltd) · Penguin Group (Australia), 250 Camberwell
Road, Camberwell, Victoria 3124, Australia (a division of Pearson Australia Group Pty
Ltd) · Penguin Books India Pvt Ltd, 11 Community Centre, Panchsheel Park, New Delhi–110
017, India · Penguin Group (NZ), Cnr Airborne and Rosedale Roads, Albany, Auckland
1310, New Zealand (a division of Pearson New Zealand Ltd) · Penguin Books (South
Africa) (Pty) Ltd, 24 Sturdee Avenue, Rosebank, Johannesburg 2196, South Africa

Penguin Books Ltd, Registered Offices:
80 Strand, London WC2R 0RL, England

First American edition 2006
Copyright © 2005, 2006 by Stellamond Ltd.
Originally published in Australia by HarperCollins Publishers

Lyrics of "I Am Woman" used with permission of Helen Reddy

Most Tarcher/Penguin books are available at special quantity discounts for bulk
purchase for sales promotions, premiums, fund-raising, and educational needs. Special
books or book excerpts also can be created to fit specific needs. For details, write
Penguin Group (USA) Inc. Special Markets, 375 Hudson Street, New York, NY 10014.

Library of Congress Cataloging-in-Publication Data

Reddy, Helen.
The woman I am : a memoir / Helen Reddy.
p.  cm.
ISBN 1-58542-489-7
1. Reddy, Helen.    2. Singers—Australia—Biography.    I. Title.
ML420.R2953A3      2006                    2005055961
782.42164092—dc22
[B]

Printed in the United States of America
1  3  5  7  9  10  8  6  4  2

*Book design by HarperCollins Design Studio*

*For Jordan, Traci, and Lily—my legacy so far*

# CONTENTS

# HELEN REDDY
# THE WOMAN I AM

# CHAPTER 1

# In the Beginning . . .

I can't say I was "born in a trunk" although I have slept on top of one. My parents, Max Reddy and Stella Lamond, were vaudevillians and one night in Sydney's Kings Cross, the four of us—my parents, my big sister, and I—all had to share a room with only one bed. My mother pulled a chair up to one end of my father's sturdy wardrobe trunk that was lying flat on the floor. Using the chair seat cushion as a pillow, the top of the trunk became my bed for the night. Don't get the idea that we were homeless, though, we were just on the road.

Before I was born Mum and Dad had rented an unfurnished two-bedroom flat on Riversdale Road in Hawthorn, a suburb of Melbourne, for two guineas a week. Knowing Dad's shopping style, I'm sure that he and Mum went to a furniture store and bought the basics in one afternoon. There was the mandatory three-piece lounge suite; a dining table with chairs; and, for the master bedroom, a suite consisting of a double bed, a dresser with a large round mirror, and two matching maple wardrobes. However, their nesting instincts were no match for the smell of the greasepaint and the roar of the crowd; my parents were gypsies to the end. Dad's maple wardrobe, wedged into a corner and empty except for two ties, stood next to his trusty cabin trunk, upright and open, with drawers on one side and hangers on the other. That trunk would be used as Max's wardrobe for as long as he lived. Although my parents would call the Hawthorn flat home for the rest of their lives, they never really moved in. It was more like a home base for two vaudevillians always waiting for their next show.

My earliest memory is of crawling from my bedroom into the bathroom of that flat; from the green floral-patterned linoleum of the room I shared with my big sister to the red-painted, cool stone floor of the bathroom. I guess even then I loved the smell of newsprint because I was after a page from the old telephone book that hung on a nail beside the toilet. Wartime rationing had made toilet paper a rare luxury. My mother was not happy to find me there, contentedly chewing away on the names, addresses, and phone numbers of Melbourne's fair residents and, with a few harsh words, I was whisked back to my room.

Another time, I remember sitting in my cot and pulling myself up to a standing position by grabbing the rails. The weather was warm—I was dressed in an undershirt and a diaper—so it would have been my second summer, making me somewhere between twelve and sixteen months of age. Mummy had put me down for my afternoon nap and I wanted to be up playing. Determined to scream and cry until Mummy came back and let me out of my cot, I yelled, and I screamed, and I cried, and then I yelled and screamed some more. Mummy finally showed up and I was delighted. My desire had been granted, I was getting up. Not bloody likely! My bottom was treated to a good spanking and I was laid down again and told to *GO TO SLEEP*. My next memory is of waking up and being furious that I'd dozed off and my mother had won.

Some call it stubbornness or obstinacy, others call it tenacity or perseverance, but it was obvious from an early age that I was a girl who was not going to give in without a fight. Maybe that was why I chose to be born during World War II.

The week that Pearl Harbor in Hawaii was bombed by the Japanese, bringing America into the war, my mother and I both came down with chickenpox. I was six weeks old and Australia, as a British Commonwealth country, had already been at war for more than two years. My father, a sergeant with an entertainment unit, was in a concert party sent to entertain the troops in New Guinea. Peter Finch, his actor friend from radio, was in the same unit. According to my father, he and "Finchie" got drunk together the night I was born. In Finch's biography, there is a photo of him in uniform in New Guinea with an unidentified Max Reddy.

Another image from my childhood is of Daddy in his

uniform, with Mummy and me in the car, driving to the place where he had to meet the other soldiers. Because of the trenches that had been dug in the big park on Albert Street near my grandmother's house in East Melbourne, I thought that this was where the fighting was going to be and that Daddy would be able to come home that night.

I can recall the blackout blinds on our bedroom windows, ration books, and Mum's sister, Aunty Lyle, coming over from New Zealand to stay with us. I remember confusing germs with Germans and looking for bacteria-sized little soldiers marching down my spoon handle.

When I was older, I would learn that when Japanese warplanes began dropping bombs on towns like Darwin and Townsville in the north, some of the Australian soldiers who were fighting with British forces in the Middle East requested permission to return home to defend their families and fight for their own country. Churchill refused. The colonies were expendable; England had to be saved. Australian women were left to protect themselves and their children against the coming invasion. Stories started circulating about the ill-treatment of Australian soldiers and nurses in Japanese prisoner-of-war camps. I was terrified when I overheard a rumor that Japanese soldiers were making a game of throwing babies into the air and catching them on the ends of their bayonets. Historically, this kind of rumor often circulates before an invasion, and is a propaganda tactic with no factual basis. However, I didn't know this and for many years I would have nightmares about soldiers pursuing me. And then suddenly General MacArthur and the U.S. Forces came to save the day. A Japanese midget submarine that managed to enter Sydney Harbour was intercepted before it could cause any damage. The tide turned, and anyone or anything American rated five stars in the eyes of Australians for decades to follow.

Like most women of my era who don't have an older brother, I know what my name would have been had I been the eagerly expected male child. Indeed, the whole Reddy family—with the exception of Nell, my father's older sister—was convinced that I was going to be a boy. My mother, the younger of two girls herself, had secretly wanted a second daughter. She found boys to be rather strange entities. Hedging their bet on the off chance that I, the babe, might be female, the name Maxine, a feminized version of my father's name, had been chosen.

When I appeared without the anticipated appendage, my mother must have decided that she would need some emotional support—she had no family of her own in Melbourne—so she quickly named me after Dad's sister, Nell. The doctor was instructed to telephone my grandmother's house in East Melbourne and inform the family that Helen Maxine had arrived. It was Aunty Nell who answered the phone and she would announce with a flushed face and trembling voice, "It's a girl and they're naming the baby after me!"

A lifelong spinster, my Aunty Nell was thrilled beyond measure to have a namesake—we were both Miss Helen

Reddy—and she would keep a special eye out for me her whole life. There were times I would need it.

I don't know if it was a legacy of the chickenpox or not, but as an infant I was covered with eczema from head to toe. When my mother took me out in public she would drape a lace handkerchief over my face so that strangers wouldn't stare at me or move away from her on public transportation. At night, my arms were tied down in splints to stop me from scratching myself. In my frustration, I would rub my itching head against the pillow until both were bloody. All this, I have been told; mercifully, I remember none of it. My mother worried that I would be permanently scarred, but the eczema left me without a mark, although it would recur periodically throughout my life.

I also developed asthma, and more than once was rushed to hospital and into an iron lung. All I recall is feeling like I was moving down a dark narrowing hallway and being squeezed as if through the eye of a needle.

The ointment for the eczema looked like yellowy-gray mud and smelled disgusting. It had to be smeared on my neck and the insides of my arms. Because the ointment stained everything it came in contact with, my limbs had to be bandaged. During the war, torn strips from old bedsheets were wrapped around my neck and arms whenever the eczema flared up.

The Hawthorn flats where we lived had been partially built with old bricks from a demolished theater. In damp weather, the odd bricks would be visible through the painted walls, and one of them was right next to my sister's bed. She woke up one morning to see little toddler me standing by her pillow, rubbing my ointment onto the wall area mottled by the brick and saying, "Poor, sore wall. Poor, sore wall." If the ointment could make my eczema go away, I reasoned that it could also make the stain from the old brick go away and then the wall would feel better.

As my intentions had been pure, I was not punished for this incident although I was advised not to do it again. By then I was old enough to appreciate my mother's sense of fairness, a quality that I have always admired in others. I adored my mother and wanted more than anything to please her. One day, at around age three, I saw a chance to do something that I thought would really make her happy. There was usually a screaming match when I was forced to swallow vile-tasting medicines. So, when I tried to eat an entire packet of chocolate-flavored laxatives, I was thinking how proud of me Mummy would be. When I showed her the box and how much I'd already eaten, instead of delight, it was her turn to scream. She immediately called Aunty Nell, who had the presence of mind to telephone the manufacturer of the product and find out what the antidote was. Unfortunately my efforts at being a good girl finished up with yet another screaming match as I was forced to drink a large glass of milk, to which was added a quantity of laundry starch powder. Yes, the kind we used to soak collars and cuffs in before we ironed a shirt! It would seem there are occasions when a good "stiff" drink is most definitely warranted.

. . .

As a child in the forties, I spent lots of time at my grandmother's house. Nanna Reddy was my only living grandparent as Dad's father and both Mum's parents had all died before I was born. And I was my nanna's first grandbaby. My sister, Toni, was already seven years old when our mother married my father, so I think Nanna felt cheated out of those baby years. Nanna loved babies and would lament in later years that her children had produced only three of them. Not only that, not one of her five surviving brown-haired, hazel-eyed children had inherited her coloring. Nanna had blue-black hair that kept its color into old age, graying only at the temples in her seventies. She had bright blue eyes, and her skin had been cream-colored in youth but had yellowed with age. Her Welsh blood showed not only in her coloring but also in her build—like their ponies and dogs, the Welsh tend to have short legs. I have fond memories of sitting on Nanna's lap in the rocking chair on the verandah being smothered with kisses. This continued until I grew too big to balance on the diminishing space between her knees and protruding stomach.

"But Nanna, you don't have enough lap," I would protest when her outstretched arms reached for me from the rocking chair. Fortunately, one of my aunts produced my first cousin at around this time, and Nanna had a new baby to kiss and cuddle.

When I was a little girl, Nanna's house still had a wood-burning stove in the kitchen and I can picture Nanna sharpening her big knife on the bluestone step outside the kitchen door. The interior of the house in those days was quite dark. (Years later, Aunty Nell would buy the place for Nanna and begin remodeling it.) Like all terrace houses, it had been built by British settlers who knew no other style of housing; there were not enough windows to let good light in, but it sure was cool downstairs during summer. On my fourth birthday, I stood on the table in that dimly lit kitchen while Nanna gave me a sponge bath before my party. (To my embarrassment, Cynthia from next door, with Tricia from down the street in tow, arrived before I was fully dressed.)

The terraces had been built in the mid-1800s, before a sewer system was available. Consequently, each house had an outhouse at the end of the backyard, next to the gate. When the city of Melbourne eventually installed the necessary plumbing, they simply connected it up to all the existing outhouses; to use the facility, one still had to go "down the yard" regardless of weather or time of day, and there was no light in the yard or inside the toilet. As the male side of the family kept a respectful distance from anything resembling a garden tool, the backyard was overgrown with weeds, and who knew what horrors lay lurking out there in the dark? For protection, I would sing "Jesus Loves Me" very loudly all the way there and back.

In today's view, East Melbourne would have been considered multicultural but back then such an idea was unheard of. Catholics and Protestants lived peacefully side by side. The family next door was Chinese, and the old grandfather wore traditional black pajamas and hat, and his long gray hair was plaited in a pigtail that reached right down his back. A few doors down lived Ola Cohn, the Jewish sculptress who had carved the Fairy Tree in the Fitzroy Gardens. She could sometimes be seen in the front courtyard of her house, which was also her studio. I was a bit frightened of Ola, a huge woman with graying frizzy black hair, always dressed in a blue artist's smock. Ola's pet magpie interested me more. It would linger by her front gate waiting for someone to pass by. Whether I ever knew what its name was or even its gender, I'm not sure, but that magpie would never fail to reward my attentions with the whistling of an eight-bar refrain in perfect tune. Another sound that echoes from childhood is that of newsboys on the corners of Bridge Road and Swan Street who yelled "Eenya–hair–uhld." I never did find out what that meant, but they all sang it out in the same singsong way.

Maybe it was because of gasoline rationing during the war, but I can recall bread being delivered in East Melbourne by horse and cart. The baker's cart was enclosed and painted bright green with yellow Victorian lettering edged in black. There was a horse trough outside the New Boundary Hotel around the corner on Hoddle Street. This was the local pub that I avoided walking past whenever possible because I couldn't stand the smell. Those were the days of the "six o'clock swill," when men who got off work at 5 P.M. had only until closing time at 6 P.M. to do their drinking for the night.

They would rush to the pub, order half a dozen beers, line them up on the counter and drink one after the other. Bars in that era—strictly for men only—were typically covered with porcelain tiles and opened onto the street. I was told this was so that the rooms could be hosed out after closing, as there were some patrons who preferred to urinate against the bar rather than lose their place at the counter. Having consumed so much beer in such a short time, some of the men would then vomit on the footpath outside the pub before heading home to their families. To this day, I am unable to distinguish between the smell of vomit and the smell of beer.

A devoted housekeeper, Nanna would sweep and wash down the footpath in front of her house every morning as she considered that to be part of her civic duty. The only girl among four boys, Nanna had been born Edith Charlotte Cox in Launceston, Tasmania, in 1878. Sometimes she would tell me stories about when she was a little girl. She had adored her father and would wait for him to come home after work, riding on his white horse and with a paper bag of candies for her in his pocket. She would also tell me about her grandmother, Charlotte Edwards, who had caused quite a stir when she first arrived in Tasmania and stepped off the ship dressed in full traditional Welsh national costume, hat and all.

To the best of my recollection, my grandmother never wore anything that wasn't covered by a full pinafore apron; we used to call it a "pinny." Once, when her niece came over from

Launceston for a visit, she was appalled that Nanna went outside her front door not only without hat and gloves on but wearing an apron! Nanna had left those social restrictions behind when she'd left Tasmania.

Having borne and raised a large family through a world war and the Depression as well as coping for decades with her late husband's alcoholic benders, I don't think Nanna cared too much anymore for keeping up appearances. Although she had never been a classic beauty, Nanna told me that as a young woman, "I wasn't pretty but I was smart." I used to interpret this as meaning that she had taken pride in being smartly dressed. Now, I believe she was probably referring to a different kind of smart.

When she wasn't baking—and I wasn't licking the bowl—I could sometimes coax her into playing the piano for me. Nanna was an accomplished pianist who had played professionally back in Launceston, and I loved it when she sat at the piano and played her favorite Strauss waltzes. All of her children had taken piano lessons to no avail, although I would discover in later years that Aunty Nell had achieved sufficient proficiency on the violin to play for company. This was before I was born, however, and when someone made an unkind remark about her playing, Aunty Nell put the violin back in its case and never touched it again. This attitude has always been known within the family as "the Reddy huff." Time would soon prove it to be an attitude that I too had inherited.

# CHAPTER 2

# Don't Put Your Daughter
# on the Stage

In 1946, shortly after the war ended, my parents, Max Reddy and Stella Lamond, had the opportunity to perform in a series of variety shows at the Tivoli Theatre in Perth for Fuller-Carroll Productions. Sir Benjamin Fuller was my godfather; when I was born, he had sent a telegram offering me a contract as Principal Girl when I turned seventeen. I was now four years old and very excited about my first flight on an airplane. It was a DC-3, and we landed first at Adelaide, to refuel, before taking off again for the long haul across the Nullarbor Plain.

Mummy had taught me how to knit, which puzzled Nanna. How was I able to knit with two needles, but was unable to master crochet, her specialty, which only required one hook?

To keep me occupied on the trip, we had brought along a project that I was working on, a blanket for my doll. One of the knitting needles disappeared into my seat during the flight and was not to be found. It upset me to learn that, with only one needle, I would not be able to finish what I'd started.

Nanna and Aunty Nell had always looked after me when Max and Stella were working. In Perth, I would have my one and only experience of a day nursery; it was a couple of doors up from our hotel. I could not understand why I was dumped in this horrible place full of strangers. Up to that point, I had had minimal contact with other children and had spent most of my time either alone or with adults. Consequently, I saw myself as a small, powerless adult rather than a child. I was also locked in my parents' world of "us" and "them"; "us" being anyone who was in show business and "them" being anyone who wasn't. So to me, other children were not only "them," they were also, well, childish.

I cried the entire morning. When my parents and my fourteen-year-old sister—all dressed up and going somewhere without me—passed by, I was holding on to the bars on the front gate crying without letup. When they did not respond to my pleas, the abandonment was compounded with rejection and betrayal. Fortunately, I never went there again but, as I spent the whole time crying, my parents were more than likely asked not to bring me back.

I had my fifth birthday while we were in Perth. A party was held in the hotel dining room, and we had red Jell-O and a pink-and-white ice-cream cake. I liked the hotel. It was right next door to the theater, and all the staff were nice to me. I could operate the elevator and enjoyed playing with the buttons, going up and down between the three floors.

Before she left for the show Mummy would put me to bed, but I would sometimes go wandering, in my nightie, in search of company. I remember hanging out with the desk clerks one night and having to hide under the counter when someone came in so that the staff wouldn't get into trouble. Another night I was sick all over my pillow and crying in the dark until another hotel guest came into my room. She was a nurse and cleaned up the mess before putting me down again. My parents then started taking me to the theater with them.

It was to be at the Tivoli Theatre that I would make my theatrical debut, singing a song that was very popular at the time:

> *There were twenty-seven babies at the baby show*
> *I can't remember where*
> *But you and I were there*
> *And of all the little babies at the baby show*
> *I couldn't take my eyes off you.*

I was small for my age and only looked to be about three years old onstage. Being able to sing in tune, therefore, made me seem quite precocious. I was dressed in a little peach-colored frock with white broderie-anglaise trim across the bodice. The ballet girls lined up behind me were wearing identical dresses. The program read: ". . . and introducing BABY HELEN REDDY." Flanked on either side by my parents on bended knee, I sang the song while the ballet girls did their dance routine behind us.

A vital part of any variety-show format is the comedy sketches. Two of them really bothered me.

One was a sketch in which Max and Stella played husband and wife. I don't remember the storyline, only that it involved an argument and that, at some point, my father would take a gun and shoot my mother. The violence of the piece, coupled with the scary arguments that had begun when Daddy returned from the war, was too much for me. I begged them repeatedly not to do that sketch, but they were not about to change the show for a child who couldn't distinguish between acting and real life. Left behind in the dressing room, I used to get in among my mother's clothes in the wardrobe, where I could smell her and cover my ears so that I wouldn't hear the gunshot. There were eight performances a week. I developed a stammer.

The other sketch that troubled me featured the comedian Jim Gerald. Jim had taken Max under his wing when he was first breaking into the business, and Jim and his wife, Essie, had been the witnesses at my parents' wedding. In the sketch, a two-hander, an artist's model poses in a two-piece bathing suit and Jim, in an artist's smock and hat, is painting, palette and brush in hand. The easel is angled so that the audience cannot see his work in progress. The punchline comes when the model asks to see the painting. He turns it around to reveal a blank canvas and tells her that he's not really an artist, he's just a dirty old man. [Blackout.]

I'm sure it's a classic burlesque bit, and the original girl was probably nude, but I was really offended by that sketch. When I told my sister, she sat me down and tried to get me to analyze exactly which part bothered me and why. I was unable to articulate my thoughts and feelings at that age. Now, of course, I see what offended me was a woman being exploited by a man. It was my first consciousness-raising experience and the beginning of my feminism, although it would be decades before I would learn that so many other women shared my views.

Still a strong tradition in Australian theater is the Christmas pantomime. Based on a different nursery rhyme each year, roles are reversed so that the Principal Boy is played by the leading female in the cast, and the role of Dame by the top banana—the leading comedian. Great license can be taken with the script. This allows roles to be modified, or created, to accommodate the special talents of whichever artists are performing in the theater's regular company at Christmastime. In the more traditional pantomimes, the dialogue is in verse form, which has created some classic moments in Australian theatrical history.

One year, the role of Cinderella was played by June Daunt, a virtuoso xylophonist. How did they work her big solo up-tempo number into the storyline? Well, after the ugly stepsisters—played by men—had gone off to the ball, poor Cinders was found sitting by herself in the kitchen. In the middle of the set was this enormous, and until now unseen, xylophone. She said,

Here I am, left all alone,
I think I'll play my xylophone.

As June was an extremely vivacious performer, Cinderella appeared to be over the moon, thrilled to bits that she was not going to the ball.

My favorite old pantomime story, though, is about Myrtle Roberts playing in *Aladdin*. Myrtle's big hit song, the one the fans would be coming to hear, was "Just a Kid Named Joe," a song about a boy who sells newspapers on a street corner. The producer must have been pulling his hair out trying to place young Joe and his newspapers into the Arabian Nights theme of the show. Finally, in a move that would threaten the boundaries of poetic license, Myrtle, playing Aladdin in the scene where she is alone under the sea, would say:

Where I am, I do not know.
But I always buy my papers from a kid named Joe.
[Cue for a song.]

That Christmas of 1946, my Nanna Reddy and Aunty Nell traveled across the desert from Melbourne to spend the holidays with us in Perth. They were also coming to see the show, of course, as all four of us were in it. The pantomime that year was *Mother Goose,* and Max was playing Dame, Stella was Principal Boy, and Toni had a speaking role. It was important to Dad that his mother validate his choice of career. Nanna had been so upset about his wanting to be a comedian that during the Depression, when work was scarce, she had scared off someone who came to the door offering a job for Max Reddy with, "Oh, you don't want him. He's not funny."

"Gee, thanks for the tip, lady," the man had replied as he scurried away.

Dad had been absolutely furious with his mother when he found out but, as she explained, "I don't want people laughing at my son!"

A regular part of any pantomime, regardless of storyline, is a sing-along segment for the little ones. This was my part of the show. The Dame would enter, a screen would come down so that the words to the song—always a nonsense song—could be projected onto it, and the audience would be invited to sing along. I would be seated in the audience close to the stage so that when Max, as the Dame, asked if there was a little boy or girl out there who would like to come up and sing the song with him, I could be up there in a flash. We would sing the song together, and then he would say to the audience, "I'd like to hear this little girl sing the song by herself, wouldn't you?"

Afterward, he would milk the applause for me and then ask, "You've never seen me before, have you, little girl?"

"No, Daddy!" I would reply, before kissing him and running into the wings where Mummy was waiting. The line always got a laugh, and I was thrilled to be part of the show with everyone else.

Excited that Nanna and Aunty Nell were going to see me in the panto, I wore my best dress and a bow in my hair. When it was time for me to run up onstage and sing, to my horror, three other children beat me to the microphone. I was outraged. They were amateurs and I was a professional. They weren't in show business. How dare they commandeer my song! I stood behind them and moved my lips but allowed no sound to escape. I was *not* singing with amateurs! My father observed my five-year-old fury and waited for the other children to finish the chorus. After the audience applauded, he said, "That was very good, children. You can go back to your seats now, but I couldn't hear this little girl singing in the back. Why don't we have her sing it again by herself?" [Music cue:]

*Chickory chick, chalah, chalah,*
*Checka–la–rohmay*
*In a bananna–ka*
*Bollicka Wollicka*
*Can't you see?*
*Chickory chick is me!*

More than fifty years after I sang this song for my grandmother, I would sing it for my granddaughter.

. . .

The trip from Perth back to Melbourne was by train and took several days. My only memories of it are when the train stopped somewhere in the desert. A small group of indigenous Australians walked alongside the carriages as passengers passed food to them. It fascinated me that one woman in a loose cotton dress kept putting the fresh fruit proffered down her bodice. As she was obviously not wearing a brassiere and had no belt on, I wondered how she kept the fruit from falling straight down.

The other thing I remember about the trip was the luggage space at the head of the top bunk where I slept. I was small enough to crawl in there and, as there was no divider between any of the baggage compartments, it would have been possible for me to crawl the entire length of the carriage and enter anyone else's space. Had I been so inclined. Which I wasn't. My respect for privacy has always been stronger than my curiosity. But it was an indication that I would soon be ready for Enid Blyton's Famous Five adventure book series.

# CHAPTER 3

# Radio Days

Mummy had taught me to read and write letters and numbers, and I can still remember her dictating to me as I wrote my first thank-you note. I was so proud of my effort but wished I knew how to join the letters together to make words by myself.

Both my parents, as was common in their time, had left school at the age of twelve. Stella had been in show business since she was only four years old and so already had the skills she needed to earn a living. Max, as the second son in a large family, was expected at that age to get a job and bring home his board and keep. Although my mother was a regular patron of our local library, neither of my parents set much store by academia. It had been decided that I would follow them into show business—what better life could there be?—and I was already learning whatever I would need to know, as they had, on the job. However, the law now mandated that all children between the ages of six and fourteen years must attend school.

I don't know why certain dates stick in the mind but I remember clearly that my first day of school was February 15, 1948. I was six years old. Aunty Nell, who was influential in all family decision making, had recommended Tintern Church of England Girls Grammar School. I will be forever grateful for her choice as the years I spent there gave me a solid academic foundation, a traditional value system, and a structure that did not exist anywhere else in my life. The school was located within easy walking distance of our flat, just down the hill, on Glenferrie Road in Hawthorn.

I spent that first morning in the kindergarten class. I must have recited my ABCs louder and more confidently than the others or the teacher discovered that I could already write because, by afternoon, I'd been moved up to a higher form. At first I was disappointed. That morning I'd already made a friend, and now I was being faced with a second group of strange girls in the same day.

Perhaps I remember the date because it was in this classroom and on that afternoon that, to my everlasting joy, I discovered phonics. Suddenly, all the letters had corresponding sounds, and when you strung them together you could sound out whole words, and when you strung those words together you could sound out whole sentences. I was in heaven. I could read at last. The woman who had given me the keys to the kingdom, my teacher, became my hero. I went home and asked Mum if I could have her diamond ring to give to Miss Elliott. I couldn't think of anything else that equaled what she had given me.

Books were to become my refuge, my comfort, and my escape from the drinking and arguing going on at home. By the time I was ten I had read every single book in the children's section at our local library and was taking the tram to the main branch, where they had a larger selection.

With me now ensconced in school and doing well, Max and Stella were motivated to stay put for a while, and their popularity on radio gave them a way to do it. Max went to work for Clemenger Advertising and began developing radio programs for its clients.

One show, called *Sports Parade,* was always broadcast in front of a live audience. Melbourne people have a love for football exceeded only by their love for beer, and the sight of some of their top players dressed in female drag, dancing and singing off-key, was always good for a belly laugh. The show aired from a different location each week, featuring a different local team and guaranteeing that the live audience would be a crowd of enthusiastic club supporters.

Another show that Max developed was *Monbulk Jamboree*— for the client Monbulk Jam. The show had a storyline and featured regular characters as well as guest artists. I can still sing the theme song Max wrote for the show.

Because he now went to work at an office in the city instead of writing at home, Mum finally had some peace and quiet and time to herself.

I can picture Mum now in our flat's tiny kitchenette. There was a hinged table that came up from the wall—it had to be folded down again to open the back door—and, for seating, the remains of my old wooden high chair. The top part had been sawn off so that the base, now painted green, could be used as a stool. When she had some quiet time, Stella would make herself a dagwood sandwich. Without fail, it would contain tomatoes and sliced raw onions plus anything else that might be sitting in the fridge. My mother loved spicy food and would always add Worcestershire sauce, mustard sauce, and lots of salt and pepper. The latest mystery novel from the River Glen Book Club would then be propped up against the two sauce bottles while the salt and pepper shakers held the pages open. Mum would perch on that little stool in that tiny kitchen, pick up her sandwich, and enter another world. I think it was the only happiness she could count on in a difficult life.

When Max wrote at home, half the dining-room table would be taken up with his typewriter and wire trays filled with script pages. I think he preferred to write at home because he was so dependent on Stella. She had the most amazing memory and could see a film and come home and repeat all the dialogue verbatim. Having been straight woman to so many of the top comics of her day, she also had a prodigious recall of every comedy sketch she'd ever seen or performed. Max was constantly calling out to her to remind him of something, give him an idea, check his spelling, or simply ask, "Hey, Stell, is this funny?"

Very few radio listeners knew that Max Reddy was the voice of Luna Park in St. Kilda. I would sometimes envy my young cousins because they lived in St. Kilda. I thought that it had to be the best suburb in Melbourne. St. Kilda had a beach with a child-sized wooden playhouse built right on the sand. It had little cafés with exotic smells, people with foreign accents, and, above all, it had Luna Park. How I loved the twinkling lights and the carnival atmosphere, the sounds and smells, and the taste of the pink fairy floss. My favorite ride was the Scenic Railway and, in time, the Big Dipper. Dad, always happy to indulge me, would buy a roll of tickets; we would sit together in the front row of the roller coaster and, without relinquishing our seats, have about six rides in a row. Clemenger Advertising handled the park's account and it was my father who had recorded the slogan: "Loo-nah Pahk—jes' fo' fun—ha, ha!"

Because Dad used a character voice for the Luna Park commercials, he sounded nothing like the Max Reddy people were used to hearing on the wireless in *Sports Parade* and *Monbulk Jamboree*.

I once heard my father tell a story about a time he was standing at a hotel bar having a drink by himself when the commercial came on the radio, "Loo-nah Park—jes' fo' fun—ha, ha!"

The solitary drinker standing next to Dad said, "I hate that bloody ad. I'd like to get hold of the bastard with that annoying bloody voice and wring his bloody neck."

Dad nodded in agreement, "I can't stand the bastard either. Can I buy you a drink?"

.    .    .

A fan of American film set décor, Max had a corner cocktail
bar specially built for the loungeroom in the flat. He envisioned something much smaller than what showed up, I'm
sure. I think we all did. The leather-topped bar with three
matching stools took up half the floor space and dominated
the room. I hated it. It symbolized the drinking that dominated
my parents' marriage, our family life, and the glorification of
drunkenness that dominates Australian society—as it still dominates British and Irish society.

On winter nights, when Mum and Dad were broadcasting
from the studio and I was left on my own, I would climb into
their bed and wait for them to come home. Their bedroom
faced west and got full afternoon sun. The pink floral linoleum
on the floor and the large dresser mirror on the south wall
reflecting the light gave the room a lovely rosy glow in the late
afternoon, and my parents' bed always seemed warmer and
safer than my own. I was never able to stay awake until they got
home though, and my soundly sleeping form would be carried
into my own bedroom.

One particularly windy night remains vivid in my memory;
I must have been around eight years old. I was sitting up in
their bed reading a scary story about a man dressed in a long,
black cape. He would envelop little children with it and they
would vanish, never to be seen again. I was more than usually

determined to stay awake until my parents got home that night.

A major storm seemed to be kicking up; the windows were rattling, and someone's cat was howling as if it were being tortured. The telephone rang in the loungeroom and I got up to answer it. There was no response to my hello and the caller hung up. I had been with Dad once when that had happened to him. He had told me that burglars sometimes telephoned people to see if they were home. If not, these bad guys would go to the people's house and rob them. I reasoned that if it were burglars who had just called, they would know my parents weren't at home because their show was airing live on the radio. The bad guys would have heard a child answer the phone, realized that the child was home alone and decided to rob the place, anyway. There would be no point in trying to hide. They already knew I was there.

I went behind the cocktail bar, where Max stored his prop guns, and got a small automatic pistol. Although it had been a functioning weapon at one time, for drama purposes the end of the barrel had been blocked up and two small holes drilled on top so that the smoke from the caps could escape. I climbed back into bed with the gun and waited in case the bad guys showed up.

The wind was now almost gale force, and the bedroom windows were rattling so badly I thought they might break. When the front door suddenly blew wide open, I was truly terrified. Dear God, they were here. I was going to have to act the part of a confident adult. I walked down the hall with the gun in my hand, hoping that they wouldn't notice there was no hole in the barrel and that I could bluff them into leaving. I kept saying in a loud voice, "Who's there? I've got a gun! Who's there? I've got a gun!"

Of course, there was no one there, and once I'd inspected all the rooms I closed and locked the front door, climbed into my parents' bed again, and eventually fell asleep. I woke up the next morning surprised, as usual, to find myself back in my own bed in my own room. I had learned a valuable life lesson, though. When we confront our fears head on, they usually disappear.

When my parents were out of town overnight or for several days at a time, I would always stay with Nanna. We would sit there of an evening, listening to the wireless while my grandmother's crochet hook created squares for many an afghan. Even though at age five I had learned to knit cable stitch, which requires three needles, I still couldn't get the hang of that one hook.

Nanna's personal pleasures were few but regularly indulged. She loved her nightly newspaper crossword that, with the help of a large dictionary, was always completed before bed, as well as her weekly housey-housey game at the local Catholic church hall. This game seems to be universal; it's also known as bingo and tombola. Her favorite radio game show was *Pick-a-Box* from Sydney with Bob Dyer, and she never missed it.

Nanna was such a fan of *Pick-a-Box* that when Aunty Nell took her to Sydney one year for a holiday, she bought tickets for the two of them to sit in the audience during a broadcast. As fate would have it, Nanna's chair had the lucky number under it and, despite trying to make Aunty Nell take her place, my grandmother found herself on the show as a contestant with Bob Dyer. He had no idea who she was, but when she told him her name was Edith Reddy, he asked if she was any relation to Max Reddy and she said, "Yes, that's my son. I'm his mother." Bob then inquired if she let him go all the way to Tasmania by himself and she replied, "I should think so. He's nearly forty!"

Nanna proved herself to be an unconsciously funny guest, and Bob enjoyed himself with her. There was a regular segment on the show in which Bob would recite a list of prizes, the contestant would say "stop" and then win whatever the *next* prize on the list happened to be. Well, as soon as my grandmother heard him mention some new cookware she fancied she said, "That'll do me, I'll have that one." Bob was so tickled with her that he let her have it.

After Nanna died, Bob Dyer, a true gentleman, sent Max a vinyl recording of the show for posterity.

The popularity of *Pick-a-Box* would extend into the television age that Nanna narrowly missed out on seeing. Then again, my grandmother had been around for the birth of the automobile and the airplane.

# CHAPTER 4

# All in the Family

My grandmother's terrace house was opposite a park, so I had a green area the size of a whole square block to play in. Facing the east side of the square was the local police station. Everyone knew the one and only constable, Cyril, who rode a bicycle and wore a bobby's helmet. If children didn't behave, their parents would often threaten that Cyril would put them in jail in that funny little wooden house. This had the desired effect on my young cousins, but Cyril seemed pretty harmless to me.

Uncle Frank, Dad's brother, who still lived with Nanna, was by far my favorite uncle. He drove a taxicab for a living and, not having any children of his own, adored his nieces and nephew. He had a happy, easygoing nature and his downstairs front room, facing the park, was always full of comic books. Uncle Frank was always a source of great fun. Once a group of us were at a football game with him when someone sitting in the stands above us emptied out the remaining tea in her cup all over Uncle Frank's head. Bursting with laughter, he called up to her, "Have you got a biscuit to go with it?"

At one time, Max and Uncle Frank were running an SP bookmaking operation out of his front room at Nanna's house. I don't think Aunty Nell knew about it because she would not have approved. There were horse races broadcast on the radio nearly every day, so the Reddy boys must have had a lucrative business going there for a while. I was made aware that this was illegal and that I should not discuss it with anyone. One busy race day they answered a knock at the door to find Cyril, the constable, standing there. There was a brief moment of panic until Cyril asked if he could "bet ten bob each way" on a particular horse. The brothers were both highly relieved but decided to end their venture as SP bookies not long afterward. If Cyril was able to find out about it, then it was only a question of time until someone not so affable did too.

Card games were popular in those pre-television days and, when Dad and the rest of his siblings were still living at home, after the evening meal the dishes would be cleared off the table and the cards dealt. Different games might be played but a basic principle applied. As soon as you won a hand you left the table; the ultimate loser of the final game was the one who had to wash, dry, and put away the dishes. Aunty Nell recalled herself as being the main recipient of that dubious honor and, knowing her brothers, was never too sure if something other than bad luck had played a part in it.

One childhood memory that all Nanna's offspring talked about fondly was the Saturday night dances. My grandmother was an extraordinarily talented pianist. You could hum any melody and she would follow along. Her party pieces, however, were the complete works of Strauss. The Viennese musical era had left its imprint on Tasmania, and the waltz reigned supreme. My grandfather, Norman Reddy, used to rent the Launceston Town Hall of a Saturday night; Nanna would spend the entire day baking the supper to be served that evening; and then, wearing her best dress, she would sit at the piano and play "Tales of the Vienna Woods" while Launceston danced and my grandfather took the ticket money at the door—two for him and one for her, according to a cousin. Afterward, when they got home, they would wake up the children, spread the tablecloth across the big bed, and eat all the leftover goodies.

The Reddy family left Launceston, Tasmania, for Melbourne in 1927. My great-grandmother, Emily Morrison Reddy, had already buried four of her six children, and when my grandfather's sister, Kathleen, died that year he became their widowed mother's sole surviving child. She was living alone in Victoria, and the decision was made to move closer to her. Max was thirteen years old.

I don't recall my grandmother recounting any affectionate memories of Norman Reddy. She said that he'd been charming and a good talker, but otherwise he wasn't spoken about too much at all. I knew that he had been a binge drinker who was prone to erratic physical behavior when he had delirium tremens. While in bed one night, he had been under the illusion that the wardrobe door was the bedroom door and he had pulled the entire wardrobe onto the bed. As Nanna could have been killed, that was the end of it for Aunty Nell. For the rest of her father's life, she locked him out of the house if he had been drinking.

Nell's decision was not popular with her two brothers and it left some residual resentment. Max and Frank had loved "the old man," as they called him, and would sometimes talk about how talented he was with his hands. My grandfather Reddy could paint and wallpaper like a professional although he worked as a hairdresser. In those days, that was a fancy term for a barber, just as today's hairdressers have all become stylists. Norman quit his job at a barbershop in the city because the loudspeaker from the radio of the shop next door drove him mad. I have supersensitive hearing, too, but in his case it may have been a hangover headache.

Norman's last years were not his best, and his sons always joked about their inheritance. "He left Max the gout and Frank the piles." Sometimes I wondered if Nanna had ever really been in love with him. In later years, when I learned that her parents had died within weeks of each other, and that she was then left with the responsibility of caring for her youngest brother, who was still a minor, I understood why Nanna might have married in haste at a time of emotional need.

My mother, Stella, had one cherished memory of Norman Reddy. He died within months of becoming her father-in-law, but she had loved him at first sight. When they met, he had instantly welcomed my sister, Toni, as his "beautiful granddaughter."

It would become clear to me why this had meant so much to Mum after my grandmother's death. I came upon a letter that Dad had written to her at the time he married my mother. Evidently, Nanna had not been at all happy about her son's marriage to a divorced older woman who was in show business and had a seven-year-old child. The letter was written by a man who was obviously besotted with his wife and convinced that his mother had only to meet his bride to love her as much as he did. It was amazing to read because I had no idea he had ever felt that deeply about my mother. My memories of my parents' marriage date from after the war, when Dad's personality had undergone a change. So many men came back from their tour of duty as strangers to their families. I wish I had known them both when they were still happy together. The only time I saw any affection between my parents was when they made up after a fight. And they only fought when they'd both been drinking.

For years, I blamed my mother's drinking on the cruel rejection she had suffered from her first husband. Mum had told me one night, when she felt the need to unburden herself, that he had gone on tour to New Zealand with a show and she had asked a girlfriend who was also going with the company to keep an eye on him and "make sure he doesn't get off with any of the ballet girls." Yup, you got it; the old story. When he came back from the tour, he was in love with Mum's girlfriend and, when forced to choose between her and his wife and child, he opted for the girlfriend.

My mother had been pregnant with my sister when they married, so it may have been that Mum was never more than a dalliance as far as he was concerned. Perhaps he resented having to marry her. We'll never know. I do know that for Mum it was a wound that never healed, and she had learned at puberty what you take for pain—a little brandy.

It was later revealed by an old girlfriend of Mum's that my mother had suffered so badly with menstrual cramps that she used to take to her bed for several days each month. As she always referred to menstruation as "tummy pain," it may be that her terminology created in her certain subconscious expectations. It also sounds like endometriosis, but between the primitive medicine of the time and "old wives' tales," a dose of brandy was often recommended for medicinal purposes and taken with milk and a raw egg. Stella's addiction had begun when she was sixteen.

# CHAPTER 5

# It's Nice to Go Traveling

I don't know when I first had the urge to travel. I do know that I was inspired by the "World Tour" Aunty Nell took in 1951. As she was born in 1905, my aunt must have been forty-six years old by then but she never disclosed her age and looked at least fifteen years younger. Tasmanian women have such dewy skin.

In Aunty Nell's day it was the custom, and still is today in some cultures, that the eldest female child did not marry but was designated to be caretaker of the parents in their old age. As the firstborn, Aunty Nell had been assigned that role but it certainly did not stop her from having a career and, after years of caring for five younger siblings, she had no desire for a family of her own anyway.

When she was only thirteen, Aunty Nell left school to study to be a secretary, which at that time (1918) was being tipped as *the* new career opportunity for young girls. It should be remembered that World War I had left a generation of women without marriage prospects. Aunty Nell had done well, working her way up from legal secretary to become private secretary for the managing director of a respected Melbourne company.

Aunty Nell's longtime "beau" I called Uncle Brad. Uncle Brad would come to the house for dinner most evenings and sit with the family afterward listening to the wireless or reading the evening paper before driving home to his flat. Once a week, usually on a Saturday night, he would take Aunty Nell out to dinner or to see a film. A veteran of World War I, he was a fair bit older than she was. Aunty Nell had several friends who had lost their fiancés during that war. Uncle Brad was still legally married to a woman who had been committed to a mental institution many years before. In those days, this was not grounds for divorce, and so Aunty Nell and Uncle Brad could never marry. That was just fine with Aunty Nell, who regarded him as "a presentable escort" but dull as dishwater otherwise. In 1951, after working for thirty-three years, investing conservatively in the stock market, living frugally, and first buying a house for her mother, it was time for Aunty Nell to *live*. She splurged on a first-class trip around the world and a lavish wardrobe.

In upper-class late-nineteenth-century England, one completed one's education by going abroad on a lengthy and extremely expensive Grand Tour. More than a century later, this life adventure, called a "gap year," is now common to all classes and usually involves working at odd jobs and living in Spartan conditions. In between these two extremes of time and travel, a luxurious form of transport—the ocean liner—would become increasingly affordable to the burgeoning upper-middle class.

It's hard to imagine nowadays, at a time when hopping on a jet is commonplace, and Australians are among the most well-traveled people on earth, but in mid-twentieth-century Australia, "going overseas" was a *big deal*. Ocean liner was the means of transport, England the usual destination, and the voyage lasted for weeks. It was also a symbol of prestige and *savoir faire*. For those traveling first class on an ocean liner, many changes of clothing were required. One dressed for dinner in formal evening wear almost every night and, while a gentleman could get by with wearing the same tuxedo, a lady needed an array of glamorous evening gowns. Altogether, it was an extremely expensive proposition and well out of the reach of the average Australian woman. I remember the whole family being treated to a fashion show one night; Aunty Nell modeled every one of her new outfits for us before sailing away. To a nine-year-old, it was all very exciting.

For one who had never circumnavigated the globe before, Aunty Nell proved to be surprisingly savvy, not to mention resourceful, in her travel style and sense of her own image. After sailing first class from Southampton, England, to New York, my aunt left the ship for a suite at the Waldorf-Astoria, at that time the city's number-one hotel. However, she only stayed for one night and, after requesting extra writing paper and envelopes, left for a more moderately priced hotel in the theater district. For the rest of her two-week stay Aunty Nell continued to write letters home on Waldorf-Astoria stationery, detailing her adventures in New York.

It was my dream to go to America. That was where I wanted to be. My parents, Max and Stella, worked with a lot of American entertainers over the years, and visiting performers were usually invited home for Sunday's roast dinner. They would always boast about how much bigger and better everything was in "the States," and I admired their sophistication and self-confidence. Mum and Dad always had American books and magazines around the house and, two or three nights a week, we used to go to the pictures after dinner.

In those pre-television days, picture theaters gave you two films plus a current newsreel, a comedy short, a cartoon and two trailers. Although I loved the grittiness and humor of British films, it was the MGM musicals that captured my heart—the singing, the dancing, the brightly colored costumes; I'd never seen anything so lavish on an Australian stage. As I didn't know about film studio soundstages, I imagined American theaters to be huge to accommodate all those different sets, shown in sweeping camera shots as all being on one stage simultaneously. Plus, no one wore the same dress twice, and the girls all had shoes to match every outfit. I thought that life in America was exactly like it was in the pictures. Like every other little girl, I dreamed of being a film star. The difference was that I had a head start; I was already in show business and knew lots of Americans who were, too. I didn't see it as an impossible dream. To me, it was viable. And, somewhere deep inside, I also knew it was inevitable.

CHAPTER 6

# Sowing a Family Tree

My show-business education was an ongoing one, and I can see now why I chose to be born into a family of entertainers. At home, the radio was always playing, and my earliest musical influences were the pop songs of the period. My first singing teacher was my mother. She taught me that what set the human voice apart from every other musical instrument was the ability to tell a story, to sing a lyric. Stella believed that the words were the most important part of the song and that, if they were unintelligible, one might as well be singing "la-la-la." I wonder what she'd think of some of today's singers who manage to get eight notes out of every syllable.

Although I don't know where she found the patience, it was my sister who taught me the time step, the basic tap-dancing rhythm pattern. We practiced in the bathroom so that I could hear the echo of each tap against the stone floor while I was learning.

When I was nine, a piano was purchased for the flat, and I started taking lessons with Miss Mona Kenafick. This pleased Nanna enormously, although she would get frustrated with me when I played anything in three-four time without a Viennese syncopated waltz feel. Having played for dances, Nanna considered the rhythmic feel of a piece to be all important and, if you didn't have that, it didn't matter how well you played, in her opinion.

Boogie-woogie was a popular musical genre at the time, and I'd discovered how to play the walking bass line on the piano, even though my fingers were still so small I needed two hands to do it. Nanna loved that; it was more her style. In her later years, she tended to mix words up, especially modern slang terms. Male teenage rebels of the time were called "bodgies," the females "widgies." Nanna somehow confused boogie-woogie with bodgies and widgies and would say, "Go on, Helen. Play some of that bodgie-wodgie for me."

Nanna also refered to the popular violinist, Yehudi Menuhin, as "Yehudi Medudi."

In Nanna's bedroom there was a large dresser that she had inherited from her mother. One drawer contained items that had belonged to her family, and its contents were the beginning of my interest in family history.

One item was an old family bible that had belonged to Nanna's parents. Inside it, her birth and those of her siblings had been recorded. As well, there was a box containing old photographs, her Cox grandparents' death notices, and her parents' marriage certificate. Her parents had married in Bendigo in the state of Victoria so the certificate included the full names of the parents of both the bride and the groom, in other words, two sets of my great-great-grandparents. The family history fascinated me. Fortunately I had memorized most of the information in the box, as it would be thrown out when Aunty Nell died.

Because Nanna Reddy was my only living grandparent and I spent a lot of time with her as a child, I knew that her English and Welsh ancestors had come to Australia as miners during the 1850s gold rush.

From Wales, Nanna's maternal family had arrived first in Adelaide, where her mother, Bessie, had been born before they moved on to the goldfields in Victoria.

From Devon, Nanna's father, Frank Cox, was just a young boy when he arrived in Australia with his parents and sisters. I can only assume that growing up on the goldfields and playing with Chinese children accounted for his being fluent in Cantonese. As an adult, he was sometimes called into court to act as an interpreter when there was a dispute involving a Chinese miner. He admired Chinese culture and customs all his life.

After their marriage, Frank and Bessie, along with her parents, moved down to the goldfields of northern Tasmania, eventually settling in Launceston, where Frank opened a printing business with a partner. Aunty Nell revealed to me before she died that Nanna's father, Frank Cox, had died in an opium den. The family had brought the body home and pleaded with the doctor to write on the death certificate that he had died in his own bed. The doctor had complied.

Along with Arthur Mee's *Children's Encyclopaedia,* Aesop's Fables, and all the stories by the Brothers Grimm and Hans Christian Andersen, I had been given a large, illustrated leather-bound Holy Bible. Inside were several pages to be filled in with family information of births, deaths, and marriages. Now I needed to get as much information as I could from Mum about her side of the family. This would prove to be more difficult.

Mum was from Sydney; her parents had died well before I was born; and her only sibling, my Aunty Lyle, lived in New Zealand. I knew that her grandfather, Tom Lamond, had been a Scottish horse trainer who had worked at Terara in southern New South Wales with Archer, winner of the first and second Melbourne Cup; Archer was disqualified from running in the third because of weight. Twenty-five years later, in 1888, Tom Lamond was a Melbourne Cup–winning trainer in his own right with a horse named Zulu. But it was a painting of Archer that hung above the dining-room door at his homestead, Zetland Lodge. The property included a private racetrack and was to become today's Sydney suburb of Zetland. My great-grandfather always claimed that Archer was the greatest horse he ever trained.

Sir Hercules Robinson, governor of New South Wales at the time, was a keen racing fan and horse owner. The Government House stables of that era would be preserved as the façade of today's Conservatorium of Music. Tom Lamond not only trained the governor's horses, he also named two of his nine children, Hercules Robinson and Nea Robinson, after the governor and his lady, indicating a close relationship between the two families.

All the Lamond grandchildren were placed atop a horse when they came to Zetland Lodge of a Sunday to visit their grandparents. My mother and her sister always distinguished themselves by crying because they were afraid of horses. Their father—my other grandfather, Colin Lamond—was the youngest of Tom and Eliza Lamond's nine children and, as he had chosen mechanical engineering for his livelihood, it was understood that his children would, naturally, be rebellious.

Mum used to speak proudly about her grandfather, Tom Lamond, but was strangely reticent when it came to information about her female ancestry. Her eyes would glaze over and she would suddenly have no memory of or interest in the subject. There were two skeletons lurking in the closet that my mother did not want me to know about. I discovered them after she died, as well as a few others I don't think she knew about.

.   .   .

Perhaps inspired by Mum's racing background or because he was tired of always losing at the track, Dad decided to invest in two racehorses. While my father had a gift for making money he did not have a clue how to spend it. I was much more impressed with Aunty Nell's approach to finances, but her brother could never have made all the sacrifices that she did in order to accumulate such large sums. Money definitely burned a hole in Dad's pocket. He was impulsive. There is a story told about my father. It may have grown over the years with the telling—who knows?—but I believe it because it sounds like him:

Max and a bunch of his mates had gone out kangaroo shooting in the bush. Don't get any mental pictures of great white hunters on safari here. An enormous amount of beer would have accompanied them, and I don't think Max had handled a rifle since the war. My mother was probably relieved that they arrived home safely without shooting each other. Anyway, at some point while driving around in the scrub, they came upon a little country pub in the middle of nowhere. Dad allegedly walked in, shot up the bar, took a wad of money out of his pocket, placed it on the counter and said, "That's for the damage. I've seen 'em do that in cowboy pictures so many times and I've always wanted to do it."

# CHAPTER 7

# The Korean War

With the onset of the Korean War, Max went back into uniform, but this time he took Stella with him. He put together a compact six-person show that could go out as a concert party to entertain the troops. The talent most prized in Australian show business has always been versatility, and my father was brilliant at putting multitalented performers together. The troupe comprised three men and three women, all of whom could perform solo in their own right.

There was Stella, of course, who could act as a feed for Max in the comedy sketches, perform one of her dramatic solo songs as well as sing harmony when needed. She also served, offstage, as Mother Superior to the two other females, who were both young, blond, and single.

One of them was June Daunt who, in addition to her xylophone skills, also played the more portable saxophone and danced at the same time. And, like Garbo, she could talk if needed in a comedy bit. While June had a wholesome demeanour, Dale Gower, the third female member of the troupe, oozed sex and sophistication. She would do her solo singing spot as well as feature in the comedy sketches. All three women could harmonize together if necessary.

Musical responsibilities rested primarily with Ted Muller, known affectionately as Betsy Pumpkin, who played piano and, more important, a piano accordion, which could fit easily on a helicopter. Ted not only provided musical accompaniment for the whole show, he was also able to act in the occasional sketch as well as perform a solo spot on the accordion, always "The Harry Lime Theme" from *The Third Man.*

Frank Cleary was the third man in the show. He made an excellent straight man for Dad in two- and three-handed sketches; they could do a little soft-shoe together; and he could also sing in addition to doing his solo juggling act.

My father really knew how to pace a show. It was fast-moving; someone was always walking on as someone else was walking off, and the constant variety and quick changes kept you wondering what would come next. The big finale, with full company, would have Ted on piano accordion, June on saxophone, and Max, Stella, Frank, and Dale singing four-part harmony and dancing.

The concert party played all over Korea and Japan. Most of their shows were performed on makeshift stages that were basically platforms atop oil drums, with tents on either side as changing rooms. They entertained troops only fifteen hundred yards from the front line—closer than nurses were allowed to go—and with Russian MiGs flying overhead. A highlight for them all was playing a show for American sailors aboard a U.S. naval vessel. Max and Stella were thrilled that their very Australian show had been understood and appreciated by the Americans, and it was the first time that anyone in the cast had tasted ice cream made from real peaches!

On their return home, a special performance of the show was presented at the Melbourne Town Hall for family members of those serving. As a backdrop, canvas and oil drums simulated a makeshift battlefield stage.

Dad took great pride in the official letter he received from the Australian Army commending him for having the best concert party artistically, socially, and morally.

# CHAPTER 8

# The Awakening

As a child I was fanatically religious. I attended church and Sunday school regularly and fervently, although I was not taken there, I was sent. No one else in the family ever accompanied me. Mum would be busy preparing Sunday's roast dinner (to which an old actor or writer with no family would always be invited). Dad favored sleeping in, as did Toni, who was working nights at the Plaza Theatre in Northcote, Melbourne's last bastion of vaudeville. My dream was to be a missionary, and Toni recalls me singing hymns in a falsetto voice around the house, to her immense annoyance.

This fervent devotion lasted until I found myself becoming disillusioned at Sunday school. No one seemed able to answer the questions I was asking, and I was bothered by the hypocrisy I was hearing. One week we were told that our religion was the only true one and that all the others were misguided;

and then the following Sunday we were celebrating world brotherhood and our oneness with those of all faiths. I was having a hard time following the plot.

The incident that finally tipped the balance occurred one Sunday when we were studying *Les Misérables*. It so happened that earlier that week I had been listening to a radio program dramatization of Victor Hugo's great novel; the actors had spoken with French accents. I had loved the story of Jean Valjean and I was excited that we were going to be studying it in class.

The teacher began by calling it "Lezz Mizz-rah-bulls" and pronouncing the hero's name as "Jeen Vall-jeen." Without thinking, I corrected her. She hated me from that moment on. Looking back, she must have been horrified to find this precocious child in her class who was not only familiar with Victor Hugo but seemed to be fluent in French. This was certainly not the case but, like my mother and sister, I can mimic just about any accent I hear.

The climax came for me when the teacher gave me seven out of ten for a four-page essay I had really worked on, while another girl, who had turned in only half a page, received the full ten marks. I bristled at the unfairness and determined that I would not return to Sunday school. In hindsight, I think the teacher was trying to encourage the other girl, a pupil she could more easily identify with, but my ego was now in the way of my faith and, with so many questions continuing to go unanswered, I became an atheist.

*Left:* My parents, at Spencer Street Railway Station, Melbourne, returning from Perth. *(From the personal collection of Helen Reddy)*

*Below:* My first appearance on radio 3XY Melbourne. *(From the personal collection of Helen Reddy)*

*Above:* With Uncle Frank. *(From the personal collection of Helen Reddy)*

*Right:* Aged 2 – this dress had pants to match and if I wet them, I insisted the dress be changed too! *(From the personal collection of Helen Reddy)*

*Left*: Perth. October 1946.
*(From the personal collection of Helen Reddy)*

*Right*: Dressed for a costume party.
*(From the personal collection of Helen Reddy)*

*Above:* Toni at 13, me at 4, wearing matching outfits knitted by Mum. *(From the personal collection of Helen Reddy)*

*Left:* Nanna after moving from Launceston to Melbourne. *(From the personal collection of Helen Reddy)*

*Right:* Aunty Nell around 1970. *(From the personal collection of Helen Reddy)*

*Above*: Dad in New Guinea. *(From the personal collection of Helen Reddy)*

*Above:* Third from left, The Folies Lovelies and 'Teacher's Pet'. *(From the personal collection of Helen Reddy)*

*Right:* Aged 17, in gold lamé, singing at the Chevron. *(From the personal collection of Helen Reddy)*

*Above:* My mother, Stella Lamond, as Molly Wilson in *Bellbird.*
*(From the personal collection of Helen Reddy)*

My atheism was to face a major challenge when I was eleven. By then I was in the first year of senior school at Tintern Church of England Girls Grammar School in Hawthorn. Our mornings always began with assembly; the entire school, students and teachers, used to gather according to their forms—which meant putting me in the second front row—and await the headmistress, Miss Wood. She would enter, wearing her academic robe, and after an exchange of greetings would proceed to conduct the morning service. We would sing a hymn; she would read something of an inspirational nature; we then finished with a prayer and filed out row by row to our respective classrooms. There were no chairs provided for assembly, and we used to stand for the duration. It seems the headmistress received a telephone call on this particular morning which had delayed her arrival, and we were kept standing an unusually long time. After she came, I was feeling a bit odd and beginning to see brown spots in front of my eyes. The headmistress was talking about Robert Louis Stevenson; I felt as if I was going to fall and had the urge to steady myself by grabbing the shoulder of the girl standing in front of me. Worried that I might startle her and cause a scene, I decided against it. The next thing I knew, with no sense of a break in time or place, I was at the back of the room looking down. I could see a girl lying on the floor and I thought, "Oh, my goodness, someone must have fainted." Because we were all dressed in identical uniforms, I wondered who it was. I zoomed in for a close-up, which again seemed perfectly natural, and found myself looking at my own face. "Oh, my God," I thought. "I've died."

I must have then gone back into my body because my next awareness is of being banged against the doorjamb as I was carried into another room by two of the girls. This jolted me back into consciousness. I was both mortified with embarrassment and overwhelmed by the now irrefutable evidence that the person who was really me existed independently of my body and therefore survived death. I had a great deal to think about.

Even though I wanted so much to discuss the experience, I knew I couldn't. They'd probably think I was a mental case and lock me up. Who could understand other than someone who'd had a similar experience? And as I'd never heard of anyone else leaving their body and going back again, maybe I was the only one?

Seven years later, I would read a book written by a yogi in which he mentioned an experience very similar to mine. He called it "astral projection." Whatever it was called, since I was eleven years of age, I have had no fear of death, nor doubt of eternal life.

CHAPTER 9

# *There'll Be Some Changes Made*

Max had begun taking his own stage show on tour. Modeled on the vaudeville/variety format, it was the usual fare of comedy sketches, musical production numbers, novelty or specialty acts, and a headliner. He had a partner in Tasmania, Arthur Benton, who handled the business end while Dad was in charge of producing the show. It was to be called the Follies (*à la* Ziegfeld), then changed to Folies (*à la* Bergère), which Dad thought was more exotic.

Stella, as usual, was the glue that held everything together. She would be straight woman to Dad in the sketches, do her solo singing spot if needed and, as stage manager, call all the cues from prompt side. The Folies company traveled around Tasmania in the spring and again in the autumn. During the southern winter, they headed north to Queensland for the warmer weather, following the schedule of the agricultural showground fairs, when country people always came into town. The summer months would be spent back in Melbourne, working on radio and putting together next season's show. My father was very proud that his company always played theaters and was not under canvas like the others. The advent of television in a few years was to change this way of life but, at that time, the annual arrival of live entertainment was eagerly anticipated by rural Australians.

In the last school term of 1953, Tintern moved its campus to a new location in Ringwood East. Now, instead of being around the corner, the school was accessible only by train or coach. As a result, I had to get up much earlier in the morning and was not returning until almost teatime. So that I could be closer to home, it was decided that I would change schools the following year. I was not happy about this. I had spent six years at Tintern; it was the only school I had ever attended, and I had a strong emotional attachment to it.

For the next three years, I was a pupil at Stratherne Presbyterian Girls School in Hawthorn, about a twenty-minute walk from our flat. Although my new school did not have the extensive sports programs that Tintern had—I would miss swimming and gymnastics—Stratherne did have an emphasis on the arts with Musical Appreciation classes as well as Drama. Jean Barklamb was our drama teacher; she took me on as a private student and taught me to love the rhythms and melodies of Shakespearean language.

Every Saturday, I was taking the tram into the city for ballet and tap classes with Miss Alice Uren, an old friend of my parents. Unfortunately, the two other rival dance schools in Melbourne were the ones that provided children for the Christmas pantomimes at the Tivoli and Princess Theatres. As the Christmas holiday season coincided with the school summer vacation period, pantomimes would open on Boxing Day and run through January. Whereas I could have had a run of several weeks in a real show in a real theater, I had to be content with a one-off amateur concert at the Melbourne Town Hall. On the other hand, I did get to sing two songs in a solo spot—"Wrap Your Troubles in Dreams" and "Sweet Georgia Brown"—for which I received an encore. That was the last time I walked out onstage as a little girl. At twelve years of age, my body was beginning to change. So was my voice. Although I might have been frustrated in my desire for more theatrical experience, I now had an adult voice, and radio listeners were not to know that the sexy French maid in one of their favorite shows was a twelve-year-old standing at the microphone in her school uniform.

At my new school I made several enduring friendships. One of my classmates at Stratherne was a girl called Robin Watson. The two of us became close despite having few interests in common; for example, Robin was a champion rider who owned two horses while I never lost my fear of them; she loved science while I preferred the arts. What we shared was a keen intelligence and a dysfunctional family background—which I respected her for rising above. I also admired Robin's courage, loyalty, and independence. We would try to arrive at school early so that we could talk before class; we would stay for an hour after classes so that we could talk again; and then we would dash home so that we could tie up the telephones and talk for a few more hours. What on earth did we talk about? I can recall the two of us having long and earnest discussions about boys and whether or not we might be kissed by certain of them. In my day, such thoughts could send thirteen-year-old hearts aflutter and be worthy of many hours of conversation. When we weren't talking about boys we were talking about clothes; we tried to wear matching outfits. And when we weren't talking about clothes we were talking about food.

On one of our school holidays, Robin even joined me on tour with the Folies in Tasmania. I enjoyed showing her one of my favorite haunts, the secret door in the orchestra pit of the Theatre Royal in Hobart. The theater, modeled on London's venerable Old Vic, was built during the convict era and some of the cells that the convict workers lived in during construction still existed underneath the theater. It was pitch black down there, and we needed a torch to see around, but the cell divisions could still be discerned among piles of old bricks. The spooky atmosphere guaranteed that we didn't stay there for too long, however.

Nanna was hospitalized in the early months of 1955. She seemed her usual chipper self when Dad and I visited her and she informed me that my sister, who had eloped a year earlier, was expecting a baby. Nanna was excited at the prospect of being a great-grandmother, having a new baby to cuddle. I didn't understand why my mother hadn't told me the news and why my father did not seem all that excited about it. After we got home, Mum told me the doctor had informed Dad that Nanna had less than a year to live, and that there was nothing they could do. So often, within families, I have seen births and deaths take place within a short time of each other, as if nature were rushing to fill the void. Nanna would die in May of 1955, without seeing her first great-grandchild, Tony Sheldon, who was born four months later.

After Nanna's death, I stayed with Aunty Nell in East Melbourne while Mum and Dad were on tour, but a problem arose now that I had reached puberty. My aunt did not get home from work until teatime and, without Nanna, I was no longer being supervised after school. After Uncle Brad caught me kissing one of the local boys in the park, Aunty Nell thought it prudent to change my status at Stratherne from day girl to boarder, before I did something dreadful, like become involved with a Catholic.

Adapting to boarding-school life was a struggle. I had always enjoyed a fair degree of independence and I was used to basic freedoms like listening to the radio and reading a newspaper, both forbidden at school. Swimming, the one sport I enjoyed, was not allowed, as the headmistress considered it "unmaidenly to appear in a bathing costume." This certainly contrasted with my school holidays on tour with the Folies. Wearing black fishnet tights and high heels I would assist the magician. Then it would be back to school again and lisle stockings, lace-up shoes, and the universally unflattering tunic. My only escape from the straitjacket of boarding school was my weekly piano lesson. Not wanting to interrupt my musical studies, the headmistress had agreed with Mum that I should take the tram once a week after school so that I could continue with Miss Kenafick. I still had a key to the flat so I took full advantage of the chance to vacate the school grounds unsupervised. I would tear out the side gate and, with key in hand, run full speed to the flat. There, I would play the radio and eat an entire can of peaches before going off to my lesson. Having my own little bolt-hole so close by also helped assuage some of my homesickness.

The vocational choices open to educated young ladies at that time were schoolteacher, secretary, nurse, librarian, or occupational therapist. Of the five, only librarianship interested me, and it was not necessary to matriculate in order to become one. In any event, I assumed I would be marrying and raising a family as soon as possible and would have no need for a career. As much as Aunty Nell was keen for me to go on to university, I simply could not handle school as a boarder any longer. I was failing exams, and the eczema had returned. Mum and Dad told me that, in the following autumn, I would be going on the road with them in the Folies, whether I liked it or not.

In the meantime, the annual summer holidays promised days spent swimming at the local public pools and long evenings of staying up late. The 1956 Olympic Games were being staged in Melbourne, and Australia had finally joined the television age in order to broadcast the Olympic events. We were the proud owners of a brand-new black-and-white television set—color TV would not come to Australia for another twenty years—and people would visit just to watch *Robin Hood* on our small screen.

My sister, Toni, and her husband, Frank, came down to Melbourne to rehearse for *The Pajama Game*, a Broadway musical that was going to be produced in Australia. For years, local producers had imported English and American actors to star in local productions of overseas shows while always consigning Australian actors to supporting roles, the implication being that we weren't quite good enough. Now, it was being acknowledged that Aussie actors were not only every bit as talented as their overseas counterparts, but that Australian audiences would pay to come and see their own. I was proud and thrilled for my sister.

As principal cast members did not receive rehearsal pay, Toni and Frank faced the prospect of rehearsing all day in the theater, then having to perform their cabaret show each night before returning to the hotel. Their fifteen-month-old son, my nephew Tony Sheldon, was going to be in need of a nanny for a few weeks, and his adoring aunt was only too happy to oblige. Like Nanna before me, I have always been baby-mad and was excited at the prospect of having one of my own for a while. Tony was a handsome and sweet little boy but, after so many different babysitters, was insecure and would scream if both parents exited the room. My sister was worried about leaving him with us as Mum and I weren't all that familiar to him. While Mum and Toni chatted inside, I took him downstairs for a little walk in the garden. He started crying as soon as he realized that his mother was out of sight, but fortunately I was able to distract him with a dandelion. Picking and blowing dandelions was a novelty to him, and by the time he'd tired of the game, my sister had slipped away and he had accepted me as a playmate. We bonded over the next two months and I had my first experience of maternal love.

It was not the only love I would experience for the first time that summer. I found myself feeling all manner of new emotions for the brother of one of my school friends. Now, more than ever, I did not want to go on the road with the Folies. How would I cope being away from the object of my youthful passion for months at a time? At fifteen years of age, however, I was not the one calling the shots. So for the next two years, I toured with my parents up and down the east coast of Australia, from Cairns in the north to Hobart in the south. And I did not like it. I did not want to be in show business. I wanted to be what all the women's magazines said a real woman wanted to be, a perfect wife and mother.

# CHAPTER 10

# On the Road Again

I started researching my future role of perfect wife and mother. One of the books I bought and read on that first tour was *Childbirth Without Fear* by Dr. Grantly Dick-Read. At a time when anesthesia was the norm, the doctor was advocating a way of giving birth which allowed the mother to witness and participate in the delivery of her baby. The theory was that fear of childbirth and anticipation of pain caused the muscles to tense, which created pain. As the practice of his theory mostly involved breathing and relaxation, I was sold. I didn't want to miss a minute of something as important as giving birth.

Six years later, I would use this method when I delivered my first child, daughter Traci. But time had dimmed my memory, and I thought the good doctor's book had been called *Childbirth Without Pain*. Wishful thinking.

.    .    .

A most welcome highlight on the Folies tour for me was the
twice-yearly trips to Launceston, Tasmania. My father's relatives on the Cox side still lived there, and even though he had
left Launceston for Melbourne in his early teens, it was still
important to Dad that he do well in his hometown. Monday
night at the old National Theatre was designated "clappers'
night," as family members got in for free if they promised to
clap often and hard. Monday night is notorious throughout
showbiz as the slowest night of the week and performers need
all the encouragement they can get!

I loved hanging out with my Tassie cousins, who were
enormous fun. They lived near the First Basin, a huge natural
pool and amphitheater, part of the Cataract Gorge. We had only
to walk down to the bottom of the road and cross the suspension
bridge to follow the narrow cliff path alongside the gorge itself. It
was quite a sight to behold in those days, before the power of the
surging river water was harnessed for Tasmania's hydroelectric
scheme. Afterward, it would be back to their house, where the
table would be spread with goodies. Tasmanian women are
wonderful bakers, and the cousins would try to outdo each other
with their Pavlovas (meringues) and sponge cakes. And then, of
course, a blanket would be spread over the cleared table and the
card games would begin. They were happy times.

.    .    .

Originally there had been eight dancers in the show, mostly hired through a dancing school in Hobart. However, one Saturday night, one of them failed to show up because, as she later explained, she "had to go to a turnout." After that, professional dancers were hired in Melbourne for the tour and, to compensate for the extra cost in transportation and accommodation, the number of dancers was cut from eight to six. During rehearsals, I would hear Dad's voice saying, "Spread out, girls, and make it look like a big show."

Dad always referred to the show's four-piece band as the Folies Orchestra. One of the regular musicians was an older man of European origin who doubled on reed instruments— clarinet, saxophone—and toured with the Folies for several years. He kept very much to himself and I don't remember ever having a conversation with him. Nor do I recall ever seeing him socializing with anyone else. One morning, another musician came upon him backstage making himself a cup of instant coffee out of the hot-water tap in the dressing-room sink. On the table was a plate of salad vegetables.

The story emerged that, as the Folies played the same circuit every year, he had found a secluded spot in each location and planted a vegetable garden. Now, as we went from town to town, he had access to fresh vegetables every day and was able to sow next year's crop along the way.

On tour with the Folies, I was mostly lonely. Not only was I younger than anyone else in the cast, I was the boss's daughter as well, and sometimes conversations would stop when I entered the dressing room.

As my father now considered me to be an apprentice, I was officially one of the Folies Lovelies and was paid the minimum union scale, which was fifteen pounds a week. Out of that, I would have to pay Dad eight pounds a week toward my board and keep. The other dancers found cheaper lodgings but I had to stay wherever my parents did. As part of my apprenticeship, I was also roped in to do anything which required an extra girl. Whether it was assisting a juggler, acting in a comedy sketch, or singing a number while the girls danced behind me, it was always yours truly who was called upon to do the honors. That may have caused some resentment among the other dancers, who were more experienced and ambitious than I was and would have welcomed the opportunity. It certainly caused resentment in me toward my father, who was not paying me extra for these added duties. I was a hard worker who didn't balk at hanging curtains or ironing costumes when we got to a new town, but I felt I was being diddled moneywise. Now I look back and appreciate training that was priceless. I was not only learning the performing arts, I was also learning how to mount and produce a show and take it on the road, knowledge that would provide me with an income for most of my working life. At the time, all I could see was that I was away from my friends and the love of my life. They were going to parties, socializing and having fun while I went back to my hotel room alone every night after the show. As well as the recurring eczema, boils broke out on my legs and body. I was miserable.

The one highlight for me on the northern tour was Townsville in Queensland. The Olympic Games had been held in Melbourne the year before and, as a big swimming fan, I knew the Australian team had trained at the Townsville pool during the winter. Going to the pool was one of the things I was allowed to do on my own. So every day I would swim my laps in my Speedos, thrilled that I was swimming where Dawn Fraser had swum before me.

Apart from professional sports, I believe that music is the only other profession in which someone goes to work in order to play. Perhaps this is why athletes and musicians are glorified in our culture.

During my second year with the Folies, I became ill at the end of the northern tour. We were on the long haul down to Newcastle by car, which took several days. I don't remember too much about the trip. I slept during most of it, wedged in the backseat between the luggage and the window so that I had somewhere to rest my head on either side. When my parents stopped for food, I had no interest in eating, stayed in the car and went back to sleep. At night, I remember only the pain in my side as if I was being held in a vise—constantly getting up to drink water and urinate, and then going back to bed again. When we reached Newcastle, Mum had a doctor friend take a look at me but, by then, whatever it was had passed and I was feeling better.

# CHAPTER 11

# I Could Go On Singing

D ad finally made his "Grand Tour" after the 1958 Folies run. He saw London, Paris, and New York before deciding that he missed Mum too much and arranged for her to join him in Los Angeles. They had friends in show business all over the world and were treated royally everywhere they went. From Hollywood, Max and Stella visited San Francisco, Las Vegas, and Tijuana before heading home via Honolulu. They'd both gone nuts at the markets in Mexico, buying serapes or shawls for everyone in the family as well as clothes for me.

Record players had become popular by the late 1950s. Huge items of wooden furniture, they were selected more for their contribution to the surrounding décor than for the quality of sound they produced. Dad had also brought me back lots of recordings to play on the turntable. From Paris, there were four songs from the score of the French stage hit musical *Irma La Douce,* with accompanying sheet music, plus a four-track EP of the legendary Edith Piaf. From the U.S., I got a 45 rpm of each song on the American hit charts. As Dad wasn't familiar with the newer artists, he simply went into a record store and bought the lot. I was thrilled to have music by Ray Charles and Chuck Berry, two artists I had never heard on Australian radio. My personal tastes definitely leaned toward jazz and blues.

When it came to singers, I felt that choice of material was every bit as important as vocal style. I bought Peggy Lee's album *Black Coffee,* which had great songs on it, and also an LP by Lena Horne. When someone made the comment that my singing sounded like Peggy Lee, I realized that I was un-consciously imitating her and decided to stop listening to female vocalists for a while. I wanted to develop my own style. I started listening to instrumentalists and big-band arrangers like Billy May and Gordon Jenkins. Because I figured it was OK to listen to male singers, I had several Frank Sinatra albums and loved his work with Nelson Riddle.

In 1973, Nelson Riddle would be my musical director on *The Helen Reddy Show* on NBC-TV. I wondered how he would handle some of the rock acts featuring on the show. He blew me away at the first rehearsal when he turned to me and said, "I love working with these young musicians. I learn so much from them."

Dear Nelson, a gentle man whose humility equaled his great talent. I learned so much from him.

. . .

A job came up singing with the band at the Chevron Hotel on St. Kilda Road. I already knew the words and music of dozens of standard songs. It was just a question of establishing what keys I sang them in and having a seamstress run up a couple of evening gowns. I also became featured vocalist (soubrette) and lead dancer in the hotel's floor show because, when the boss asked me if I could sing in French, I answered in the affirmative. Of course, I then had to go to a record store, buy every available recording in French and learn as many songs as I could phonetically.

Recordings of live performances were becoming popular, and one album I played over and over was *Marlene Dietrich at the Café de Paris*. I found that I most admired performing artists who were able to carry an entire show on their own. It seemed that developing oneself as a solo artist offered a performer not only a great challenge but also total artistic freedom, or so I thought. Certainly, no Australian that I had ever seen was working in that format. I would also buy, when they became available, recordings of *Noel Coward in Las Vegas* and *Bobby Darin at the Copa* for examples of what was on show in American nightclubs. At that time, I was still considering tailoring my talents toward cabaret/nightclubs. The concept of working as a solo artist in theaters and concert halls around the world had not yet crystalized in my mind.

What I did know was that I needed to carve out a space that was my own and would not put me in competition for a job with anyone else in the family.

In March 1959, after a night of sleepless agony, I had to wake my parents and ask them to take me to a doctor. This time I was immediately hospitalized with an abscessed kidney. Exploratory surgery revealed that my left kidney was swollen to the size of a football. It would have to be removed. And not a moment too soon. The abscess burst, sending my temperature to over 41°C (106.5°F) and the nurse rushing from the room. Again I experienced the sensation of moving down a dark, narrowing hallway and being tightly squeezed, as if through the eye of a needle. On the operating table, the kidney ruptured as soon as it was touched. By some miracle—my doctor was Catholic, and it was St. Patrick's Day—I survived, although I required private nursing around the clock until the risk of infection had passed.

When I came to after the surgery, Mum was sitting by my bed. Immediately, she told me that I had lost one of my kidneys. I was only seventeen. I remember bursting into tears and saying, "I'll never dance again. I'll never have children," and sobbing bitterly.

Long months of convalescence followed. Although I would have to concentrate more on singing and acting, I would dance again onstage, television, and film. And I would give birth to two beautiful, healthy children.

. . .

In September of that year, after six months of recuperation, I flew to Hong Kong via Darwin and Manila. Aunty Nell was on another world tour and she had invited me to join her at her final port of call, Hong Kong, as an advance eighteenth-birthday present. The plan was that she would be arriving by ship from Yokohama while I would fly there from Melbourne; we would stay at the Peninsula Hotel for a week and then sail back to Australia together. It was to be my first trip overseas and my first extended ocean voyage. I'd taken the overnight trip to Tasmania many times aboard the old *Taroona* but being at sea for weeks would be entirely different. It turned out, however, that we would not be able to arrive in Hong Kong on the same day. The flight from Australia that was closest to my aunt's arrival time put me in Hong Kong three days ahead of her.

Concerned about my being in Hong Kong for three days on my own, Dad arranged for some Chinese friends who lived there to keep an eye on me. One of them had a brother who introduced me to all the nightspots. Every club had a Filipino band, and two popular songs they all played were "Story of Love" and "Dahil Sayo." We hung out at the Golden Phoenix until it closed at 3 A.M. and then moved upstairs to the Highball, which stayed open until 4 o'clock. I had a wonderful time.

After Aunty Nell arrived, the emphasis was more on shopping and sightseeing than night life, but she was terrific fun to travel with. Both of us were embarrassed by the way a lot of

Westerners treated the Chinese, and Aunty Nell refused to barter with people who so obviously needed the money. She would pay rickshaw operators double the fare and took much delight in being sought after as a customer in return, as hagglers in Panama hats were abandoned whenever Aunty Nell appeared.

The voyage home was a pleasant one on a ship with a small first-class clientele. Aunty Nell and I shared a twin cabin and, as the nameplate on the door listed us both as Miss Helen Reddy, someone started a rumor that I must be Aunt's love child. She refused to confirm or deny this and I suspect she was secretly thrilled that anyone would believe she had ever been involved in any sort of romantic intrigue.

In December 1959 I was chosen as the opening act for Sammy Davis Jr. at the Melbourne Stadium. I had previously seen him in concert at the same venue with Diana Trask as his opening act. She had been discovered by Frank Sinatra, who had made it possible for her to work in the United States. She went on to feature as a regular vocalist in the enormously popular U.S. weekly television series, *Sing Along with Mitch*.

Diana Trask had inspired me. Although originally from Melbourne, she had moved to Sydney and been one of the stars on a regular musical series on Australian Broadcasting Commission (ABC) television. She seemed head and shoulders above anyone else on the show, and when I had seen her perform in person, I thought she had not only a lovely voice but also good choice of material, great stage presence, and she carried herself like a star. When I learned that her vocal coach was Jack White, a Canadian who had settled in Melbourne, I signed on as a pupil. Jack taught me how to use my instrument properly and kept setting the bar higher whenever I thought I was making progress.

Sammy Davis Jr. was the kind of act that Australian audiences could understand and appreciate. He was versatile and multitalented and right on the verge of major stardom. He was also personally excited that he was going to be making a movie with his buddies Frank Sinatra, Dean Martin, Peter Lawford, and Joey Bishop, or the Clan as they called themselves; not the Rat Pack, which is a media myth. Sammy had a copy of the script on his dressing-room table; the picture was going to be called *Ocean's Eleven*. He was charming to work with and, considering I was merely the opening act, most gracious in inviting me and my parents to join him for dinner after the show. Dad was doing some of his shtick for Sammy afterward in his hotel suite and Sammy commented on the bond between performers that transcends country of origin.

Although it was to be almost a decade before I would see him again, Sammy and I worked together several times after I achieved success in the United States, and our families holidayed together in Hawaii.

# *If It's Magic*

When I was a child, I had seen the stage hypnotist Franquin perform his show at the Princess Theatre in Melbourne. I regarded his act the same way I regarded any magician's act; very entertaining but based on trickery. After all, I had been an "audience plant" myself. I found it hard to believe regular people would do such ridiculous things onstage in front of their friends.

In my late teens, I toured Tasmania in the same show as John Calvert. Formerly an American B-movie actor, he was now working as a stage magician and hypnotist. Every night I used to watch his act from the wings and study how he chose and tested his subjects. Obviously, some people were more suggestible than others. The others always got sent back to their seats.

The chance to try out my new knowledge came in a social situation in one of the towns we visited. Although I drank nothing but water, there was nowhere to hang out but in the bar of the hotel where we were staying. One of the local lads, let's call him Bill, was telling a story about a time he'd been out in the bush and had fallen asleep with his head against a log. Bill had woken up to find a snake staring at him. He was unable to move or look away from the snake and found himself paralyzed. I recognized a highly suggestible subject. If a snake could hypnotize this guy, then I should have no problem. With his permission, I put him under with ease, used some deepening techniques, and planted a posthypnotic suggestion that he would go under again whenever I snapped my fingers a certain number of times. Bill was a most willing subject and responded well to my suggestions as he went in and out of hypnosis.

Afterward, he moved down to the other end of the bar to be with his mates. The room was filling up with noise as more customers arrived. The people I was still with had been quite impressed with the demonstration they'd just witnessed. Frankly, so was I. I felt like a kid who's just lit a match for the first time—empowered but scared. In a replay discussion with the others, I could still see Bill out of the corner of my eye engrossed in conversation with his friends at the far end of the bar. When I demonstrated the click combination that had triggered him going back into hypnosis, I saw Bill suddenly slump at the other end of the bar. He could not possibly have heard the clicks over the din in that noisy room, nor was he facing me. Immediately, I had to go and bring him out of it. It seemed I was dealing with some form of telepathy. I was terrified. This was not something I wanted to play with.

I longed to be able to discuss what I was discovering with someone who could answer my questions, but the only hypnotists I knew were showmen who had no interest in metaphysics. It was not until I read *The Search for Bridey Murphy* (1956), based on the fascinating recorded interviews of a middle-class American woman while under hypnosis, that I became aware of the use of hypnosis as a research tool and of the possibility of reincarnation.

This revelation gave me much food for thought and impetus for further research. Reincarnation struck me as a theory that made sense out of many inexplicable things in life, and it seemed to be above the petty jealousies and hairsplitting differences dividing organized religions. It also appealed to my sense of fairness, order, and justice.

So many of us feel guilt after a loved one has passed and think, "I should have said this" or "I should have done that." Reincarnation means that in reality, nothing is ever truly left unsaid or undone. Life is eternal, and other opportunities will be given to right all wrongs.

A truly memorable experience was the time that I would first witness a hypnotic subject being regressed to a past life. A lifelong fascination with research in this field would follow. Had I known that, almost half a century into the future, hypnotherapy would be an accepted branch of science or that I would be practicing as a clinical hypnotherapist, I'd have been thrilled.

. . .

When a conversation turns to reincarnation I am invariably asked, "If we have lived before, why don't we remember our past lives?"

Earth is like a school for the soul, and we don't remember because life is not an open-book exam. We are here to be tested on what we have already learned and retained to the extent that it has become second nature and part of our true character.

Conscious awareness of our past lives would also clutter our minds with too much information and emotional baggage. We need to be able to focus on the here and now when we are in body. It is the life presently being lived that is the most important one.

# CHAPTER 13

# Melbourne to Sydney

I was forced to face the fact that I would never have a future with the young man who was my first love. He made that as painfully obvious as he could, and I didn't think I could ever again feel that intensely for anyone else. I resolved not to date the same man twice in future and to concentrate instead on building a career that could provide me with a decent livelihood and give me a chance to see the world.

Singers I admired, such as Diana Trask and Lana Cantrell, were having their success out of Sydney. There they seemed to be free to choose more modern material to sing. In Sydney, there were several genuine nightclubs featuring full production shows, while the Melbourne nightlife was pretty much confined to hotel floor shows or a three-song set in a café. Frustrated with the limited opportunities available in

Melbourne, and believing that greener pastures awaited me in the larger city to the north, I decided to move to Sydney.

Shortly before my scheduled departure, reality caused a crack in my confident veneer. In Sydney, I had no family or friends and no job prospects. I was being driven by ambition and blind faith. What if I couldn't get work there? What would I do? That night I went to bed with these thoughts in my head and had a most peculiar dream.

I was in a church—no, it was a recording studio; no, it was a church; no, it was a recording studio. The images seemed to meld, as they do in dreams. And I was singing a duet with Peggy Mortimer, a well-known soprano. The dream was unusually vivid, and I remember waking up and thinking how strange it was. Not only did the two different settings seem at odds with each other but for me to be singing a duet with someone I hardly knew, and a soprano to boot, was highly unlikely.

I arrived in Sydney on June 1, 1960. I was eighteen. My first job, which I landed because I could sight-read music, was on a radio program for the Australian Broadcasting Commission and I was instructed to appear at Studio 226 in Bourke Street for the taping. I arrived at the address to find an old colonial church that had been taken over by the ABC. Inside everything had been preserved—the pulpit, stained-glass windows, and so on—however, pews had been removed in the middle of the church to make room for recording equipment, microphones,

and music stands. My first assignment was to sing a duet with
Peggy Mortimer!

Most of the work available in Sydney was in the private clubs
and, as I recall, there were more than a thousand of them in
New South Wales at that time. They all had poker machines
and bars and served food as well as presenting live entertainment on the weekends. Whether it was a workers' club, a
returned servicemen's club, or a sports league establishment,
membership in one of these clubs allowed the average
Australian male to drink and gamble to his heart's content
without breaking the law.

For performers who were "sight acts," such as acrobats,
jugglers, and the like, who transcend language but are
essentially one-trick ponies, these clubs were a godsend,
because they were able to set down roots and live in one place
rather than travel around endlessly with various circuses. By
the time these performers had played all those clubs, they
would seem like a fresh act on the circuit again. Sydney
was the only city in the world that allowed this, and performing families who had been caravan dwellers for generations became property owners.

Because agents represented the clubs and not the artists, it
was necessary to "do the rounds" of all the agents' offices, with
diary in hand, to secure bookings. The biggest agents were
those who either represented the largest number of clubs or
the more prestigious ones. For some reason, my stammer was

much worse when I was on the phone so I was better off calling on agents in person. Because I had no car and walked so much, it wasn't long before I had to line my best shoes with cardboard every time I went out, as I had worn holes in the soles. I envied American performers and their system of agents and managers who represented the artists themselves. How wonderful it must be to have someone who believed in you and could speak on your behalf.

Working as a singer, I found the clubs to be tough going. Each club had a band of sorts or at least a pianist, but there simply wasn't the necessary number of experienced musicians available to staff so many clubs. To make matters worse, there was never a rehearsal beforehand. You handed out your music charts to whoever was in the band and "talked through" the arrangements before you went on. By the time you discovered that these weekend musicians couldn't sight-read music, it was too late. You were already out there with a spotlight on you.

Before coming to Sydney, I had paid one of Melbourne's top jazz arrangers good money for six hot small-band musical charts and had had some new evening gowns made. I'd envisioned myself singing my "new act" in one of Sydney's most glamorous nightclubs. Instead, I found myself working in beer halls for lousy money, with musicians who knew only three chords in one key, and audiences who were more interested in drinking, talking, and gambling than entertainment.

I fantasized about what it would be like to have my own band that traveled with me. I thought that this would be the ultimate luxury. Eventually I would tour the world for two decades with my own band, but that was still many years in the future.

Gradually I started playing a better class of club and did a season at Chequers for Dennis Wong, one of Sydney's top nightclub entrepreneurs. I was the soubrette, singing in front of the line of girls for their two dinner shows per night, as well as being vocalist with a small jazz group for the late show. It was during this period that I would have my first experience of racism American style.

Having grown up in show business, I had worked and traveled my whole life with people of every shade, faith, and sexual orientation. Because they were performers, they were "us," and it was the civilians, those who could never understand our profession, who were "them." I had always assumed that performers worldwide shared this bond. I had heard and read about racism in America but believed it was confined to a place called the Deep South and a handful of civilians who could be recognized by their red necks.

On the evening in question, I was seated in one of the booths in the club with several other people, including an American couple I had just met. The husband was a nightclub entertainer recently enjoying enormous popularity on Australian television. I saw a trumpet player I knew across the room and, as he was American, I beckoned him to join us. It had not registered on my radar that the couple was white and the musician was not. I assumed that the American couple would be glad to see someone from home who was a fellow performer. I was wrong. The wife informed me that she and her husband were from the South and didn't sit with n----rs.

I wish I had gotten up and walked away instantly but, for several minutes, I couldn't move or even breathe. I felt as if I had been punched in the stomach. You can read about it, you can hear about it, but until you actually witness racism first-hand, you cannot comprehend its ugliness. Those who live with it every day of their lives, and still smile at the sky, bear witness to a courage I can only imagine.

Before leaving Melbourne for Sydney—with no plans to return and therefore no chance of involvement—I had overlooked my one-date-only rule and more than once had seen an older, divorced musician. He was dating someone else as well, and when she announced their engagement, I can't say I was heartbroken. On the contrary, I felt relieved that I could now leave Melbourne with no loose ends. Imagine my surprise when he followed me to Sydney not too long after, having broken up with his fiancée.

I was subletting a small single room in Kings Cross, and he suggested that much larger accommodation would be affordable if we shared. He'd found a charming two-bedroom, fully furnished flat in Double Bay, close to the water. There was just one tiny problem. In 1960 a single man and a single woman could not lease a property together—we would have to pose as man and wife.

# CHAPTER 14

# Sydney to Melbourne

I was playing in the Silver Spade room at the Chevron Hilton, the newest and most glamorous nightspot in Sydney, unfortunately still as a soubrette. By now I was nineteen years old and America seemed increasingly out of reach. Not only was the airfare way beyond my limited finances but it seemed that every Australian performer I knew who had tried to break into American show business came up against the need for a "green card." American immigration still operated on the old quota system; only one hundred Australians per year were granted the precious card, without which employment was impossible, and there was a ten-year waiting list. I'd seen too many Aussies try to crack the American market, hit a brick wall, and come home with a chip-on-the-shoulder attitude. I didn't want to be one of them.

In those days, you were not legally an adult until the age of twenty-one, unless you were married. I was chafing against those legal restrictions placed on me and longed for the autonomy of adulthood. I'd been self-supporting since I was fifteen and living away from home since I was eighteen. I resented having to ask my parents down in Melbourne for their signature on documents or permission to do something like get married. (See where this is headed? I wish I had.)

And I was getting older. More than anything else, I wanted to have a baby. In the early sixties, women were advised to complete their families before age thirty, while their eggs were still fresh.

On top of everything, I was feeling obliged to legalize what had become, in essence, a common-law marriage. Several people, with my best interests at heart, tried to talk me out of it but to no avail. On January 7, 1961, my father escorted me down the aisle in the little Presbyterian church in Cross Street, Double Bay—now the boutique mall, Chapel Court—and I got married. I was nineteen; my bridegroom was thirty-three.

Marriage, I had thought, would mean that I wouldn't have to wait another two years to be free of my parents' legal jurisdiction. What I had not anticipated was that I was now legally under my husband's for the rest of my life. What's more, I had jumped from the frying pan into the fire; I had married an alcoholic.

Knowing what I know now about alcoholism as a disease, how it impacts on the family, and what enabling and codependency are all about, I realize that, given my family history, it was inevitable that I would marry an alcoholic. If I had walked into a room with a hundred men in it and only one was an alcoholic, he's the one I would have been drawn to, like a moth to a flame.

Exactly when we returned to Melbourne or why, I don't remember, but it was within a few months of our marriage. All the contacts I'd made and the goodwill built up in the time I'd spent in Sydney went out the window and I had no job to come back to. The recession of 1961 seemed to have hit Melbourne first and hardest: I was out of work for many long months. Fortunately, we were able to stay at my parents' flat in Hawthorn while they were away on tour. My musician husband found two regular band gigs but balked at giving me housekeeping money and told me to get a job. I was glad my parents kept such well-stocked cupboards.

I was hired for a regular spot in a weekly TV variety show called *Sunnyside Up*. While I appreciated the paycheck each week, I did not find the work to be artistically satisfying. I had no say in the selection of material and was forced to perform embarrassingly corny songs some weeks instead of the smoky, nightclub jazz tunes that I preferred. It was not the sort of exposure likely to lead to more sophisticated personal-appearance bookings. However, I did get to act in the occasional comedy sketch—a piece of film survives to keep me eternally humble—and it was a friendly cast. I enjoyed the camaraderie. Marriage had turned out to be a lonely experience, and it was wonderful to be out of the house and with other people, if only for one day a week.

Seeking solace in religion, and still looking for answers to my many questions, I had begun studying Catholicism. It was while I was in *Sunnyside Up* that I learned the baby I had been praying for at the Church of St. Francis was finally on its way. Mine was an era in which pregnant women were not acceptable on television unless they were standing behind a credenza, a large potted plant, or both of the above. It was understood that I would quit the show as soon as I "started to show."

Although I hadn't planned on ending up a single mother, life takes its own turns sometimes, and we have to go along. Two years after my wedding, at the age of twenty-one, there I was eight and a half months pregnant, living with Aunty Nell, and facing single motherhood.

I'd heard rumors that my husband had been physically abusive with his first wife and had, allegedly, pushed her down the stairs, causing a miscarriage. When I had asked him if it was true, he had denied it most vehemently. I had believed him, and there was no problem while we were living together. However, after we were married, he became mean and nasty on several occasions when he'd been drinking. Something about "pregnancy" must have been threatening for him because that was when he became physically abusive. Once was enough for me. I'd seen my mother put up with that nonsense for years and I was not going to tolerate it; the Church might preach that the husband was the head of the house, but I would not risk losing the baby I had prayed for. Aunty Nell took me in, as I knew she would, and I lived with her for the next year and a half.

As I had been forced to leave the marital home, I was considered a deserted wife and therefore entitled to the Widow's Pension (?!) for six weeks before and six weeks after the birth. For that period, I received nine pounds every two weeks (there was no increase in the Widow's Pension for more than twenty years). Dad made up the difference by giving me five pounds every week, and Aunty Nell would sometimes slip me a few shillings to proofread legal documents for her. She used to make extra money toward her overseas trips by doing typing on the weekends for a lawyer, and I learned not to be intimidated by legal language.

Like most women during their first pregnancy, I went through a period of wondering whether the baby was going to be OK and how would I cope, as a single mother, if I should have a child who required special care. Worst of all, would I be able to love it and keep it? Only weeks before the birth—I could barely fit my stomach behind the steering wheel—I was sitting at a red light at the corner of Collins and Swanson Streets, watching the pedestrians crossing in front of me. One of them was a woman with an older Down's syndrome child. In that instant, I knew, and to the depth of my soul, that nothing could ever make me give up my child and that I was going to love it, no matter what.

When I went into labor, I found myself not wanting to give birth; not because I was afraid of the pain, but because I couldn't bear the thought of my baby and me never being that close again. We were one body about to become two, and I was experiencing separation anxiety. I'm so glad that I decided to breast-feed, not only because of the multiple benefits for any infant, but because it allowed me to gradually wean myself from my physical attachment to her. Mother Nature knows what she's doing.

Although I had no knowledge of it at the time, my daughter entered the world 175 years to the day after our First Fleet ancestor, his ship safely at anchor in Botany Bay, stepped onto Australian soil for the first time in 1788. What I did figure out, however, was that my little Aussie bub had been conceived on Anzac Day (April 25)!

Her father and I had verbally agreed on a name if the baby was a girl, but there had never been a discussion of the spelling. I had wanted the old English form of the name, Tracey, but when I received her birth certificate I saw that my husband, who had registered the birth while I was still in hospital, had spelled it Traci. As it would have required a deed poll to change it legally, Traci it became and has been ever since.

The same month my daughter was born, a hot new English musical group burst forth on the radio. They were called the Beatles, and their sound and images filled the media. I bought one of their four-track EPs during those early months of motherhood. While I was living at Aunty Nell's, with her willingness to babysit of an evening, Dad was able to get me a job singing with the combo at a hotel where he was doing his comedy act. It was seven nights a week but only three hours a night, from seven to ten; ideal for a young mother who needed to be with her baby all day.

I was also starting to get work as a studio singer doing commercials. Although the money was poor—they paid no royalties or residuals in those days, and one of my commercials ran for twenty years!—I did appreciate the chance to keep up my sight-reading skills. I used to resent it when an ad agency rep would come into the sound booth with me to make sure that I pronounced every syllable in the name of his product. Even so, it taught me to have good enunciation, and becoming familiar with recording equipment gave me skills that I would put to good use in years to come.

When I was living with Aunty Nell, our shared name gave rise to an interesting situation. Sometimes, a phone conversation would go like this:

"Hello."

"Hello. Could I speak to Miss Reddy, please?"

"Which one?"

"Miss Helen Reddy."

"Which one?"

"The singer."

# CHAPTER 15

# Melbourne to Sydney, Take Two

By the time Traci was walking, I realized that I needed to move on. I was not a child anymore. I was an adult with a child for whom I had to provide a future. Although Aunty Nell would have been happy for us to continue living with her forever, and was upset when we left, it was time for me to grow up. I had come to terms with the fact that there was still no future for me in Melbourne, either in show business or out of it, and there never would be.

For my twenty-first birthday, Dad had bought me a vintage Morris Minor. It had had two previous owners but sported the original leather upholstery in good condition. I can picture Traci's little car seat with its plastic steering wheel and horn, tied with cord to the bucket seat next to mine; the trunk and backseat loaded with as many of our possessions as would fit. I would have to leave behind my daughter's cot and high chair—she had already grown out of her pram—but I found room for her stroller. My parents were there when Traci and I left, and despite my assuring Dad that everything would be fine, he pressed some money into my hand as we set off on the two-day drive to Sydney. I'm so grateful that he did as, never having driven that distance before, I had naïvely assumed that one tank of gas would suffice to get us to Sydney. I had considerably underestimated my cash needs for the trip.

In Sydney, it was back to the beginning of the game for me professionally, but at least I now knew how the game was played. Or I thought I did. No one in Sydney could care less about a Melbourne television show in which I'd been a regular, but some of the agents remembered me and gave me club gigs. There was also occasional work doing background vocals, but I could not get a foot in the door either in television or voiceover commercial work. It seemed that in those two areas, the jobs consistently went to the same people, and it was very "cliquey." There was a small recording industry in Sydney but their only interest was in "bubblegum" music by artists who appeared on Australia's version of *Bandstand*. And forget movies; at the time, there had not been a film industry in Australia since the 1930s.

Max had a one-line speaking role in a George Wallace film from that era. The only time he saw the picture was on a ship from New Zealand to Sydney. Because his friends all cheered as soon as he appeared on-screen, my father never got to hear his one line!

I was in Sydney in 1964 when the Beatles came to town. Ringo had to join the tour later due to illness, but John, George, and Paul were seen in person waving from the balcony of the Sheraton Hotel. I know because I was among the crowd standing below in Macleay Street waving back. Within a decade I would have met them all and dined with John and Yoko at the home of a mutual friend.

It was also in Sydney that I saw Marlene Dietrich perform her one-woman show in a theater, with an as yet unknown Burt Bacharach as her musical conductor. During her performance, I took down at least twelve pages of notes. From her striking entrance to her lighting, which was a marvel, to the carefully crafted musical arrangements, to the way she took her bow, it was a master class in stagecraft. I dared to dream that I might one day present myself in a one-woman show. For the first and only time in my life, I waited outside a stage door for a glimpse of a true star.

My mother had felt that way about Ruth Draper, a mono-loguist of her era. Mum had the talent to be a great solo performer but her dreams were cut short at an early age. Stella Lamond had started as a child performer in pantomime with her older sister, Lyle, playing *Babes in the Wood*. When you're playing the title role at age four, where do you go from there? Mum graduated to comedy solo numbers and was known for a while as the Woop Woop Girl. This must have been a country bumpkin–type character, as Woop Woop, in the vernacular of the time, referred to any one-horse town in the outback. She also accompanied herself on the ukulele.

By the age of sixteen, Stella was working in the Australian production of the show *Hellzapoppin'* with Olsen and Johnson, a famous American comedy team. They were both so impressed with Mum's comedic talents that they wanted to take her back to the United States with them. Her mother said that she was too young to go, and that was the end of that. It was an opportunity that would not come around again.

I have a theory that many of us fulfill the unfulfilled dreams of our parents, whether or not they have been verbally expressed. Sometimes one's heart simply feels what the other's heart has yearned for. In any event, I had always had a strong attraction to America and a feeling that I would end up there as a star.

# CHAPTER 16

# *The Contest*

I began sharing a flat with another singer, Jan Porter, who was also working the club circuit. Jan had fallen in love with my daughter and was a tower of strength for me during this period. Working conditions on the club circuit hadn't changed a bit. Jan told me about a club she sang in where the drummer had only a stand-up snare drum. When she asked him where his bass drum and high hat were, he replied that he was still taking lessons and was only up to the hands, he hadn't gotten to the feet yet! Nonetheless, he had a union card and was working.

The affection between Jan and Traci was mutual, and volunteering to share some of my parenting duties, Jan began taking Traci to preschool on alternate mornings. Better still, she was a great cook, and I love to iron, so it was a harmonious living arrangement that moved from Woolloomooloo to

Summer Hill to Randwick, and lasted until I left for America. I wish Jan lived closer now, as I don't see her for years at a time and I miss her kind, generous spirit. She was a truly loving, giving friend at a time my daughter and I needed one.

In 1965, out of frustration, I entered a talent contest, Bandstand Starflight International, cosponsored by the Australian Nine Network, Pan Am Airlines, and Mercury Records, USA. This was the second year that the contest was being held so I figured it had to be legitimate. The winner of the first contest in 1964 was Sharon Black, a vocalist with a warm, personable manner and a stunning smile. Sadly, Sharon was destined to die young before her talents could be fully realized.

First prize was a trip to New York and a chance to record there. America was still where I longed to be but, as I had yet to earn a three-figure salary per week, the cost of the airfare was way beyond my reach. A round-trip airline ticket Sydney—New York—Sydney was US$1,246—more expensive than today, nearly forty years later! If I won the contest, not only would my airfare be covered, but I figured that a major American corporation would have no problem sponsoring me for a green card.

The second prize in the contest was a recording contract in Australia. Either prize would give me the longed-for chance to make a record. At the very least, I would have the opportunity to be seen on television on *Bandstand,* which might lead to more work. Altogether that year there were 1,358 contestants competing for the grand prize.

I was advised by some of my showbiz friends not to enter the contest. They pointed out that it was essentially an amateur affair and, even though the rules did not prohibit a professional from entering, if I lost to an amateur it would be the kiss of death for my career. They had a point. One other professional singer also entered the contest that year. After failing to reach the finals, she dropped out of the business for three years before returning under a new name.

Despite the warnings, I was willing to take the risk. I was already twenty-three years old and had a child to support. This was my one chance to go to America and I was confident of both my talent and my ability to win. But I had work to do. During the six months that the contest ran, every morning I would get up, look at myself in the mirror, and say, "Helen Reddy—you are going to win that contest!"

I won't say that there weren't times when doubts crept into my mind but I would push them aside. I survived the semifinals and the finals but as the Grand Final loomed ahead, I was becoming increasingly anxious. I bought a copy of *Variety* magazine so that I'd have some knowledge of what was going on in American showbiz. It wasn't in English! It was full of unintelligible phrases like "Box Sox Jox Vox" or worse. I wondered what on earth I was getting myself into. Perhaps I'd be better off staying in Sydney. I was finally beginning to break into the market there for commercials and television work. What if I couldn't survive in America?

My body could not bear the brunt of all that repressed fear, and I had a full-scale anxiety attack one morning when I was home alone with Traci. I thought it was a heart attack. I had to crawl to the phone to ring an ambulance, and my two-year-old had to come with me to the hospital. Jan was doing an out-of-town gig, I had no family in Sydney, and I couldn't leave my daughter alone. Fortunately, Jan got back into town that afternoon and was able to take Traci home with her. I was released from hospital that evening but the experience had shaken me and left me feeling vulnerable. I was gambling our livelihood on this contest.

The choice of song for the Grand Final was critical. It was my one chance to convince the judges. Should I sing a ballad or would an up-tempo tune be a wiser move? Which would impress the judges more? How could I know?

For a month, I haunted record stores listening to album cuts in the soundproof booths provided, before I finally found "the song." It was on a Petula Clark LP, written by Tony Hatch and Jackie Trent, and called "Strangers and Lovers." The first half of the song—about strangers in the city—was slow and sad, then suddenly the drums kicked in, the trumpets blared, and the second half—about lovers in the city—was upbeat and joyful. I'd found a song that was both a ballad *and* up-tempo. Perfect!

Now, what was I going to wear? I saw myself in something long, white, and floaty and found just the thing in a store downtown that specialized in evening gowns. I had it altered so that it fitted perfectly. This was the mid-sixties, and big hair and heavily made-up eyes were *au courant*. I decided to go all the way with three pairs of false eyelashes and two extra hair pieces attached to my red wig. They were dyed three slightly different shades of red but, as Australian TV was still black-and-white, I didn't think it would matter; my hairdresser added white flowers to the assortment of hair as a distraction, just in case. And, to leave absolutely nothing to chance, I encased my bosom in a padded, push-up bra. With all my perceived inadequacies now covered and out of sight, I had only to think about singing one song. Once again I began feeling confident about my chances.

The morning of the Grand Final, there was a knock at my door. It was a young man I had worked with back in the Folies days; he had wooed and wed one of the Folies Lovelies. Surprised to see him, I invited him in for a cup of tea. He told me he had felt compelled to warn me about the contest. He was a cousin to one of the judges and he had heard that the decision had already been made to give first prize to the girl who impersonated Ella Fitzgerald. He wanted me to know so that I wouldn't be disappointed when they announced the results on camera. It was a heavy blow, but the contest was not over yet, the Grand Final had not yet taken place. I resolved that I was going to be so good on the show that night, there would be a public outcry if I didn't win.

.   .   .

It would be a long time before I found out what was actually happening in the judges' booth on the night of the Grand Final. All I knew, then, was that after all sixteen finalists had finished videotaping their songs, we sat in the studio, in make-up and costume, and waited for the judges to make their decision. As the five judges were in a soundproof room with a glass wall into the studio, their deliberations were seen, but silent for the two hours we sat, watched, and waited for the verdict to come in. The Grand Final was being videotaped that Wednesday evening for broadcast on the coming weekend.

I had promised Mum and Dad that I would call once I knew the result, whatever the outcome, so that they wouldn't have to go through the torture of waiting for the show to air. They must have been conflicted. On the one hand, my winning would give them enormous parental pride and me the chance to fulfill Mum's thwarted dream; on the other, it would mean that I would be going a long way away and taking their only granddaughter with me.

When I dialed the number in Melbourne, Mum picked up immediately. She must have been sitting right next to the phone. I could hear the trepidation in her voice:

"Hello?"

"Mum—"

"Yes?"

"I won."

"Oh no! Oh no!! Oh no!!!" And then her voice dropped. "Are you sure?"

Mum was alone. Unable to stand the suspense, Dad had gone out drinking, leaving her to wait for the call by herself. After we'd hung up and needing to share the good news with someone, she went downstairs to the neighbors in the flat below for a celebratory drink.

Dad waited until he felt sure that the contest was well over before wending his way home. As he pulled his car into the driveway, he saw that there were no lights on in the upstairs windows. Taking this to mean that Mum had gone to bed already, and reasoning that she would have waited up for him if I'd won, he started up the stairs feeling disappointed but relieved that at least he now knew one way or the other. Suddenly, a window in the downstairs flat flew open as Mum and the neighbors called out, "She won! She won!"

As the Grand Final show did not go to air until the weekend, and the results were not publicly announced until then, my father had three days to go around the pubs in Melbourne placing bets on his daughter to win. I'm told he cleaned up.

Anticipating public loss, I had so steeled myself to have no emotional response when the result was announced that my only reaction, when I heard my name, was an involuntary blink. I appeared to be so composed that some people concluded that I knew I was going to win—the whole thing must have been fixed!

As I was eventually to learn, the judges had been divided— two for me, two for the Ella Fitzgerald impressionist, and one undecided. The undecided judge was Bruce Gyngell, and as he would tell me over lunch nearly thirty years later, he cast his vote in my favor because, despite my being one of the oldest contestants at twenty-four, he thought I would be the one to make the most of the opportunity. He was glad that time had proved him right.

After I won the contest in December 1965, I started putting my affairs in order so that I would be ready to leave at a moment's notice. I stopped taking performance bookings as I didn't expect to be around to fulfill them.

I kept calling to find out my date of departure for the United States but was always told they would let me know. Weeks and then months began to go by, and my finances were becoming perilously low. On February 14, Australia switched over to decimal currency—from pounds, shillings, and pence to dollars and cents. Ten shillings of the old money would equal one dollar of the new. Finally, I was given a departure date, April 14, 1966.

Traci had turned three in January so she could no longer fly for free. I would have to pay half-price for her, which amounted to US$623. The prize money that came with my ticket had been announced on air as AUD$400. In reality, I received US$350, which was considerably less at the rate of exchange in 1966.

GTV9 flew me down to appear on *In Melbourne Tonight* on the eve of my departure for America, so I was able to say goodbye in person to my parents and Aunty Nell, and let them see Traci one last time. She and I then returned to Sydney the next morning as our flight was due to leave midafternoon. As I watched my father, through the airplane window, slowly walking back to the terminal, I wondered if I would ever see him again. If I were successful, I would be staying in America, and if I were not? I didn't know if my pride would allow me to return.

Either way, I was not planning to come back, and we could only take with us what would fit in our two-suitcase limit, so crucial decisions had to be made that afternoon regarding toys. Clutching my three-year-old with one hand and my purse containing my remaining US$230 with the other, I boarded the plane for America.

# CHAPTER 17

# Coming to America

As luck would have it, the singer Bobby Rydell and his manager, Frank Day, were also on the flight. I had met them both briefly when they were in Australia. I was too excited to sleep on the plane so Frank came and sat next to me and we talked all the way to Honolulu. One thing I remember him telling me was that scientists were developing computers that would one day compose music by themselves!

Traci and I were staying overnight in Los Angeles with some friends of my parents while Frank and Bobby flew on to Philadelphia. We agreed to keep in touch, and I promised Frank that I would contact him if I ran into any trouble. Frank Day was to be the one responsible for my eventually getting a green card. I'm so glad I had the chance to let him know, before he died, how grateful I was for his friendship and faith in me.

My first night in New York, I turned on the TV to watch Johnny Carson on *The Tonight Show*. Who should he have on as a guest but Lana Cantrell! I took that as a very encouraging sign. I admired her work. She sang beautifully that night, and every Aussie who did well in America opened the door for others, as far as I was concerned.

I showed up at the headquarters of Mercury Records on Fifth Avenue the following day, with Traci in tow, and was told I would be taken to lunch by someone in the sales department. I don't remember his name or the name of the restaurant, but I do recall that it was on the top floor and, through the window, I could see a large red neon sign with three sixes. Now, there was a sign! When I inquired over lunch when I might expect to sign my contract and start recording, the gentleman informed me that I must have misunderstood. First prize was not a recording contract but an audition for one. I asked how soon I could audition and was told that it would not be necessary. A tape of me singing had already been sent from Australia and, while he was sure that I sang very nicely, they had really wanted a male group. Everyone hoped I would have a nice time while I was in New York and I shouldn't forget to call and say good-bye before I returned to Australia.

They say there's no such thing as a free lunch. Sometimes that's all there is.

.   .   .

From a business perspective, at a time when the American hit music charts were overwhelmingly dominated by a male-group sound, at a time when radio stations allotted only one space on their play lists for "a female record," Australia had sent female soloists to America two years in a row. The executives at Mercury had been so disappointed they had never even bothered listening to my tape. With the benefit of hindsight, having lived in America for more than thirty-five years and run my own production company, would I have made the same decision in their place if a contest winner appeared from another hemisphere, dragging with her a small child, and expecting to become an American recording star overnight? Probably.

Looking back now, I marvel at my naïveté and my trust. I have always trusted in the future. As far as I was concerned, I had already achieved the impossible by getting my daughter and myself to America; the rest was supposed to be a breeze.

Without a green card, I was not allowed to work in the United States. However, as a member of the British Commonwealth, I would be allowed to work in Canada, so my short-term plan was to work for a few weeks in Canada and then use the money to live on for a while in New York. There, I could do the rounds of the agents and maybe pick up an occasional weekend gig outside the city, while waiting for someone to give me my first break.

I was able to secure two weeks' work at a nightclub in Winnipeg, Manitoba. It was a perfect gig. The showroom was in the hotel where I would be staying, so accommodation was taken care of and a car unnecessary. There was even a park and playground within walking distance. Meals were also provided, and the hotel had a list of reliable babysitters. So I would be able to clear most of my salary. My major expense would be transportation for us both from New York to Winnipeg and back. When I looked at a map I could see the two cities were quite a distance apart. We would need to fly to Winnipeg via Toronto but, as there was no rush to return to New York and I wanted to see some of the United States, I decided to take the bus back; it was much cheaper than flying.

The engagement turned out to be an enjoyable two weeks all round. Traci liked her babysitter, and I found the staff at the hotel to be a friendly lot. I was paid in full after the final show on the Saturday night, and we were packed and ready to leave on the bus early Sunday morning.

Dawn was just beginning to break and breakfast was not yet being served at the hotel or the bus station when we left. Traci and I would have to wait for the first rest stop before we could eat. When we reached Fargo, North Dakota, just across the U.S. border, I fronted up to the café counter and ordered a full breakfast. As I started pulling money out of my purse to pay, the waitress said, "We don't take Canadian dollars."

I had been paid in cash on Saturday night. It was now Sunday morning. There had been no opportunity between then and now for me to exchange the money for American dollars. I asked her if there was anywhere I could change some money. She said, "No."

I told her I was willing to pay extra if she would accept the Canadian money. She answered, "We don't take Canadian dollars."

I looked in my purse. At the bottom were some American coins. They amounted to nine cents. I looked up at the menu board. The last item on the list was milk—ten cents. I showed the waitress my coins and said, "I have nine cents American. Can you let me have a glass of milk for my little girl?"

"Milk is ten cents," she replied.

I then asked her, "Can you pour one cent's worth off the top and give me a nine-cent glass of milk? My child hasn't had breakfast."

Once again, she responded, "Milk is ten cents," and moved on to the next person.

I was outraged. Here I was with hundreds of dollars in my purse and my daughter was being denied a glass of milk because I was one cent short in American currency.

I went to the bus driver and complained. He kindly loaned me some money so that Traci and I could eat. When we reached Philadelphia on the Monday morning, I was able to get to a bank, change my money to American dollars, and repay him. I have never forgotten his kindness and I have never forgotten that waitress. I'm so grateful that she was not my first impression of the United States and, no, I didn't leave her a tip.

I had presumed that I would have an advantage looking for work in America. After all, I was a fresh face backed up with years of experience. I found it hard to understand why New York agents, when reviewing my résumé listing credits as singer, dancer, actress, and so on, would ask me, "Are you an actress who can sing or a singer who can read lines?" or "Are you a dancer who can carry a tune or a singer who can move?" What on earth were they talking about? I'd been trained to do it all.

It seemed the United States had embraced specialization. And if you were a jack-of-all-trades, then to their minds it followed that you were master of none. In Australia, versatility was valued above all else when it came to employability. Versatile performers were also regarded by their peers as being more naturally talented. I was about to discover that America's obsession with specialization went beyond the entertainment industry.

After Traci was born in Melbourne, I was given a government-issued booklet before I left the hospital and told to take it with me to my local Baby Health Centre when I took my infant daughter for her routine check-up. Every community had a local Baby Health Centre, staffed by a registered mothercraft nurse. She was available to demonstrate bathing and changing a newborn, advise on breastfeeding and nutrition, and provide regular check-ups and necessary vaccinations. At each visit, the nurse would note in the booklet the baby's weight, length, and other relevant data and also record the child's vaccination dates. This service was provided by a government with a vested interest in a healthy populace and was a boon to first-time mothers.

When we left for America, three-year-old Traci needed only

one more booster shot for diphtheria, tetanus, and pertussis (whooping cough) to complete her records. When the due date came around, I was staying in New Jersey. I asked a neighbor for directions to the equivalent of the local Baby Health Centre. She looked at me as if I was from another planet. She'd never heard of such a thing. When I explained to her what I needed, she informed me that I would have to make an appointment to see a pediatrician. Now it was my turn to be aghast. I was expected to pay a hefty fee to a specialist for a simple shot that any registered nurse could give? What a waste of a doctor's time, and what on earth did poor people do?

It was a drag not having a home base and having to restrict our belongings to what I could fit into our two suitcases, but another booking that helped me survive financially was a few weeks at a club in Akron, Ohio. I got billing above the belly dancer but way below the BARBECUED RIBS! Nevertheless, I found Midwesterners to be a kindhearted lot and I enjoyed the chance to see more of the United States. Traci and I were staying at an old, old hotel that seemed to house mostly Social Security recipients; in other words, it was affordable accommodation. One of the younger women there was a former schoolteacher with multiple sclerosis. Despite having no discernible handicap other than a slight limp, she had been tossed on the scrap heap by the Department of Education and was considered unemployable. I asked her if she would consider a job as Traci's babysitter while we were there. She was delighted and I was thrilled at the prospect of being able to get some sleep during the day while I was working at night.

In the meantime, little Miss Three had captured the heart of the elevator operator, an older gentleman of color, and was going up and down from floor to floor with him, taking it all in. This quickly became a favorite pastime of hers. I was told that an elderly lady got in the elevator one morning and asked Traci, "What do you know about God, dear?"

"What floor does he live on?" she responded.

Obviously, I had neglected my daughter's religious education; mostly, it was because I didn't know how to explain my philosophy to a toddler. How could I impart to her my belief that the same core truth is at the heart of all religions? When she was four, she showed me the way herself. She asked me, "Mummy, when you're not with me and there's no other grownups around I can ask, how can I tell if something is right or wrong?"

It was the perfect opportunity to teach her the Golden Rule. I said to her, "You have to ask yourself, is this something I would want someone to say to me or do to me? Always try to think about how you would feel if you were the other person. And if it's something that would hurt your feelings or make you feel bad, then don't say it or do it."

She understood, and I am so grateful that both my children have grown up to be adults who are kind and of good character.

# CHAPTER 18

# New York, New York

In the months leading up to my departure for America, I had been given quite a few contact numbers by friends who had lived or worked in New York. Lillian Roxon was a name on more than one list and a name that was familiar to me; I had seen it in print many times. She wrote fashion, beauty, and society columns for an Australian weekly women's magazine and, now that she was based in New York, she penned a gossipy showbiz column for a Sydney newspaper. I think she was the last person on the list that I called. Actually, I dreaded meeting her. My confidence was at a low ebb from all the rejection I'd received since I arrived and I was not about to be eaten for breakfast by an Australian journalist.

From all the fashion and beauty columns that bore her by-line, I pictured Lillian Roxon as an elegantly dressed, brittle New Yorker with perfect hair and nails, who would proceed to pick my appearance to pieces. Finally, I think, it was the need to hear an Australian accent that made me call her. She sounded pleasant on the phone and invited me to her office in the *New York Times* building so that we could meet in person. I dressed in my newest outfit, a plaid wool miniskirt with boots in matching fabric, girded my loins, and went to face the dragon.

The woman walking toward me couldn't possibly be Lillian Roxon. She was well beyond plump and wearing baggy clothes. As she got closer, I could see that the remains of at least one meal decorated the front of her sweater. Her hair was thin and fine and hung limply around her face. But what a face! Not a smidgen of makeup covered one of the most beautiful complexions I have ever seen. She had flawless, luminous skin, large eyes that radiated kindness, and a warm smile as she greeted me with, "Hello, darling. Would you like a cup of tea and a biscuit?" I threw my arms around her and hugged her. I'd found a friend in New York.

As I would quickly learn, Lillian wrote about fashion and beauty because, being female, she was confined to the women's pages. Women were not allowed to cover or report on anything close to general news—that was a man's job. Lillian was bright and witty and a good writer who was frustrated by the limitations imposed on women journalists. She was particularly interested in the experimental music that was coming out of New York's hippest area, the Village, and the bands that were breaking the barriers and setting the boundaries. She believed that a whole new art form was coming into being, not only the music but the literature it was spawning. She was the first to see that rock journalism was going to be a huge force in American culture.

When I was living in a budget hotel in Greenwich Village with limited funds and an even more limited wardrobe, Lillian wrote for her Sydney column that "Helen Reddy has been a chiffon lady at all the best New York parties this season." When I protested that I hadn't been seen anywhere, nor did I own anything chiffon, she told me that it was important to keep my name alive and who would know the difference? It was Lillian who encouraged me to write when I lived in New York. It was Lillian who listened to my poetry without judgment when I moved to Chicago. It was Lillian who became my muse as well as my best friend. And it was Lillian who, in a roundabout way, was responsible for my meeting my second husband.

I had given some serious thought to the subject of marriage—what had gone wrong with my first one, what I wanted to look for in a man the next time, and what I needed to avoid. First and foremost, he had to be a nondrinker, this was paramount for me; I was not going to make the same mistake again. I also wanted someone with a compatible career, like a manager or a producer but, please, not an actor. Being "Mrs. Somebody" had no appeal for me; I would feel more secure if I were the "somebody."

I also saw acting as a job, not a way of life. I had never been one to play the game of acting all fluttery and helpless when a man was around. Nor was I willing to deliberately lose a game, in sports or cards, so that the man could win, as the women's magazines of the time advised. The thought of being in a relationship, in which I had to pretend to be less than I was, was abhorrent to me. I wanted to be the best that I could be. I decided that the kind of man who understood this, and encouraged me in this, was the only kind of man I could be happy with.

Lillian knew just about every Australian in New York and would try to hook us up whenever she could. She introduced me to Martin St. James, who was working in America as a stage hypnotist. Having recently discovered Edgar Cayce in a book on psychic healing, I was keen to converse with someone pursuing metaphysical research as well, but any discussion on the subject with Martin was useless. He was strictly a showman.

Martin and his wife, Lee, had a child close in age to Traci and as the St. James family lived only four blocks from us in Greenwich Village, we socialized and exchanged babysitting favors fairly often.

Our proximity to Washington Square Park provided Traci with daily access to a playground, which was a godsend. It was our first New York summer and we were sweltering in our corner suite—two furnished rooms and a bathroom—on the top floor of a rather old and tired hotel.

During the months we lived there, I experienced two events which would shake me up. I no longer recall the sequence in which they occurred, but both left me feeling helpless and vulnerable.

One was the death of an elderly woman, a longtime resident of the hotel. I didn't know her but she had been dead for several days before the smell alerted someone in management. As our suite was on the eleventh floor, we always used the lift. I had the misfortune to enter it immediately after the stretcher had exited and I will never forget the smell as long as I live. Was that how I was going to end up? Dying old and unwanted in a cheap hotel? It was a shattering thought and made me question the wisdom of leaving my family in Australia.

The other experience was far worse and involved an envelope that arrived from Melbourne. The contents were a letter and a bundle of press clippings with a note attached, in my mother's handwriting, telling me to read the letter first.

My sister's husband had committed suicide. She was devastated, and the family had closed ranks around her. The press reportage was speculative and insensitive. I felt guilty that I was so far away and not there to hold and comfort my now fatherless nephew. Tony had turned eleven only days before.

The last time I had seen them all together as a family had been at their new home. My brother-in-law had worked his way up the ladder and was now producing Melbourne's top TV show, *In Melbourne Tonight*. He was in a position which gave him a good salary, respect, and an outlet for his creative talents. I had spent that last afternoon with Toni sewing some curtains for her while she prepared the evening meal and waited for her husband to come home. After dinner I had left in a taxi and, as the two of them waved good-bye at the front door with their arms around each other, it occurred to me that my sister had been blessed with everything I could ever want.

What on earth had gone wrong? Should I be there with her now? Would it be of help if Traci and I returned to Melbourne? What was the right thing to do? A phone call to my mother assured me that everything was under control, and while she missed me and hoped to see me soon, there was no reason to cut my trip short. The funeral was over. It would serve no purpose for me to come back. There was nothing I could do.

Things were no cheerier for me in the employment department. An occasional check from Aunty Nell, usually when it was least expected and most needed, helped keep me going, but with my twenty-fifth birthday looming, I had to face some hard facts. I was doing the odd gig here and there and, thanks to Arthur Frommer's *New York on Five Dollars a Day*, we were surviving, but only just, and the work was dispiriting.

One date I played was at a club in Rhode Island where the comic and I had no audience at all. Only one man had shown up, and he was sitting at the bar with his back to the stage, watching a ball game on TV. I figured the show would be canceled that night, but the club owner insisted that as we were being paid we should do the show anyway. I sat in the audience for the comic and laughed, and he sat in the audience for me and applauded. Now I realize the club was probably a Mafia money-laundering operation.

I still had our return tickets to Sydney, and it was looking very much like I would have to swallow my pride and use them. How ironic that I had finally been getting work offers back home before I left. The exposure from the contest had opened doors for me in Sydney that I'd been trying to break down for years, and I had given up everything to come to America. Going home now, I would have to start all over again.

Martin St. James and his wife, Lee, decided to throw a surprise/rent party at their place for my twenty-fifth birthday. Entrance at the door was five dollars toward my rent, and the surprise was that I truly did not know about it. I'd have been mortified. One of the guests was a gate-crasher who'd overheard someone else being invited; on top of that, as I later learned, he didn't pay the five-dollar entry fee. That should have been my first clue.

He had come with a friend. The two of them spoke jive together and, as I had yet to hook up with any other American musicians, this was literally music to my ears. He was a non-drinker and very knowledgeable about jazz. I was pleasantly surprised when he told me he managed Oscar Brown Jr., who'd hosted a half-hour jazz TV series that had been popular with Australian musicians. The show was fairly avant-garde, and he in turn was pleasantly surprised that I was familiar with it. Oscar was currently starring in a long-running stage pro-duction in Chicago and would not be needing him as a manager for many months. Consequently, he was using the free time now available to him to learn more about the internal workings of a business he'd gotten into by default. For a modest salary, he was working as a secretary at a major talent agency in New York.

I was impressed that he wanted to improve himself, recognized education as an ongoing part of life, and was willing to take a big cut in salary and prestige to gain specialized knowledge. Had I known he was lying about his age, this should have been clue number two, but he was fun, he was funny, he was bright, and he was the best-looking guy at the party. Although I was tempted to spend more time hanging out with him and his friend, my one-date rule was still in effect.

I didn't give him my phone number, but he managed to track me down at my hotel the next evening. After putting Traci to bed, I set up the chessboard and challenged him to a game. I checkmated him in six moves, and he left soon after. I figured that was that.

The following evening he showed up again, and again we played chess. This time he anticipated some of my moves, and it took me longer to beat him.

The evening after that was Halloween, which is not celebrated in Australia but would become my favorite American holiday. He insisted we take Traci trick-or-treating around Greenwich Village. With my three-year-old daughter wearing a borrowed lion costume topped with a Frankenstein mask, we did just that. Afterward, once again, the chessboard was set up and this time, to my surprise and delight, he beat me. Obviously he had gone to the library, checked out some books on chess, and boned up on some slick moves. This was intriguing. Here was a man who not only wasn't threatened by an intelligent woman, he found me a challenge! Someone like that, I reasoned, would always keep me at my best.

The next night, uninvited and unannounced, he was standing at my door with his suitcases, having left his mother's home in the Bronx for the bright lights of Manhattan. I wasn't looking for a roommate but it was late and it was cold. I let him stay the night. I figured we'd straighten things out in the morning, right? Wrong. For the next fifteen years, he would dominate my life, and I would be the one who was eventually forced to leave.

He was working at the William Morris Agency in the personal-appearance department, so he often had tickets for concerts by artists on their roster. As I had always been a jazz fan, I tended to dismiss rock or folk artists as three-chord wonders who couldn't change key without a capo. In other words, I was an elitist musical snob. Now I was seeing and hearing rock musicians like the Blues Project, who were fusing genres, electrifying acoustic instruments, and knocking down musical walls I hadn't known were there. This was what I had come to America for—to be stimulated by innovative ideas and be immersed in a creative atmosphere where I was away from the "knockers."

That autumn I would also see Simon and Garfunkel in concert and be impressed with the purity and simplicity of their performance. I would have taken any job that came along at that time but the idea of appearing solo in a concert format was beginning to take form and shape in my mind.

He found a nice little furnished apartment in Chelsea's London Terrace that was being sublet for four months. It would be a better environment for Traci than where we were staying now—there was a preschool on the roof, and the building had an indoor pool, to list only two advantages. Of course, we would have to pose as a family unit to get the lease. Didn't I see this movie before? Traci was already calling him Daddy.

Had I known he was only twenty-two, maybe I'd have thought harder about what was happening, but I wouldn't find out his true age for months—and then, only by accident. In any case, I was not in a bargaining position. I had already been visited by two people from immigration wondering why I kept going back and forth to Canada and how I was supporting myself. Fortunately, a large chec k from Aunty Nell had arrived shortly before they did; it was sitting on the tabletop; and Traci was extremely adorable that day. I had no desire to repeat the experience, however, nor could I afford to keep going back to Canada in order to renew a visa which was about to run out again. I needed to move on.

Did I mention that the four months' rent for the apartment had to be paid in advance? And in order to accomplish that, he cashed in our return plane tickets. That should have been clue number three, and by now, my alarm bells were clanging but it was too late. There was no longer any question of going home. I was stranded in a foreign country with a three-year-old, no other family, no job, and no visa. He had me right where he wanted me. By the time our four-month lease was up, another apartment had become available on the other side of London Terrace, and we moved across the courtyard.

# CHAPTER 19

# *Chicago*

After Number Two was fired from two jobs in a row, it seemed that the best option for him was to take a position he'd been offered in Chicago. Maybe there would be a chance for me to do something there too. I was not impressed with the work I was being offered out of New York. Dates in the Catskills didn't seem to be any better than the club circuit in Sydney, and I hated having to follow comics whose jokes kept getting bluer when they didn't get any laughs.

Showbiz was changing with the influence of sixties music and fashions, and America was becoming increasingly polarized. The baby boomers, the generation that followed World War II, were now in college. Many of them were souls who had reincarnated after dying in that war and they were determined not to have their lives cut short again so soon by another one. The opposition to an increasing military presence in South

Vietnam was passionate, and the growing divide in the United States was political, generational, and cultural.

In September 1967, we moved to Chicago, and I didn't know where I fitted in. I had been too young to be a beatnik and now I was too old to be a hippie. Musically, I was turned on by the newer singer-songwriters like Tim Hardin, Van Morrison, Kenny Rankin, and Buffy Sainte-Marie. Introducing this sort of material into the old nightclub format would be different, but I didn't see why it couldn't be done.

I was still legally married to my first husband. Between the five-year mandatory separation period, filing procedures, waiting for a court date, and then the wait for a decree absolute, it took about seven years to get a divorce in Australia in those days. Number Two had already told everyone that he and I were married, and he was pressuring me to make it legal.

One option was to go down to Mexico and get an uncontested divorce there, which would be valid in the United States. However, there were two problems with this solution. One was that I would not be able to re-enter the United States from Mexico because I had already overstayed my visa. The other was that a Mexican divorce was not recognized in Australia, and if I went back there, I could be charged with bigamy.

The long-awaited green card finally became a reality, thanks to my friend in Philadelphia, Frank Day. We had kept in touch. He found me an immigration lawyer and acted as my sponsor;

then, following a Mexican divorce, Number Two and I flew to Las Vegas and were married at City Hall by a justice of the peace. Our two witnesses were the official's secretary and the cabdriver. We then went and saw some shows. After I couldn't stay awake any longer, he left me in the room and spent the rest of the night gambling. Some honeymoon.

By the spring of 1968 I was working in a revue at the Happy Medium Theater on Chicago's Rush Street, with Tom Patchett and Jay Tarses. They would go on to become a successful writing team in television and movies but, at that time, they were still hungry young comics, eager to make it. I had been hired to do a three-song set in the show, and two other girls were hired to work in the comedy sketches. One of them had no previous stage experience. She was hired simply because she had enormous breasts, which Jay thought were enormously funny. I think he was less amused when she failed to show up one Saturday night and was never heard from again. Her clothes were left hanging in the dressing room unclaimed. She took her breasts with her.

Fortunately, the other woman in the show and I were stone professionals and we both ad-libbed our way through the evening, splitting up the absent girl's lines between us and, where necessary, referring to one of her characters, Dorcas, as being in another room. When the other girl also left, I was left having to do her lines as well—now with two characters offstage. We had started out as a cast of five in a show called

*Four on the Floor* and ended up as a cast of three in what became a tight, ultra-low-budget, but still good little revue.

Tom and Jay were both married with young daughters, and Traci sometimes played with Jamie Tarses, Jay's eldest. We decided to try and see if Jamie was ready for her first sleepover at our place. All was well until bedtime, when little Jamie wouldn't stop crying until her parents came to pick her up again. As an adult, she was one of the first women to run a television network in the United States.

I heard it on the radio during intermission of the revue one night. The year 1968 was an election year, and I was avidly following the political news. President Lyndon Johnson had announced that he would not run again, nor would he accept his party's nomination for President of the United States. This left the race wide open, and I fervently hoped that Senator Robert Kennedy would be the Democratic candidate. I believed that if he won the election, he would put an end to the war in Vietnam, a war that was deeply dividing the American people. The Democratic Convention was to be held in Chicago.

At that time in my life, I was practicing hatha yoga and meditating on a regular basis. Our apartment looked out over Lake Michigan, and I always found that being near water surrounded me with psychic energy.

This particular day, I had been thinking about the upcoming election before drifting into an alpha state. I saw the date June 6 edged in black and understood that it was for Bobby

Kennedy. It signified that he would be out of politics forever on that date. My conscious mind was unable or unwilling to face the significance of the black border and, because I knew that the California primary was around that date, I interpreted the vision to mean that Bobby would lose the election in California, retire from the race, and never again run for political office. This vision was followed by three days of paralyzing depression. I had no desire to dress, brush my hair, or move out of a chair. After the black cloud passed, I wondered what on earth had caused it.

The California primary came around, and I sat up to watch the election returns on television. Bobby had clearly won and, with his wife Ethel by his side at the Ambassador Hotel in Los Angeles, he thanked his supporters gathered in the ballroom for their efforts. He closed by saying, "Now it's on to Chicago and let's win there!" as he flashed the peace sign and left the podium. I flipped off the television and went to bed thrilled that he had won the primary and that my prediction had been wrong.

The next morning I opened my door to find the newspaper blaring headlines about Senator Kennedy being shot. I had turned off the television and gone to bed only moments before all hell had broken loose at the Ambassador. Bobby was in critical condition with a gunshot wound to the head. I was glued to the TV set waiting for further bulletins from the hospital. Once it was confirmed that he was already brain-dead, his family decided to have him taken off life support.

The primary had been on June 4, he had been shot on June 5, and his heart had stopped beating on June 6. My vision had been accurate, and I now understood why I had been so deeply depressed for three days. If hatha yoga and meditating made me this sensitive, I wanted no part of either one, and I stopped the practice of both for a while.

# CHAPTER 20

# California, Here I Come

The following month, July, we moved to Los Angeles. Having survived a Chicago winter, I was looking forward to the warmer climate.

Number Two had taken a job with a new management company in Beverly Hills, and I was hoping to get work in Los Angeles. While I was in Chicago I had been signed to the William Morris Agency by Harry Kalcheim in the New York office. However, I found it meant absolutely nothing to the William Morris guys in the West Coast office. The young agent who had been assigned to me suggested that I try to get myself a gig at one of the little clubs around town so he could come and see me work. He had to be kidding. I was already a client. This was his town. Wasn't it his job to procure work for me?

. . .

After I moved to California, Lillian Roxon continued to send me news clippings and articles about the rising feminist tide. I had read Betty Friedan's book, *The Feminine Mystique* (1963), and understood how women had been conquered and divided, each isolated in our own little kitchen—the room which was once the center of the home, where generations of women had labored side by side. After lying dormant for nearly fifty years, the seeds of the feminist movement were bursting into life again. Thoughts and feelings I had harbored in secret, for years, were now being articulated by other women. Some of it I found trivial, like the Miss/Mrs./Ms. issue. "Mr." and "Ms." still divided humans by gender, so what was the point? Nevertheless, since I was a child I had deeply resented the domination and exploitation of women by men. It was wonderful to know, at last, that I was not alone.

When I thought about the women in my family, I realized that they had always been the strong ones, keeping the family together through two world wars and the Depression. It was the women who had held jobs and done their own housework. My mother could pluck a chicken, skin a rabbit, and repair electrical equipment. It was Mum who had taught me, when my grandmother died, how to prepare the body for burial. Nowadays, such functions are always handled by personnel in funeral homes, but to women of the older generation it was the last act of devotion one performed in this life for a departed loved one. She had instructed me in how to wash the body and plug up all the bodily openings using cotton wool and tweezers. Then the jaw would be strapped up before the body was dressed and groomed for showing. I had grown up surrounded by capable, resilient women and what a blessing this had been for me.

If women could only look on all other women as their sisters, what a difference we could make. We could transcend all barriers of country, continent, creed, and color in creating a new world. A world in which true family values are honored, and children, education, the elderly, and health care are given priority over developing weapons of mass murder. It was heartening to think that if women could unite, we had the power to make the planet a safer and saner place. First, however, it would be necessary to build up women's self-confidence, and I needed to start with my own.

In Los Angeles, I was having a hard time of it. It was not helping matters at home that Number Two had a job requiring him to find work for other artists, some of whose talents were questionable, or that he was on the road so much. It placed quite a strain on the relationship.

The music business had begun to split into different factions, and there weren't too many openings for a singer. With the amount of acting work available, especially in film and television, I thought I might have a better chance of employment if I sought work as an actress. However, I didn't have the kind of "look" that casting agents seemed to go for and often drove home in tears.

After nine months of fruitless auditions and constant rejection, I decided to go back to school to try to develop a more marketable skill. My inability to get work in show business puzzled me. Even if I was completely without talent, surely all those years of experience should count for something? But, if I wasn't going to make it in show business, I needed to find something else which I could do well enough to earn a living. I had to be good at something.

After taking a night school class at Hollywood High to accustom myself to American higher education, I began taking courses through the University of California at Los Angeles Extension. I was re-entering academia at a level that was three grades above the one I had failed to complete thirteen years before. The difference was that now I was motivated to learn. Also, the life experience I had acquired along the way gave me a much larger frame of reference for what I was learning. I started with courses that had no prerequisites and moved up from there. It was gratifying to discover how high educational standards had been in Australia; I'd received the best foundation possible. I loved being back in school and being able to study subjects that interested me.

As well as a psychology class, I signed up for UCLA's first-ever course in parapsychology with Dr. Thelma Moss. I'd read about the work that Dr. J. B. Rhine had pioneered in extra sensory perception (ESP) at Duke University in North Carolina, and I was curious. I was not the only one. After hundreds of people enrolled, it became necessary to move the course from a classroom to an auditorium. Our first assignment was to write about a psychic experience, if we had had one. I decided to write about my out-of-body experience at age eleven. From the hundreds of accounts that were submitted to her, Dr. Moss read three of them out loud to the class. I was stunned that mine was one of them.

Going back to school had been the right decision. After all those months of rejection, I loved that I could set a goal, work hard, and achieve a result, something certainly not guaranteed in show business. Attending the University of California and getting straight A's gave me back the confidence I'd lost from being out of work for so long. I started writing again; I wanted to get a message across about what I'd learned so far in the battle to survive; I wanted to give other women hope. After all, if I could do it, so could anyone.

# CHAPTER 21

# Capitol Gains

With the new decade of the seventies came the return of the solo performer, especially the singer-songwriter. Artists like James Taylor and Carole King were recording hugely successful albums. This was good for women, as we have more often tended to be soloists. Why is that? Record companies may not have been throwing the doors open for us, but at least the doors were no longer being slammed shut.

The comedian Flip Wilson had become a good friend and respected colleague when I was based in Chicago and he was playing at Mr. Kelly's, the city's top nightclub. After I moved to California, our families would sometimes get together for weekend barbecues. Flip was responsible for a major breakthrough in my performing career; in fact, he was involved in a second big break for me too. When he was filling in for Johnny Carson as host on *The Tonight Show,* Flip invited me as his guest on the show, and I was spotted by Artie Mogull, head of Artists & Repertoire at Capitol Records. He offered me a contract to record two songs: two sides on one 45-rpm single.

Absolutely everything was now riding on this small opening into the record business. I had to find a song that sounded like a hit, one that hadn't already been done to death by other artists.

I was watching a late-night talk show when Mac Davis, a rising young singer-songwriter, came on and sang a new song he had written called "I Believe in Music." The song had a catchy hook and an upbeat attitude, and I thought it sounded perfect for me. Okay, I was set for the A-side; now I needed something for the B-side.

Artie Mogull suggested that I sing the ballad from *Jesus Christ Superstar,* the newly released rock opera album. I was not in favor of the idea. As well as the original album version of the song being available, another singer had already released it as a cover single. My reasoning was that I would be third in the race, radio probably wouldn't play a female ballad anyway, and why would I want to waste this opportunity on a whiny song structured around a vocally awkward major-sixth musical interval? I was persuaded that if I really wanted to record at all, I had better get on with it. Besides, no one ever listened to the B-side anyway.

• • •

I remember that recording session as if it were yesterday. It was held at A&M's studios at La Brea and Sunset in Hollywood. This location had originally been Charlie Chaplin's studio, where he had made his first silent films. That evening I was unusually nervous and felt terribly pressured. I was already twenty-nine years old and was trying to get into a young person's game. I had waited years for this shot and I didn't think there would be another one. Tonight was my last chance for a hit record.

I stood in the control room and listened to the playback in utter dismay. My nervousness permeated the track, and "I Believe in Music" sounded more like "I Believe in Terror." With a sinking heart, I began listening to the B-side. Strangely, all the emotions I had been feeling that night worked for the ballad. The self-doubt had given my voice a plaintive quality that made the lyrics more believable. There was no question that it was the stronger of the two tracks. The decision was made to release "I Don't Know How to Love Him" as the A-side. I figured that was the end of that. Well, at least I'd had the chance to record.

WDRC, a little radio station in Hartford, Connecticut, began playing my version of "I Don't Know How to Love Him." In those days, you could telephone a radio station direct from anywhere across America without the receiver knowing the caller's point of origin. WDRC began receiving a lot of calls from Los Angeles, California. My fifteen-year-old nephew, actor Tony Sheldon—who was visiting from Sydney and already adept at different voices and accents—made quite a few calls. So did other friends. I confess I may have made a call or two myself. The station began reporting that it was getting heavy phone requests for the Helen Reddy version of the ballad from *Jesus Christ Superstar*. The snowball began rolling. Two other stations went with my version. Product started moving in the stores. I hit the charts.

Where Capitol Records was concerned, I was now in a unique position. Record companies back then looked on hit singles primarily as marketing tools to sell albums, which was where they really made their money. Capitol suddenly found themselves with a hit artist and no product. The race was on to get me into the studio and an album into the stores as quickly as possible. First, they had to sign me up to a new contract—I was going to record an album at last.

I was overjoyed at the opportunity I'd been given. I had witnessed the power that song lyrics had to inspire social change. The protest songs of the sixties had certainly illustrated that point. On my album I wanted music that not only showcased new, young songwriters but also songs that reflected my evolving consciousness.

I searched for lyrics that reflected the pride I felt in being female and descended from so many strong women. Where were the songs that celebrated that? It seemed there weren't any. There were lyrics like, "I am woman, you are man. I am weak, so you can be stronger than," or a truly dreadful song called "Born a Woman" with the lyrics, "When you're born a woman, you're born to be lied to, cheated on and treated like dirt . . . but when your man comes home you're glad it happens that way, because to be his woman no price is too great to pay." Young girls were being indoctrinated into accepting domestic abuse as if it were a man's divine right. This was something that not only had to be stopped, it had to be reversed.

It dawned on me that I would have to write what needed to be said myself. Did I feel up to the task? Not really, but I remember lying in bed with the phrase "I am strong, I am invincible, I am Woman" going over and over inside my head. I wasn't even too sure what invincible meant, so I decided the phrase must be inspiration from above. The rest of the song I had to work for.

Even though I was only one voice, I knew I spoke for many women. To express that singular collective, I chose the words, "I am Woman, hear me roar" to start the song with what, I thought, was an obvious reference to the roar of the crowd. How easily we can be misunderstood. Although the phrase has long since passed into the lexicon, I hope it's not too late to correct the impression that some still have of me as Jungle Jane with delusions of leonine grandeur.

I wrote lyrics for two verses and two choruses but was not happy with what I was coming up with melodically. "I Am Woman" was sounding like something John Philip Sousa might have written and I had no plans to record with a marching band. Deciding that I was too close to the material, I cast around for someone with no emotional involvement to take a crack at it, preferably a male.

An Aussie band called the Executives was trying to break into the music scene in L.A. Instead, the band broke up as some of its members pursued solo careers. In the meantime, they were a lot of fun; I remember playing a game of water polo in their hotel pool, involving wives and girlfriends, that was hilarious and reminded me so much of home. I chose Ray Burton, a guitarist with the group, to see what he could come up with melodically for "I Am Woman." I also gave him the lyric sheet for another song I'd written called "Best Friend."

I really liked what Ray composed for "Best Friend," a lovely, lilting melody that flowed along and seemed to capture the mood of the lyrics very well. A few years later I would sing it as Sister Ruth in the film *Airport '75*. However, I found the melody he wrote for "I Am Woman" had the same problem as the one I had come up with and concluded that the fault lay in the words.

Capitol Records informed me that my first LP was to be titled *I Don't Know How to Love Him* in order to capitalize on the popularity of the single. For the other nine slots on the album, I was advised to record the nine highest-rating songs currently on the charts, as "name recognition" would guarantee sales. The chance to make an album was something I had waited a long, long time for and, over the years, I had accumulated a list of songs I hoped to record one day. That day had finally come, and I was not about to be told what songs I should sing. This would probably be the only album I ever made. I wanted to be proud of it.

And I would be.

The album cover photo of me in a long red dress, surrounded by green ivy, was taken under a Hollywood freeway underpass up the street from the Capitol Records tower on Vine Street. Although album liner notes, once *de rigueur,* were hardly seen anymore, I wanted some for my first album. Lillian Roxon, by now the published author of *Rock Encyclopaedia,* agreed to write a blurb for the back cover. She began with, "There is a certain sort of woman who is remarkably without artifice and remarkably without fear. . . ." Lillian knew me better than I knew myself.

When the first box of LPs arrived at my house, I slept with one under my pillow that night. It had been five years since I first arrived in New York with a three-year-old, two suitcases, and $230; and twenty-five years since I used to run up onstage at the Tivoli Theatre in Perth. I'd earned it.

With my success, my husband finally decided to become my full-time manager. Now we could truly be a show business team; I would be responsible for the show and he the business. I was sensitive to the fact that some of his friends were giving him flak over the feminism issue and I admired him for being confident enough in his manhood to ignore it. I always stressed that we were equal partners in a career venture.

.   .   .

In the first four months of 1972 I went back and forth to Europe three times. I had dreamed of being in Paris for so many years yet in real life it was almost a nightmare. The representative from the French record company who had been assigned to look after me fancied himself as a Lothario and I was not amused by his running his car up over the sidewalk while he leaned out the window making disgusting sounds at female pedestrians. Dinner on the first night seemed inter-minably long, and I couldn't wait to get away from him. I was not accustomed to the European style of eating late and lingering over several courses nor, after a long flight, did I want to sit at all. What I wanted was to walk the streets of Paris and smell the city—every city has its own smell—not see it through the backseat window of a car. I pleaded a headache and got back to my hotel as quickly as I could.

My husband and I had gone to bed and I was lying there still fuming when I suddenly asked him if he was awake. When he answered me, I said, "I'm not going to let that fool spoil my first night in Paris. Come on, let's get up and get dressed and go out again."

It was January and freezing cold so we bundled up and set off down the Champs Elysées on foot. It was almost midnight, and nothing seemed to be open except for one little sidewalk café that was getting ready to close up. We each had a cup of hot chocolate before walking back to the hotel again. I was now happy. I'd swapped a bad memory for a good one and felt like the captain of my own fate once more.

.   .   .

In the United States I would have a second Top 30 hit off my first album with Van Morrison's "Crazy Love." That combined with the success of "I Don't Know How to Love Him" in the UK, France, Holland, Germany, Sweden, Denmark, and Belgium, meant that, in me, Capitol Records had an artist on their roster who was a guaranteed moneymaker. Six months after I'd recorded my first album, I was back in the studio to record a second. One of the songs on that album, "No Sad Song," also made it into the Top 40 and I would record it in French—"Plus de Chanson Triste"—as well as English.

By the time of my third trip to Europe, in April, I would be in the first weeks of pregnancy. Between that and the constant flying, jet lag from the eight-hour time change, and having to hit the ground running as soon as I arrived, I was nearing exhaustion. In Amsterdam, when I was about to board the short flight back across the Channel to our base in London, I started to hemorrhage. After we were airborne, my husband informed the flight attendant. She told the pilot, who requested and received permission to fly at a lower altitude— you bleed more at higher altitudes—and radioed ahead for an ambulance to meet me on the tarmac. By now I was convinced that the baby was already dead. I was highly emotional.

On landing, I was taken immediately to the medical facility at the airport, and the doctor there suggested he perform a D and C on the spot. My husband, whose father and grandfather had been obstetricians, wanted a second opinion from someone who didn't have frayed cuffs. He asked for the name of the Queen's obstetrician and ordered an ambulance to take me to St. Mary's Hospital in Paddington. There, I was given a massive dose of folic acid and tests which showed that the baby was still alive.

Although I was suffering from exhaustion and would require days of badly needed bed rest, the pregnancy was safe.

# CHAPTER 22

# If at First You Don't Succeed

obin Morgan, a leading American feminist writer, had compiled a collection of women's writings into book form and called it *Sisterhood Is Powerful*. Bernard Slade turned it into a screenplay and called it *Stand Up and Be Counted*. It was produced as a film by Mike Frankovich for Columbia with a great ensemble cast. I was invited to an advance screening as there was interest in using my recording of "I Am Woman" over the credits. I loved the film and the fact that its strong feminist point of view was softened by some lovely comedic moments. Given that the media had been branding feminists as humorless, that was a definite plus factor.

The decision makers at Capitol Records thought that, in case the film was a hit, they should release "I Am Woman" as a single. Although the song was included on my first album, the musical arranger hadn't known what to do with it, either. It clearly was not hit-single material and got no airplay at all. I used it as an opening song whenever I performed live, and it was always well received: I also noticed that the song was being singled out for mention in fan mail.

The problem was that I had only written and recorded two verses and two choruses; the song was way under the three-minute mark, the length of the average single. I would need to write an extra verse and chorus and rerecord the song and, as long as this was happening, why not do a new arrangement as well? Jay Senter had the fresh ears and new approach that the song had been needing, and his choice of Jim Horn as arranger for the trombone charts was inspired. Now the song had spunk and style.

As events unfolded, it was the original recording of "I Am Woman" that was featured on the soundtrack of *Stand Up and Be Counted*. Touted as a "women's lib comedy," the movie opened and closed the same week. The new version of "I Am Woman" was to head up my third album for Capitol and it became a number-one hit single. Previously, I had had three single recordings make it into the Top 40, but "I Am Woman" would be my first number one. It was also the first in five years for Capitol Records, which had not had a number-one hit single since Bobbie Gentry's "Ode to Billie Joe."

In the seventies—before music videos and MTV—music was still very much an audio medium. A record lived or died by radio airplay, which is how payola—the paying of cash or gifts in return for airplay—was born, and promotion men got to be so powerful. When my revamped version of "I Am Woman" first came out, I wasn't getting any radio exposure—DJs and program directors hated "women's libbers." I had to turn to television. The prime-time television variety shows of the era favored nightclub performers over contemporary recording artists, with rare exceptions. While I sang "I Am Woman" nineteen times on different television programs, women began calling radio stations and requesting the song, thereby forcing airplay.

With "I Am Woman," I had touched a nerve, and women were responding. Through the medium of popular music, I was able to connect with all kinds of women—women who had been initially turned off by some of the more strident feminist voices; or women who believed they were already liberated. ("My husband lets me do whatever I want. I only have to ask.") They might be listening to the car radio driving to the supermarket or picking the kids up from school, and the positive message in "I Am Woman" would seep into their subconscious. The acceptance of female equality was reaching a critical mass. Remember, this was back when newspaper classifieds still listed jobs by gender; when a woman could not get a credit card in her own name or obtain a mortgage. Usually, the reason given for this financial strangulation was that, "If the wife falls pregnant, she won't be able to keep up the payments." As I was both pregnant and the breadwinner, that was hardly going to be happening in my case. I pressed the issue and became one of the first women in the United States to have a credit card in my own name and a mortgage. Many others would soon follow suit. "I Am Woman" had entered the Top 100, moved up to 99, then to 98, then 97, and then dropped right off the charts.

I was around five months pregnant and playing at a little club called Marvelous Marv's in Denver.

My husband, wearing his manager's hat, decided to fly back to Los Angeles and see if he could rekindle interest from the promotion team at the record company. It worked. And so did I. I spent most of my pregnancy on the road and made my last television appearance only two weeks before giving birth. My opening act in Denver was Alex Harvey, a singer-songwriter who collaborated with Larry Collins. Sometime later, I would go on to record two of their songs, one of which was "Delta Dawn." It would become a number-one pop hit for me.

The year 1972 was an election year in the United States and an exciting one for women. A black congresswoman from New York, Shirley Chisholm, was running for president and, though it was highly unlikely that she would be nominated at the Democratic Convention, she could potentially gather enough delegates to have a voice in the decision making. Perhaps women's issues, like equal pay for equal work, education, childcare, care of the elderly, and health care, might find their way onto the party platform. The possibility galvanized women. Although 53 percent of the American population was female, those numbers were not reflected in the population of the Congress, which was overwhelmingly male and white. I admired Shirley Chisholm's courage enormously and thought she had taken a giant leap forward for women.

Ultimately, it would be the male members of the Black Caucus who would block her. Most successful women of color I know claim they have experienced more prejudice because of their sex than their race. Let's not forget that the abolition of slavery after the Civil War only gave all *men* the right to vote. Extending this right to any *woman* had to wait for the twentieth century and the female suffrage movement.

If you had told me thirty years ago that in the United States in the year 2004, no female presidential candidate had ever been nominated by either of the duopolistic parties, that there was not even a vice-presidential candidate currently under consideration, or that the only female to have thrown her hat into the presidential ring would be a black Congress member, I would not have believed you.

It is hard to believe, in the twenty-first century, that the United States of America has yet to ratify the Equal Rights Amendment, first proposed in 1923, which would include women in the Constitution. Then again, back in the old days, they weren't in a hurry to give women the vote, either. New Zealand and Australian women could vote well before their American sisters. One of the arguments trotted out at the time against women's suffrage was the threat it would pose to the stability of the

American family. If the wife supported a different candidate from her husband, it was felt that this would lead to dissension, divorce, the disintegration of the family unit, and the end of known civilization. If, on the other hand, a husband and wife agreed on the choice of a candidate, well, the husband was already representing his little lady at the polls now, wasn't he?

American women would face similarly ridiculous arguments in 1972, some of them from their own gender. One woman, a paid political lobbyist, flew all over the United States appearing on TV interview shows decrying the dangers of female equality. It would lead to horrors like unisex toilets, she would say with a shudder. She extracted a lot of mileage out of that one. Unfortunately, none of the interviewers thought to ask her if she had ever located a ladies' room on any of the commercial aircraft she was flying around in. Unisex toilets have been a fact of life on airplanes for as long as I've been flying. They're called restrooms, and they offer the individual a lot more privacy than stalls. Her argument had a hole in it that you could, frankly, fly a plane through, but no one ever called her on it. The Equal Rights Amendment was defeated by only a few votes and, as of this writing, has yet to be reintroduced.

Words have great power and a word like "sex" conjures up all manner of things in people's minds. I believe that a simple change of the Amendment's wording, substituting the word "gender" for the word "sex," would have seen it be ratified.

·  ·  ·

How do we recognize sexism and how do we eliminate it from our lives?

Because our society has become more aware of racism, the usage of racist terms has become socially unacceptable. We now recognize the power that words have to divide us. Well, prejudice is prejudice in any form. If you are unsure as to whether or not a statement is sexist, all you have to do is give it the race test. Simply substitute "white" for "male" and "black" for "female," and the prejudice becomes obvious.

One thing we can choose to do is use terminology that is inclusive rather than divisive, for example "children" instead of "boys and girls," "siblings" instead of "brothers and sisters," "spouses" instead of "husbands and wives," "people" instead of "men and women," and "Good evening, everyone" instead of "Good evening, ladies and gentlemen."

As a moral issue, abortion will be debated as long as humankind is able to debate. I respect all points of view as being valid to the holder. What concerns me is abortion as a legal and political issue. I am against all reproductive laws for the same reason I am against the draft. I believe that legal ownership of one's body is the most basic civil and human right. Without it, we are all slaves to whatever government is in power at any time.

One of Adolf Hitler's first actions, on assuming control of the German government, was to outlaw abortion and institute the draft. With one stroke of the pen, he controlled the bodies of women and men and, through them, power over life and death. Hitler would go on to create breeding farms for humans who were of favored Aryan stock while sending to their deaths millions who were not.

President Ceaucescu, in Romania, decided that every Romanian woman should have at least four children. Birth control was outlawed, and any woman wishing to leave the country, for whatever reason, had to undergo a gynecological examination to determine if she was pregnant before being allowed to depart. If she was pregnant, she would be examined again, upon her return, to make sure she hadn't had an abortion while she was gone. Any woman unfortunate enough to have a miscarriage could be charged with murder.

China's leaders, on the other hand, want to reduce their country's population, and millions of women have been forced to abort their pregnancies. China and Romania appear to have had opposite policies but, in fact, they were the same. Whether forcing women to bear children against their will or forcing them to abort their pregnancies against their will, both governments were Communist regimes that considered women's bodies, and the product of women's bodies, to be the property of the state. As is the body of any soldier drafted and forced to kill or be killed.

I will say it again—legal ownership of one's own body is the most basic civil and human right. Without it, a free society cannot exist. We need legislation that will protect our individual, sovereign rights against all enemies, foreign *and* domestic.

# CHAPTER 23

# The Best of Times;
# the Worst of Times

Many people assumed that 1973 was the best year of my life. Little do they know. I would say it was the most eventful; it was certainly the longest. Framing it were a birth in December of 1972 and a death in January of 1974.

After nine months of slowly and steadily climbing the pop charts, "I Am Woman" finally reached the number-one slot in December of 1972. However, the unquestionable highlight for me that week was the arrival of my son, Jordan. In my mind, the overwhelming joy that comes with the birth of a much-wanted child far outweighed any career triumphs. The joy was tempered, however, by the fact that my parents in Australia were 9,000 miles away and unable to see their grandson.

There was certainly a huge difference in the circumstances in which my two children, born ten years apart, came into the world. When my daughter was born, I was unemployed and collecting a pension. Her bassinet was purchased secondhand at auction for three pounds and repainted; an oddment end of tulle was used for a new mosquito net. Her entire layette, including blankets, was handmade by me. When my son was born, I was on the verge of making my first million and able to shop for whatever was needed at the best stores in town. I still made his baby blankets myself, however. The love was the same.

In May 1973 I became the first Australian to win the Grammy Award for Best Female Vocalist at an award ceremony televised from the original Grand Ole Opry in Nashville, the heart of the Bible Belt. I caused quite a stir when I closed my acceptance speech by saying, "I want to thank God because She makes everything possible."

Do I really believe that God is a woman? No more than I believe that God is a man. I believe the life force that brought us into being is beyond human form and without gender. I agree with Spinoza, who wrote, "God is not He Who is, but That Which is."

During the summer of 1973, Flip Wilson, by now the toast of network television with his own one-hour variety show, gave me another big break. He turned his time slot over to me for the show's eight-week summer hiatus period. This was the second big break Flip facilitated for me. While I was thrilled to have *The Helen Reddy Show* Thursdays at 8 P.M. on NBC-TV for eight weeks, a writers' strike left all of us having to write, rehearse, and film eight hours of variety television in front of a live audience in only three and a half weeks. And I was still breast-feeding.

While all this was going on, a simple consultation with an interior decorator about a bedspread had somehow turned into a major home renovation. For almost five months, I was without a kitchen. As it was time to start weaning the baby, I found myself heating bottles in a little machine plugged into an electrical outlet on the living-room floor. There's nothing like feeling as if you're on the road in your own home.

I will always be proud of the new ground we broke on NBC-TV. I was fortunate to inherit a lot of Flip's crew for the summer and so, I became the first woman on American television to have a show with a black director and a female producer. We also had the first woman handling camera cables on the studio floor. As for guest artists, we certainly weren't limited to the nightclub-type acts that were seen on most of the variety shows. I had a manager with a knack for spotting offbeat talent, and some of the acts the show featured that summer had never been seen on prime-time variety television before—people like the Pointer Sisters, Cheech and Chong, the Eagles, and Jim Croce, who was killed only weeks later. Also appearing were some of my favorites—the Modern Jazz Quartet, B.B. King, Chuck Berry, the Temptations, and Gladys Knight and the Pips.

Three more number-one hit singles would follow "I Am Woman"—what I would come to refer to as my trio of crazy ladies: "Delta Dawn," "Angie Baby," and "Ruby Red Dress."

"Leave Me Alone (Ruby Red Dress)" was a number I had to be talked into recording. I was not all that keen, as I thought the song was too much like "Delta Dawn" in storyline content. To me, the song was also overly simplistic in structure and the choruses mindlessly repetitive. Radio stations around the country were to run contests offering two free tickets to one of my shows to anyone who could call in with the correct answer to how many times I sang the phrase "Leave me alone" on the record. The answer was forty-three. When it became a hit, I was surprised.

"Angie Baby" was written by Alan O'Day, who would go on to have a vocal pop hit himself with another song he wrote, called "Undercover Angel." If I were going to teach a class on hit songwriting, I would use "Angie Baby" as my textbook. It had every element. First, it's a song about a girl and her relationship with her radio. What DJ or program director isn't going to go for that concept? They started playing the song on air as soon as they heard it. Second, the storyline is intriguing and deliberately obtuse, so listeners are free to draw their own conclusion—a mark of great art, some say. Many times I was asked what really happened at the end of the song and I would always counter by asking the inquirer what they thought happened. I heard some pretty wild answers, most of which told me more about the inquirer than they did about Angie. Third, the song had that all-important "hook," a repetitive melodic phrase that catches the memory. I would have to add that Joe Wissert, my producer, knew exactly what to do with the song and made a brilliant recording of it.

"You and Me Against the World" would become my second most-requested song after "I Am Woman." The first time I heard this song, written by Paul Williams and Kenny Ascher, I knew I was listening to a future standard. Kenny had written a haunting melody, and Paul's lyric sentiments were timeless. I wanted to sing it right away but there was a slight problem. Paul had written it as a man-to-woman love song, and when I tried to sing it as a woman-to-man love song, it sounded wrong. There was a paternalistic attitude built into the lyric which would not work with gender change. I was still determined to sing the song, however, so I had to take a different approach. It occurred to me that Paul's words would work perfectly for a parent-child love song and when I thought about how many of those there were, I was hard-pressed to come up with much except "Matelot" and "Mighty Lak a Rose." Stevie Wonder had yet to write his classic song of paternal pride, "Isn't She Lovely?" To me, it was an idea whose time had come around again. In order to clarify my intent and make the song even more moving, my producer, Tom Catalano, suggested that my daughter, Traci, speak on the recording at the beginning and end of the song. During the years I had been a single parent, it truly had been the two of us against the world.

To this day, I still receive mail from people who have lost a parent or child who tell me "You and Me Against the World" was "their song." I am always touched by these letters.

As well as the songs I chose, I also turned down the opportunity to record a few songs which would prove to be hits for other artists. The demo of "Killing Me Softly with His Song" sat on my turntable for months without being played because I didn't like the title. I protested that I couldn't sing "Don't It Make My Brown Eyes Blue"—even though I recognized it as a great song—because I didn't have brown eyes (?!). I rejected "I Honestly Love You" because I didn't feel comfortable, as a married woman with a jealous husband, singing a song about infidelity. And I found a demo of Barry Manilow's "Daybreak" at the bottom of a box. Across it I'd written "Could be good for TV production number."

One factor I had to keep in mind when touring was which songs were hits where. Local branches of the record company used to choose the tracks to be released as singles in their market, and when performing in those countries, I would have to remember to include in my show certain songs that may not have been hits anywhere else. Places with large Hispanic populations, like Mexico and the Philippines, tended to go for romantic ballads, for instance, while Italy turned out to be a tough market to crack. My tenth chart hit in the United States, "Angie Baby" was my first to finally score airplay on Italian radio.

.   .   .

When my sister called me in early July and asked if I was sitting down, I knew immediately one of our parents had died. I simply asked, "Which one?"

It was Mum. When I had last spoken to her, on the previous weekend, Mum had been depressed on the phone and full of complaints; she was cold, she was lonely, and so on. My suggestions—things like having her heater repaired, ringing up friends—were met with negative excuses. She was too into her depression to be reasoned with, and the call lasted no more than fifteen minutes. After I hung up the phone, I realized that I hadn't told her I loved her. It wasn't something that was said in our family. But the thought had occurred to me and I didn't act on it. How I wish I had called her right back and said those three simple words. Now, it was too late.

I took the first available flight to Melbourne. My mother had died at the height of the Australian winter, and because it was fogged in, we were unable to land at Melbourne airport. The plane landed instead at an old, disused army airfield about sixty miles from the city. All passengers were informed that we would have to wait for a bus to drive up from Melbourne through the fog, collect us and our baggage, and drive the sixty miles back again. Mum had been dead for several days before the neighbors noticed the newspapers outside her front door and called the police. Health laws demanded proper disposal of a body within a certain time limit, and the funeral had already been postponed until after my scheduled arrival. Fortunately, my husband at the time, a most resourceful man, was able to access a telephone and find a local cabdriver willing to take us to Melbourne right away. I had been awake for almost twenty-four hours and I hadn't cried yet. That would have to wait until afterward. For now I needed to stay strong to get through what had to be done.

There is a quality that actors have that sometimes enables them to rise above the limitations of the physical body. Stella Lamond had that quality. Someone who worked on the set of *Bellbird,* a long-running TV soap opera, related that one day on location, Mum had the shakes so badly, she couldn't put her makeup on. Some of the cast didn't know how she was going to get through the scene that was coming up. When the camera's red light went on, Mum's shaking stopped instantly. She gave her usual sterling performance and not until the red light went off did she start shaking again.

I had asked my mother on several occasions to come to California and live with me and her grandchildren. There was still hope in my heart, with alcoholism now recognized as a disease and not a character flaw, that once she was in America, Mum might be willing to accept help. But she would always answer, "I can't leave your father, Helen."

Dad was in an Army psychiatric hospital, suffering from dementia, and was kept heavily medicated in an effort to control his violent fits. He had been hospitalized nearly two years before and wasn't ever coming home again. Mum could not possibly manage him on her own without help. She no longer drove and depended on her in-laws to take her for hospital visits. I suspect another reason she wouldn't come to America. She still had her career. Although they might only use her once a month now, Stella Lamond was still Molly Wilson on *Bellbird*. She had been an actor since she was four years old and her self-worth and reason for being depended on her having a job.

I met my sister at our mother's flat and we embraced. Toni had been working in Queensland when she received the news. I had not cried and was determined to keep as busy as possible. I started clearing away some of the clutter that had built up around Mum in her last years. Her energy still lingered, and I could feel how isolated she had been at the end. My mother, the woman who had given birth to me, had moved out of the master bedroom and into the room my sister and I had shared. She had died in my bed. On the dressing table was one of the black-and-white photo postcards of Mum as Molly Wilson that the *Bellbird* publicity department sent out. She had been trying to sign it but had obviously abandoned the effort as her hand was shaking too badly. Suddenly I got the whole scenario. Mum used to carry these cards in her handbag to give to fans when she was recognized. She had been trying to autograph some in advance so as not to be embarrassed when she was asked for an autograph in person. My heart ached for her.

I had told Mum that I would come down and help her move out of the old flat and into something smaller and more modern. This was scheduled for November, when I was going to be in Australia for a concert tour and planned to bring both children with me. She had died in July without ever seeing my son. She had seen me win the Grammy on television and knew I had my own series in the States, for which I am thankful, but she did not live to see her younger daughter walk out on an Australian stage as an international star.

The loungeroom was cluttered with furniture—the original 1940s three-piece lounge suite, the huge cocktail bar with stools almost bisecting the room and, with its back to the fireplace, the convertible sofa bed I'd been given for my eighteenth birthday. Trying to immerse myself in a flurry of activity to keep my emotions under control, I was conscious that I had a funeral to get through. When I looked behind my old sofa bed into the fireplace, I could see a large, dead bouquet of flowers still wrapped in cellophane with card attached. They were the flowers I had sent her for Mother's Day. That did it. The dam burst, and I broke into racking sobs.

Some of Stella's fans, who knew and loved her as Molly Wilson, braved the chilly weather to attend her funeral service in the unheated church, Cairns Memorial, in East Melbourne. Maurie Fields, who had appeared in *Bellbird* with Mum, gave the eulogy, and I was glad to see friends of hers in attendance whom I had not come across in years.

The memory of the last time I saw my mother is something I will always cherish. It was the day that Traci and I were leaving to go back to the States after one of our trips home. And I wonder if she knew she was seeing us for the last time and that's why she'd made the effort. As the door opened and she walked down the hall toward me, I noticed that Mum was stone-cold sober. When she hadn't been drinking, she always looked years younger. She'd also taken time with her appearance; she was smartly dressed and wearing fresh make-up. The biggest difference however was her outlook; instead of the "poor me" victim attitude that I'd lost patience with years earlier, she was smiling and upbeat and the beautiful woman I remembered from my childhood. And that is the picture of her that I will hold in my heart forever.

While I was in Melbourne, I visited Dad in the hospital. I had been warned that he might not know me, as he had never asked after me. That was probably because he was aware only of whoever was in front of him. He recognized me as soon as I walked in the door and also greeted my husband by name. It shocked me to see that his hair, which had always been so curly, was now completely straight. He had not been told Mum had died, and I did not mention her name. When I showed him some photos of his infant grandson in America his face lit up. Mum had told him that I had had a baby, but he had thought she was talking about Traci. Holding in his hands the photos of me with both Traci and a baby, it penetrated that I now had two children. He kissed the photos and held them up to show one of his fellow patients in the visitors' sitting room. I had brought with me Dad's old pianist, Ted Muller, and although Ted didn't know any of my songs, he bravely played along as I sang for my father. It was to be the last time I would see Max Reddy. Ten weeks later, come September, I would be back in Melbourne for his funeral.

Dad might have lived on for many years in his own twilight world but the doctor told him, in a moment of lucidity, of Mum's passing. Dad had been under the illusion that he was in a convalescent hospital and that he was going home soon. The realization that there was now no home for him to go back to hit him hard. He lost the will to live and faded away quickly.

At my father's funeral, I found out how low tabloid journalists were prepared to go. As I was speaking with mourners leaving the church, thanking them for coming to pay their respects, a reporter came up to me, with pad and pen in hand, and asked if he could interview me. I told him it was hardly the time or the place for an interview. He persisted. My husband told him I would be returning to Australia for a concert tour in November and that we'd be happy to give him an exclusive interview at that time. He protested that he wanted to do the interview while I was in Australia on my current trip. I explained that I was leaving the church for the crematorium, after which I would be driving directly to the airport for my flight back to the States. He suggested that he go in the car with me so that he could do his interview in the back seat. At this point, my husband told the guy to f--- off and stop harassing me. In his subsequent piece, a "review" of my father's funeral, the reporter described me as being uncooperative with the press and my husband as using language which could not be printed in a family newspaper.

In between my parents' deaths, I lost my cherished friend, Lillian Roxon. In fact, the last time we spoke was when I told her of my mother's passing. The following month she would be gone herself, dying of an asthma attack at age forty. Being out on tour, I was unable to attend her memorial service. Instead, I wrote a heartfelt letter to her which was published in the magazine she had worked for. What would she think if she were alive today to see how the profit motive has corrupted journalism, a profession she was so proud to be a part of? I'm sure it would have saddened her.

Lillian never married and had no children, but her legacy lives on in her brother's daughter, Nicola Roxon, who lives in Melbourne and, as I write, is Australia's Shadow Attorney-General. She's one to watch.

My parents' funerals had been exactly ten weeks apart and 9,000 miles away, at a time in my life when I had dozens of people dependent on me for their livelihoods. If I had taken time off, I would have put them out of work as well as broken million-dollar contracts. Above all, I had been raised to regard the saying "the show must go on" as holy writ. There had been no choice with both deaths but to fly down to Melbourne, attend the funerals, and fly straight back to the United States.

There was virtually no reportage of my parents' deaths in the American press, and in Los Angeles, where I lived, I could count on the fingers of one hand the number of sympathy cards I received. Instead, I was constantly being patted on the back by people telling me how lucky I was to be having all that success. It seemed every time I released a new single it went to number one. What they didn't know was that every time the phone rang, I would wonder who else had died.

In October, a month after Dad's death, my band and I were heading home to California from Philadelphia on a leased private jet when the plane hit a storm cloud, known as a thunderhead. A few minutes before, I had been playing Scrabble with some of the musicians when my husband, who had an uneasy feeling, suddenly told everyone to put the game away and tighten their seat belts. It was said with such authority that we all instantly obeyed; only moments later, it felt as if we had hit a brick wall. With a high-pitched whining noise, the plane started going down.

Everyone's faces were becoming distorted from the G-force. Cabin baggage was floating, and interior paneling started to snap out of its moorings. One of the musicians began screaming, another was praying; my husband and I declared our love and said good-bye to each other. This was the first time our son, who was now crawling, had not come on the road with us. I was grateful that my children would survive me. I affirmed my faith in the Almighty and then I started to lose consciousness.

The two pilots were able to pull out of the downdraft and regain control of the airplane, and we made an emergency landing at a little airfield in Moline, Illinois. They told us later that the jet would not have crashed. We had been within seconds of reaching a G-force level that would have caused the small plane to implode. We wouldn't have made it all the way down in one piece.

The following month, November, I returned to Australia for a concert tour as planned. I had already been told that Aunty Nell had advanced cancer, and there was nothing the doctors could do. This was to be the last time I would ever see her.

If not for Aunty Nell's moral compass and steady hand at difficult times in my life, I might have turned out to be a totally different person. She had a finely developed ethical sense and assumed that everyone else did also. One experience of Aunty Nell's to which I was privy defined her rather well, I thought.

On one of her regular overseas trips, she had visited South America and while there, she had bought some semiprecious stones. On her return she had one of them made into a ring, a large aquamarine, set in platinum and surrounded by small diamonds. It was clearly her favorite ring, as she always wore it, but because of its weight and her tiny hands, the aquamarine tended to slip around to the palm side of her finger. Aunty Nell had dealt with this problem by wrapping some surgical adhesive tape around the inside of the ring to hold it in place.

Subsequently, after a massive family gathering, Aunt's ring could not be found. She always took it off before she peeled the potatoes and she kept it by the sink, but it was not there. Nor did a thorough search of the potato peelings produce any sign of it. It seemed that every inch of the property was scoured, but there was no ring to be found anywhere. If Aunty Nell had any suspicions, she never voiced them and, after several weeks had gone by without the ring turning up, she filed a claim with the insurance company.

Six years later, with another family gathering coming up, my aunt decided to do some spring-cleaning. She got a stepladder and climbed up to bring down from the cupboard some of the big serving dishes she used only on special occasions. When she pulled down a large soup tureen, she noticed something sparkling on the rim. It was the ring! It appeared that Aunty Nell had been wearing it when she put the tureen away and, as she had stepped down, the surgical tape must have adhered to the china rim, pulling the ring off her finger without her feeling it.

She was so excited it had been found, she said, when she wrote and told me about it. She'd had the ring adjusted so that it wouldn't slip anymore and she was so happy that it was back on her finger again. She closed by telling me how kind the man at the insurance company had been when she'd informed him of the ring's discovery. He was allowing her to repay them in three monthly installments!

How very proud I am to carry on this woman's name.

The Australian tour sold out in every city except Melbourne. I had made the mistake of insisting that my show be at the Melbourne Stadium, where I had performed with Sammy Davis Jr. fifteen years earlier, even though I was advised to play instead at the newly built Dallas Brooks Hall. Allowing sentimentality to override my business judgment was a mistake. My audience did not care for the industrial-area West Melbourne venue and would have preferred the much smaller, but newer and more modern East Melbourne concert hall with its better acoustics and safer parking. And I would have filled it with ease as opposed to the stadium, which was three times larger. Although attendance was respectable, the fact that I did not sell out on that one night gave the press license to label the whole tour a flop. It wasn't; the promoter made money. All I really cared about was that my beloved Aunty Nell was sitting in the front row that night. She was only weeks away from death and seemed terribly frail. Nevertheless, she was still head of the family and wouldn't have considered not being there to represent my parents at my homecoming concert.

While I was visiting, we had discussed her death calmly. She knew it was imminent and didn't want me to have to make the long trip back and forth again for the third family funeral in six months. We agreed that we would say our good-byes before I left, and although she had always planned to make me her heir, I advised her that my future was well provided for and suggested that she bequeath her estate to those who were less fortunate. We had been as close as mother and daughter; in fact, when my mother's illness overtook her, our relationship became exactly that. Aunty Nell had been my rock and my safe haven, the lighthouse in the stormy sea, and her death on January 4, 1974, left me bereft.

In the space of thirteen months, I had given birth, had three number-one hit records and my own television series, won a Grammy, lost both parents, my aunt, and my closest friend, and faced death myself. On the stress scale, I was off the chart, but it was my husband/manager who was unable to handle the pressure. As bullies tend to do, he took advantage of my vulnerable state and, four weeks after Aunty Nell's death, he became verbally abusive. I did not have the emotional resources to cope. I was also without a support system. Other than my young children, I had no family in the United States.

The future had become scary and unpredictable; the present was almost unbearable; only the past was safe—it had already happened.

# CHAPTER 24

# Growing a Family Tree

Every culture has its rituals to perform whenever there is a death. These customs not only honor the person who has passed on but also provide a path to healing for those left behind. It would be several years before I came to realize I had been denied the normal grieving process. I had not attended the wakes, commiserated with family and friends, or cleaned out the family home. I had paid for the funerals and cremations, but my sister had borne the burden of handling all the arrangements. With my mother's death, I had gone from midsummer in California to midwinter in Melbourne and back again in seventy-two hours, and the experience seemed almost unreal, as if I might have dreamed it.

I was haunted by all the questions I had never asked and that now could not be answered. I wanted to know more about these two people who had gone into making me. What had gone into making them? There was so much to learn. Unwittingly, genealogy would prove to be the key to healing my grief.

I began flying down to Australia, whenever I could take time off, to do research, and started interviewing people who had known my parents.

In Sydney, I visited an elderly man whose father had been best friends with my mother's father, Colin Lamond. This old gentleman had been in and out of my grandparents' home on a regular basis when he was a young boy and he gave me some valuable insights into my mother's childhood and her parents' marriage. Patterns were beginning to emerge. Both of Mum's parents had been alcoholic, and her father abusive when under the influence. As my understanding deepened, I would learn that forgiveness follows of its own accord.

Mum's father, Colin Campbell Lamond, as well as tinkering with engines, loved to sing and would occasionally perform professionally at private functions. Colin's favorite sister, Nea (named for Lady Robinson), had inherited a Surry Hills terrace house, which she rented out to a family. Young Colin's assigned task of picking up the money each week led to his meeting my grandmother, Stella Pearl, when he came to collect the rent.

A budding romance with the landlady's brother blossomed into a proposal, and Stella Pearl began a new life as Mrs. Colin Lamond. While she did piecework sewing at home for a tailor, Stella Pearl yearned for a theatrical career and sometimes she sang and acted in small parts at Sydney's Majestic Theatre. After her daughters—Aunty Lyle and Mum—were born, my grandmother's frustrated ambitions were transferred to the two of them.

Discovering that Stella Pearl had been illegitimate and passed off at birth as her mother's younger sister explained to me why Mum had been so reticent to discuss her family tree. There were more surprises to come.

Given the close connection between the Lamond and Robinson families—Sir Hercules had been Tom Lamond's patron when he became first an alderman and then mayor of Waterloo—and the common family names, I had assumed a familial connection. Not so; it took some digging, but my great-grandmother, Elizabeth Robinson Lamond, had the most interesting background of all.

Eliza Robinson was born in Sydney in 1841 to John Robinson, proprietor of the Boundary Stone Inn, and his wife, the former Ann Wade. Realizing that the Robinson family was established in Sydney in that year, I felt as if someone had lit a fire under me, as anyone with an ancestor living in Sydney in 1840 has a 50 percent chance of finding a convict forebear. The hunt was now on. By the time I reached back to the First Fleet, I had found three of them.

Genealogy is addictive; it begins as an interest, becomes a hobby, then a passion, and finally an obsession. Not only with each generation uncovered does the number of people to investigate double but so too does the desire to understand the forces that shaped them. I was now fascinated by the history of my country. In the still colonial Australia that I grew up in, we were not taught Australian history or, for that matter, Australian geography; the emphasis was on English history and English geography. I knew about the Fens and the Firth of Forth but bugger all about Bendigo or Ballarat. Becoming aware of my ignorance about the land in which I had been born and raised was disturbing, but it spurred me on my voyage of discovery.

Family research is painstaking work. After establishing that there were eight different men by the name of John Robinson living in Sydney in 1840, I had to keep nine separate files; one for each John Robinson and one to hold incoming information not yet allocated. By using facts already established such as place of birth, names of children, siblings, and so on, I built a dossier on Eliza's father, John Robinson, by weeding out data relating to the other seven men.

John Robinson, of the Boundary Stone Inn, died in 1857 at the age of fifty. He married Ann Wade in Hobart in 1832, and had been born in England (c. 1807), but when and how did he get to Australia? There was no John Robinson—neither military, nor convict, nor settler—on any shipping manifest within twenty years of the right age. It became even more confusing on learning that John Robinson had been named for his father, who had died in Tasmania.

Aunty Lyle had spent time with me in California after Mum died and told me lots of stories about her side of the family. As a schoolgirl, my aunt had compiled a family tree for her teacher and she presented me with her old exercise book, containing the assignment. On the inside front cover she had written "John Robinson, Quaker from Kent," a space was left and then underneath that she had written "John Robinson, came to Australia with his sisters Rachael and Elizabeth." I had assumed that both entries referred to the same man.

The pieces would fit together when I read an entry from the Van Diemen's Land Muster of 1822. It recorded that John Robinson, a free settler, had arrived per *Minstrel* in 1812, with one male and two female children. It hadn't occurred to me that Eliza's father, John Robinson, might have come to Australia as a five-year-old boy, but there they were: John Robinson, father and son with his sisters Rachael and Elizabeth. '

It was fascinating to find out that both my parents had a Tasmanian connection and I would become one of the founding members of the Tasmanian Genealogical Society.

Aunty Lyle's old exercise book, would also reveal that Isaac Robinson, Eliza's brother, had gone to Norfolk Island as U.S. Consul during the whaling days of the Third Settlement. Isaac had married a local girl and raised a family there. An elderly cousin of Mum's could recall Isaac and his family staying at Zetland Lodge and told me that it caused a lot of talk among the Lamond girls when their Robinson cousins came to visit. It seems the islanders were used to running around barefoot, and loved to roll down the hill behind Zetland Lodge. The Lamond girls—always dressed in starched white frocks with black stockings and trained to assume ladylike positions in all situations—were shocked.

Aunty Lyle's records came to a stop at World War II, and the two branches of the family lost touch. Curious to know if any of Isaac's descendants still lived on the island, I placed a full-page ad in the Genealogical Society's magazine. I received a reply from an Anglican minister who was also a keen genealogist. He put me in touch with one of my cousins on Norfolk and I resolved to visit the island one day.

Traditional genealogy has tended to follow the patriarchal model, and researchers are trained to focus on male last-name lines. For instance, English-speaking students of genealogy usually begin by drawing up ancestral charts of the British Royal Family. They're not only the best documented family, they're also all so splendidly inbred. Reference is sometimes made to Queen Elizabeth and Prince Philip both being descended from Queen Victoria. In fact, they have more than a dozen mutual direct ancestors. The Hanoverian behavior of their offspring, not to mention Anne's physical resemblance to George II, is easily understood when one sees that the Queen has three separate lines of descent from George II while Philip has four, giving their children seven separate lines of direct descent from this one man.

Without exception, I brought a female perspective to my research. I believe family history is truly women's history. In the days before cloning and surrogate mothers, the maternity of an infant was unquestionable. As a feminist, eager to trace my mitochondrial DNA—which is inherited only through the mother—I found myself following matrilineal lines.

The challenge for those researching maternal lines is that in each generation the last name is lost when a woman marries and takes on her husband's name; unless you are lucky enough to have Scottish forebears on your mother's side. Scotswomen kept their own names for life as Scottish records show, but in most Western cultures, once a woman married she ceased to exist in her own right and became Mrs. John Doe. A woman's first name often became lost as well, as her children and grandchildren remembered her only as Mum or Granny. Sometimes, in order to learn the first name, you need to find a distant cousin who still remembers dear old Great-aunt Mary. Collateral cousins are often a good source of old photographs and of correspondence that yields first names; wills are excellent for revealing the married names of female relatives, too. Given that women frequently died in childbirth in earlier times, men would sometimes have two or three wives over the course of a lifetime. The wide diversity in first names for females was not as common then as it is today. Two wives would often have the same name: for instance, Henry VIII of England married a Catherine and two Katherines and two Annes. So be doubly sure to cross-check all your dates of birth, marriage, and death.

.   .   .

Over a period of twenty years, my research was to take me around the world and into libraries and archives in Sydney, Hobart; Wellington, New Zealand; San Francisco, London, Bristol, and Dublin. Whenever possible, I would combine research with performing engagements, for example, by going to London a week ahead of a tour and using the time to comb through microfilms and old registers. I became such a regular visitor to the Latter-day Saints' genealogical Family History Library in Salt Lake City, Utah, that they invited me to be one of the guest speakers at their Tenth International Genealogical Congress in 1991. The subject of my talk was Australasian and Matrilineal Research.

Although I became a qualified genealogist, I didn't delude myself that I would ever be able to support my family on something that paid so poorly. At different times I engaged the help of professional genealogical researchers but I would estimate that, over those two decades, the long-distance travel and all the accommodation would have been my greatest expense. However, I gained priceless knowledge and understanding.

In the meantime, I was still the mother of two children, had a husband/manager whose mood swings were becoming increasingly erratic, and I was at the height of a demanding career.

# CHAPTER 25

# Starry, Starry Nights

W hen I thought about it, I realized that I had come along at a particularly good time in American show business history. A lot of the old stars were still alive and I was to meet and, in some cases, work with people like George Burns, Jack Benny, Lucille Ball, James Cagney, Edward G. Robinson, Cary Grant, Rosalind Russell, Greer Garson, and Gloria Swanson. I would always think how thrilled my parents would have been to meet some of these giants from their generation.

I became friends with Frank Sinatra because of the problems he ran into in Australia in 1974, thanks to a favored tactic of yellow journalists—provoke someone until they retaliate and then write a nasty story about them. This approach was used to great effect when Frank Sinatra visited Australia. By deftly using an American slang expression for

whore—unknown in Australia—to describe Frank's wives, a
newspaper provoked a reaction and then wrote a headline
about "Cranky Frankie."

I happened to be a guest on *The Tonight Show* with Johnny
Carson during the period when Frank was being denied hotel
room service or fuel for his plane. Johnny couldn't resist asking
me, as an Australian, how I felt about what was going on.
Although I'd never met Frank, I defended him and I told
Johnny I was ashamed of the gutter standards in journalism
that were giving Australia a bad reputation. Coincidentally,
Frank's daughter Tina was watching the show. She called her
father in Sydney and relayed my remarks. The next day I
received a dozen yellow roses from Frank Sinatra with a note
saying, "If anyone ever hits you, call me." If Frank thought you
were on his side there was nothing he wouldn't do for you.

Later that year, I was invited to perform with him and Gene
Kelly at the huge Universal Amphitheatre. What a thrill! It was
a fundraiser for Cedars-Sinai Hospital—my husband and I
had earlier underwritten the cost of building the outpatient
clinic there—and the audience was a who's who of Hollywood.
Jack Benny was the master of ceremonies for the evening and
introduced me as the opening act and only female on the show.
I was followed by Gene Kelly who would, for the first time "live
and in person," re-create his "Singin' in the Rain" musical
number. From above, wires had been strung across the entire
stage with sprinkler hoses attached, and the stage crew was
dressed in yellow slickers and hats when they came on to sweep

*Above*. A hug from Frank Sinatra – backstage at the Universal Amphitheater, Los Angeles.
*(From the personal collection of Helen Reddy)*

*Above*. With the Bee Gees on *The Midnight Special*. *(Reprinted courtesy of Photofest)*

*Above:* After a concert with George Burns at the Shubert Theater, Los Angeles. *(From the personal collection of Helen Reddy)*

With a youthful Sylvester Stallone ... *(Reprinted courtesy of Photofest)*

... and an even younger Billy Crystal. *(Reprinted courtesy of Photofest)*

*Above:* Jane Fonda fulfilled a lifelong ambition to sing when she joined me on *The Helen Reddy Special.* *(Reprinted courtesy of Photofest)*

*Above:* Singing 'It's Easy to Say', the song nominated from *10* at the Academy Awards in 1980, with Dudley Moore. *(Reprinted courtesy of Photofest)*

*Above.* With jazz great Ella Fitzgerald. *(From the personal collection of Helen Reddy)*

*Right.* I wanted Jim Henson to go away so I could really talk to Kermit. *(Reprinted courtesy of Photofest)*

*Above:* Olivia Newton-John and friend at a party at my Brentwood home. *(From the personal collection of Helen Reddy)*

*Above:* 25 October 1976 – dinner on my 35th birthday with a fellow Scorpio. *(From the personal collection of Helen Reddy)*

*Above:* A happy moment filming *Pete's Dragon.* *(Reprinted courtesy of Photofest)*

up afterward. We all knew we were witnessing a once-in-a-lifetime event and Gene, ever the perfectionist, was magical. For the second half, Frank did his complete show, and as I sat there watching him, I thought back to the little girl who had gone to the pictures to see Frank and Gene in *On the Town* and *Anchors Aweigh*.

I never told Frank this but, when he had come to Australia in 1955 for a concert tour, I saw his show at the Sydney Stadium. Max and Stella were playing a season at the Tivoli Theatre at the same time; I was on school holidays and had nothing to do except hang around backstage at the theater. I was pleased that Frank Sinatra had brought his daughter Nancy to Australia with him. She was only a year older than I was, and I wished we could meet, as I figured she didn't know anyone else her own age in Sydney, either.

The show was in the round, and I had a seat in the second row. As Frank walked up onto the stage I could see that he was trembling with nerves. He was coming off a rough spot in his life following the very public failure of his second marriage; his career had also hit a slump, and some critics had dismissed him as not being able to sing anymore. I hadn't imagined that big stars still got nervous but I knew what helped me when I was nervous and that was a smiling face in the audience. For his entire show, I sat there with an ear-to-ear grin trying to project love and approval. At one point, he did a double-take when he noticed the thirteen-year-old with the Cheshire cat expression—it was probably during a ballad—and my face ached afterward, but the critics were wrong in their presumptions. The man could take a song, wrap his voice around it, and make it his own. And that voice—a unique and instantly identifiable timbre. Frank used to say that Vic Damone was a better singer than he was and, technically, this may have been true; but you could hear Vic sing an entire song on the radio and not know it was him until the announcer told you. Frank only had to sing one note for you to recognize his voice.

Another memorable evening for me was a glittering event in Washington, D.C., honoring American women of achievement. Some amazing women were celebrated that night, including Dr. Virginia Apgar, who developed the ten-point test given to newborns. The evening was to be hosted by Rosalind Russell, the movie actress first associated with roles portraying strong successful women and, later in her career, star of *Auntie Mame*. When I got to rehearsal, I asked someone if she had arrived yet. They pointed out this little old lady sitting in a chair with a scarf around her head mammy-style. She was hunched over, seemingly crippled with arthritis, and her puffy face bore the unmistakable sign of heavy cortisone use. My heart sank in sympathy for her. There was no way this poor soul could host a tea party, much less a gala evening with thousands in attendance.

That night, while I was standing in the wings waiting to go on, I felt a presence standing next to me. It was Roz. Her hair was upswept and perfectly coiffed, her makeup flawless; she wore a stunning full-length, form-fitting, long-sleeved white beaded evening gown. She stood erect with her head held high and, when her name was announced, she walked out onstage as the star she undoubtedly was.

My exposure on television had made going out with the children a problem. One night, I took them to the circus and we ended up leaving with my little boy in tears. So many fans had been standing in front of us and staring at us instead of the show that he wasn't able to see a thing. It was his first time at a circus; he'd been given a big build-up about how much he was going to enjoy it; and the evening had been ruined for him. To my regret, I had to face the fact that if my children were going to enjoy some of the things that most kids enjoy, I would not be able to accompany them.

I used to think that a writer like Neil Simon was in the ideal position. The success of his plays meant he would earn royalties as long as he lived; he had a famous name that any maître d' would instantly acknowledge with a reservation; he had the respect of his peers; and he could go most places without being recognized.

The best one I've ever seen at handling fans in a public place was Paul Newman. Once I was on the same flight as him and he was traveling alone. As he moved through the airport, people were coming up to him and asking for his autograph. The number-one rule for a celebrity is keep moving. If you stop to sign anything, a crowd will gather. Paul would say to each one, as he kept walking, that he didn't sign autographs but, "I'll shake your hand, and the next time I see you, I'll have a beer with you." Then *whoosh,* he was gone, leaving behind a more than satisfied fan with a story to tell back home.

One of the highlights of my stay in Sydney during a concert tour was receiving a telephone call from Marlene Dietrich. At first I thought that someone was playing a joke on me; but no, I had listened to that live performance album too many times not to recognize the unique Dietrich style of speech. It was amazing to me that she knew who I was. I told her about playing her live performance album to tatters, taking all those notes at her concert, and waiting to see her leave the stage door afterward. She told me that the reason she was calling was to tell me to keep my chin up and try to ignore what was being said about me in the Australian press. She said that they had been cruel and hurtful to her, too, and that she would never return. She is not the only overseas artist I have heard say the same thing. How many Australians have been deprived of the opportunity to see a professional of international standard because of this attitude?

# CHAPTER 26

# *You Can't Go Home Again*

Despite having been in the United States for almost eight years, I had stubbornly clung to my Australian citizenship. Now, I began to question the wisdom of this decision. I realized that my parents and Aunty Nell were the main reason I had retained it, and now that all three of them were gone, I did not have the same incentive to keep returning to Australia anymore. Nor was I up for being rubbished when I did.

The reality was that my life now was in America. That was where my career was based, where my home and family were located, and where my talents were freer to flourish, away from the naysayers. I was married to an American, my son was American, and my daughter, although born in Australia, had lived in the United States since she was three years old. Most important, I did not like it when our family had to be separated at immigration and customs because my daughter and I had a different nationality from my husband and son. We were a family, and I wanted us to stay together as a family. We became an American family.

The Australian press reacted to my change of citizenship as if I had committed treason. The Murdoch press was particularly vicious—although it would be remarkably restrained when Rupert did the same thing—and, to this day, various magazine or newspaper articles in Australia will refer to "the furore" caused by my action. In reality, I received a total of *one* letter, sent to me by someone who had recently become an Australian citizen. It was a charming letter, empathizing with the difficulty in making such an emotional decision and wishing me well for the future. So much for press propaganda—I guess "furores" sell newspapers.

When the Australian law later changed to allow dual nationality, I renewed my Australian citizenship.

In 1975, I undertook a world concert tour. The United Nations had declared it to be the Year of the Woman, and I was delighted that they had chosen "I Am Woman" as their official song. However, I would receive an honor that year which surpassed anything else.

I began the European leg of the tour in Holland, where I had previously enjoyed a great deal of popularity and appeared in several television specials. It was Sunday, my day off, and I wanted to take the children somewhere I could push a stroller. It was decided that an outing to a tulip farm would be colorful and educational. I had no idea that the following day something very special and very secret involving a tulip had been planned for me. My arrival at the farm unannounced, I would later learn, caused consternation behind the scenes. I was not aware of this and assumed that the guided tour my family and I were given was a standard courtesy. In fact it was a plot to keep me away from a certain plot of tulips. At one point, I remember admiring a bed of bright scarlet blooms. The nameplate identified them as General Eisenhower tulips, and I remarked how marvelous it must be to have a flower named after you, little knowing that the next day I would be presented with the Helen Reddy tulip.

It was a reddish violet hue and I recognized it immediately as Aunty Nell's favorite color. How thrilled she would have been to know there was a bloom that bore our name. Reflecting on how she had walked from East Melbourne every morning, through the Fitzroy Gardens, to her job in the city, I decided that I wanted to donate some beds of tulip bulbs to the gardens in her memory. To my disappointment, I was subsequently told that the bulbs were held in quarantine and they died there. To the best of my knowledge, Helen Reddy tulips are still unavailable in Australia.

In Japan I received a rapturous reception and was delighted to see that female journalists were getting the chance to interview me and carry the banner for feminism.

Jordan, not yet three, was confused at first while watching television because his favorite characters on *Sesame Street* were speaking Japanese. I was hoping that there were not too many English speakers at our hotel as I walked through the lobby holding his hand. He was singing at the top of his lungs, "Old MacDonald had a penis, ee-eye-ee-eye-oh." Max would have loved it.

When I arrived back in Australia on the last leg of the 1975 tour, I was mobbed at the airport by reporters and cameramen. I was leading my toddler son by the hand and I had to scoop him up quickly into my arms so he wouldn't get trampled. He was terrified. I can only presume that not one of the reporters or cameramen was a father.

I had taken Peter Allen around the world with me as my opening act. I loved his music and used to leave my dressing room and go to the wings every night to watch him sing "Tenterfield Saddler." I was also personally fond of him and wanted him to have the chance to go home in style. Instead, the Australian press turned on him and was merciless in its homophobia. On the flight across the Tasman to New Zealand, he was in tears because of this cruelty.

I understood how he felt. One journalist had written that if my father were alive, he would be ashamed of what a big-head I'd become. Fortunately, a friend told me that when I'd had my first hit, she'd asked Max how he felt about his daughter, now that she was a big star. He had replied, "She was always a big star to me."

While Peter Allen would eventually reach recognition in his own country with his song "I Still Call Australia Home," it was not until after his untimely death that they would fully embrace him as "the boy from Oz." If only a few people could have been nicer to him while he was still around to appreciate it.

# CHAPTER 27

# *Leaving Las Vegas*

Some offers are too good to refuse—which is how I ended up working in Las Vegas for an extended period. They have a saying in Vegas, "Show me a gambler, I'll show you a loser." Life itself has always satisfied my gambling instincts and I have never felt the need to bet my hard-earned money against the house.

One of the things I would quickly learn about Las Vegas is how everything is geared to making the customer gamble. For example, the layout is such that you have to walk the length of the casino to get to any of the restaurants. The worst part for me was staying in the hotel suites for any length of time; they were usually decorated in color combinations that make the average person uncomfortable, drawing them back downstairs to the casino. On one memorable two-week stay my suite had purple carpeting with orange armchairs, a hot pink couch, and curtains in a vivid print employing all three colors. Unable to deal with the desert climate, I was stuck in the suite all day long and I found myself feeling nauseated. I asked the hotel staff to exchange the orange chairs for some green ones, and that gave my eyes some relief. On my next engagement there, I was provided with a larger suite that was all beige! Don't tell Dame Edna!

So that the children's regular schedules would not be disturbed, I began commuting back and forth between Los Angeles and Las Vegas by private jet every night. This meant I could have breakfast in the morning with both of them before they left for school, play with them after school, and we could have an early dinner together before I left for the airport to fly to Las Vegas. I needed to be in my dressing room by 7:30 P.M. for the first show at 8 o'clock. The second show started at midnight, and by leaving immediately afterward I could be in the air by 2 A.M. and back home by 3 A.M. Then, it was up again to see the kids off to school a few hours later. I would try to sleep during the day while they weren't home, but my fatigue was such that I didn't trust myself driving them to and from school any more.

To reach the backstage dressing rooms at the MGM Grand, it was necessary to climb a two-story staircase that went straight up without a landing. I used to stand at the bottom of those stairs some nights and wonder how on earth I was ever going to make it to the top. I always would, of course, and then go out and walk across a stage in high heels for two hours, but my fatigue was showing. Some of the reviewers began commenting on my lack of energy in performance.

The strain of the deaths of multiple loved ones, one after another in a short space of time; the constant verbal abuse from my spouse; working seven nights a week; and trying to be a good mother—it was all taking its toll on my health.

# CHAPTER 28

# Is There a Doctor
# in the House?

I was getting thinner and thinner, and the specialist I was seeing didn't seem to be helping me at all. I would find out later that for two years he had been giving me placebos and telling my husband that I should see a psychiatrist because I was—erroneously, in his view—convinced that something was wrong with me. I was at the point of despair when I finally met Dr. Elsie Giorgi.

It was such a relief to talk to a female physician who didn't think all women were hysterical. As soon as I told her I had lost a kidney many years before, she asked me if the adrenal gland had also been removed. I had no idea. Given that the kidney had ruptured on the operating table, Elsie assessed that they would probably have removed anything in the surrounding area. She looked at the patches of discoloration on my face, which was now permanently tanned, and concluded that I probably had Addison's disease, a rare disorder linked to malfunctioning adrenal glands. Within days, tests would prove her right. I was lucky to have found a doctor who had seen and treated this unusual condition before. Addison's disease is incurable, and fatal if not treated, but it can be managed with cortisone medication, in the same way that diabetes can be managed with insulin. I was immediately given massive doses of cortisone and felt well again for the first time in years. It is an extremely difficult disease to diagnose, however, because not only do the symptoms mimic many other illnesses, but different patients can manifest different symptoms. The one universal seems to be the darkening of the skin. Unfortunately, because we all tend to look good with a tan, Addisonians appear to be radiantly healthy while they're dying, and many sufferers are not diagnosed until the autopsy. Those of us who are living with the disease believe it would not be so rare if more doctors were familiar with the symptoms and more sufferers were diagnosed while they were still living. To that end, we are pushing for medical information and current research to be made available at all public libraries in Australia.

John F. Kennedy is the most famous Addisonian, a fact that his family tried to cover up for many years. Their efforts would muddy the tracks for assassination conspiracy theorists when information from his autopsy report disappeared. His sister Eunice Kennedy Shriver also has Addison's disease, and one other family member, now deceased, may have had it also. The roots of the Kennedy family reach back to County Wexford in Ireland. Oddly enough, this is where my Reddy ancestors originated. I suspect there may be a genetic link involved with Addison's disease, although current research has yet to confirm this.

I had spent many years of my life raising large amounts of money for research into various diseases but, because it was so rare, never my own. I am thrilled that there is now, in the new millennium, a support group for people with Addison's disease in Australia.

Are you tired, weak, dizzy, craving salt, getting thinner, and has your skin darkened? Seek out more information at www. addisons.org.au.


Maybe it's because I was born under a water sign that when I'm troubled, I'm drawn to water. Whether it's a river, a pond, a lake or the ocean, I find comfort near water. When I lived in southern California, I would often head for the beach if I needed to be alone and think. There is something soothing, almost hypnotic, in the regular rhythm of the waves. I talk to the universe and open my heart to receive counsel. I always leave feeling at peace—or nearly always.

One day when I was at the beach during a crisis of faith, I prayed, "It's not my faith in You that is in question, because my faith in You is unshakable: it's Your faith in me that I'm questioning. I need to know that I'm on the right path, headed in the right direction. I guess what I need is reassurance." And then to my mother, "I miss you so much, Mum. I know you're watching over me and I know you love me but I wish there were some way you could reach down and tell me that I'm a 'good girl.'" I sat there for a while but the usual feeling of peace eluded me. Nor did I receive any counsel or wisdom. I was disappointed but accepted it and prayed, "It's okay. I understand that things are very busy today and there are other people with problems far greater than mine. I'll try again another time." With that, I pulled my car onto the Pacific Coast Highway and headed for home. I couldn't have been driving more than a few seconds when I noticed that the car in front of me had a personalized license plate. It said: GUD GRL.

# CHAPTER 29

# *Movin' On Up*

In 1974, my family and I moved to the exclusive Brentwood Park section of Los Angeles. The area was more rural then than it is now, and some of our neighbors kept a horse or sheep on their property. The place we bought was sprawling and comfortable with a pool and a tennis court and lots of room for the children to grow. I had told my husband that if the verbal abuse didn't stop, I was ending our relationship. He promised a fresh start with the new house.

Knowing only too well the fluctuating fortunes of show business, I insisted on paying cash for the home as I didn't want to be saddled with a mortgage that I might have trouble keeping up sometime in the future. I also didn't want to pay 1970s inflated interest rates. My husband seemed to settle down with the move, and for a while there, life looked like it was getting better.

The house had an interesting history. One previous owner had been Dore Schary, when he was the head of MGM studios. He used to sit in the screening room of an evening, watching the dailies—the film footage shot on the lot that day. It certainly gave me a buzz sitting there in my own home theater, watching two films I had appeared in, for the first time.

The MGM musicals that I had adored as a child were no longer being made. However, a film genre that was popular in this era was the all-star disaster movie. After all those years of seeing stars in glamorous costumes on screen, in my first film, *Airport '75*, I would be outfitted by multi-Oscar-winning designer Edith Head—as a nun. A flying, singing nun or, if you prefer, a singing, flying nun. I was later offered the role spoofing myself in *Airplane!*, but the makers of the original film claimed that it would be a violation of copyright. I'd thought the original was a spoof! Maureen McGovern was wonderful in the part, and I'm glad she had the chance to do it.

While I loved having the opportunity to dance onscreen in my next film, *Pete's Dragon*, and it was an education to work with screen veterans like Mickey Rooney and Shelley Winters, I didn't fare any better in the glamour department. Although a musical, it was set in America's Victorian era, and I played the daughter of a lighthouse keeper on the coast of Maine. I consoled myself by thinking about all the gorgeous designer gowns I could now wear onstage in Las Vegas.

In the early getting-to-know-you days of rehearsals on *Pete's Dragon* I would sometimes have lunch in the Disney commissary with our English director, Don Chaffey. He told me a wonderful story about an actress he had once made a film with. The scene they were shooting on that particular day was the rescue of the leading lady, who had been shipwrecked at sea. According to Don, everything was set to go in the big tank, with cameras in position and actors playing seamen standing by, ready to pull her out of the water and up the rope ladder. When called to the set, she appeared perfectly coiffed, not a hair out of place, her makeup and clothes immaculate. Her assistant held a glass of water with one hand while dipping her fingers in the water with the other and flicking the droplets at the leading lady. Don asked her what on earth she was doing. The actress replied that she would need to look wet when she climbed up the rope ladder. Don then told her that she had to be completely immersed in the tank; that her character had been swimming for her life, and that she was supposed to look like a drowned rat.

"Oh, I couldn't do that," she said.

"What do you mean? Of course you can do that," Don said. "You're an actress."

"No, I'm not," she exclaimed indignantly. "I'm a film star!"

Even though I fulfilled my girlhood dream of starring in a Hollywood musical, I found film work to be boring. I loved rehearsals and being able to spend so much of the day dancing, but once filming started on *Pete's Dragon,* I would be waiting, waiting, and waiting, sometimes for twelve hours a day, in order to shoot a three-minute scene. While sitting on the set all those months, I needlepointed a piano-seat cover and knitted a bedspread. At least I was able to keep my hands busy!

# CHAPTER 30

# *Family Ties*

Because of my interest in genealogical research, I had joined both the British and Australian Genealogical Societies and I frequently used professional "genies" to look up specific information for me. This was before the advent of computers and the Internet, back when someone needed to be in a particular place to look up something in a particular file. I will never forget the day I learned that my mother's side of the family went all the way back to the First Fleet. I was so excited that I literally jumped up and down like a child. Now I had a family history that paralleled the history of Australia as a nation, and enough stories and characters for an entire book. Following is a brief outline.

Richard Morgan, my great-great-great-great-grandfather, was sentenced to transportation for seven years. As there was no transportation provided back to England at the completion of time served, it was, in effect, transportation for life. In January 1788, he arrived first at Botany Bay and then Sydney Cove aboard the *Alexander*, the largest of the transport ships in the eleven-strong fleet. He would subsequently be sent to the settlement on Norfolk Island, where he met his lifetime companion and the woman who would become my great-great-great-great-grandmother, Catherine Clarke. Also a convict, while still in her teens, Catherine had been sentenced to seven years' transportation for shoplifting. Their firstborn, also named Catherine but known as Kate, was born on Norfolk Island on February 15, 1792.

Bringing a mother's perspective to my research, I noted that although little Kate's date of birth was recorded in the *Norfolk Island Victualling Book* (Mitchell Library, Sydney), she is not shown as drawing rations from the public store until nine months later. This indicated to me that Catherine had breast-fed her for that period of time. As weaning stimulates ovulation, the fact that the next child was born nine months after baby Kate went on stores would seem to confirm it—I love it when dry facts come to life. Kate, my great-great-great-grandmother, would grow up on Norfolk Island as the eldest of eight children. Upon the government's decision to close down the island's First Settlement, the entire colony was shipped off to Van Diemen's Land, now Tasmania, where Richard would be compensated for the loss of his land on Norfolk Island with a land grant at Kangaroo Point. His farm would eventually become the Rosny golf course, and I believe the house he erected in 1806 still stands.

Richard Morgan received a full pardon when documents sent out from England revealed that he had been what we would call today a "whistle-blower" and the victim of a miscarriage of justice. He had reported fraud taking place where he worked and was then quickly transported on trumped-up charges to prevent him from testifying against someone of influence back in Bristol.

Morgan had been one of the Norfolk Island settlers who had staunchly supported Governor Bligh. After the Rum Rebellion in Sydney, when Bligh sailed to Hobart seeking support from the lieutenant governor there, Richard Morgan was one of a handful of settlers who risked charges of sedition by going to Bligh's aid and supplying his ship.

Richard Morgan outlived his wife, Catherine, and died in Hobart in 1837. His grandsons went on to be pioneers in New Zealand and California, and one of his great-grandsons would become an archbishop in the Church of England. I have traced around seven hundred of his descendants thus far, including nine who died at Gallipoli. Lest we forget, innocent or guilty, the Australian nation was built on the blood and sweat of those First Fleet convicts.

Backtracking to 1804, the new settlement which would become Hobart was started with the arrival of the *Calcutta*. One of the convicts aboard the ship was John Wade. I know it's what they all say, but John Wade was also innocent of the crime for which he had been transported; sometimes it's true.

A cursory glance at the court calendar on the day of his trial makes it obvious what had happened. A shoemaker with his own horse and cart, John Wade had given a lift to a woman attempting to carry more than she could manage. It turned out that what she was carrying was stolen goods. As her trial immediately preceded that of John Wade, the judge had already sentenced her for theft before his case could be heard, in other words, she never testified at his trial. Although he was a man of trade, property, and good reputation, John Wade, as with all defendants, was given no opportunity to defend himself. He was tried as an accomplice and sentenced to seven years' transportation.

It must have been obvious to his jailers that he was not the criminal type, as he proved to be popular and was entrusted with responsibility almost immediately.

By the time the Morgan family arrived in Hobart from Norfolk Island, John Wade was a free man, and sixteen-year-old Kate Morgan caught his eye. In later years, John Wade served as high sheriff of the southern half of the island during the outlaw days of the bushrangers and he gave colorful firsthand accounts of run-ins with some of them. His obituary would begin by describing him as having "a great deal of original wit and humor." John Wade and his wife, Kate, produced four daughters and three sons. I am descended from their second daughter, Ann Wade, who was born in Hobart in 1810.

Ann's three brothers, Johnny, Henry, and George Wade, would end their days in three different countries. While Henry, the middle brother, would stay behind with Kate, their widowed mother, Johnny, and George Wade, would cash in their inherited land and be the first to take cattle, horses, and whaling gear across the Tasman Sea to the new settlement in Wellington, New Zealand. There, Johnny would take up auctioneering, as well as acting as a shipping agent, and the brothers would buy a large tract of land, subdivide it, and sell off the lots for housing. Today, Wadestown is all that remains in Wellington of the Wade family. George Wade would drown during a storm while crossing Cook Strait and Johnny would further seek his fortune in America.

Johnny Wade was certainly of an adventurous and entrepreneurial nature; when he saw an opportunity, he took it. Following the Wellington earthquake of 1849 and the news that gold had been discovered in California, he and his family left for America, settling in the area that would become San Francisco. He took out American citizenship, opened a law office on Montgomery Street and, according to his obituary, "campaigned for Abraham Lincoln." Many of his letters home to his sister, Annie, are still in the family's possession.

Unfortunately, the fire that followed the San Francisco earthquake destroyed a great many records, but those that remain can make fascinating reading for those, like me, who love history. I remember going through the San Francisco census returns from the mid-nineteenth century and feeling as if I'd taken a time machine back to that era. Reading the names and descriptions of the occupants of each house in a particular row was like walking invisibly down the street and entering the front door of each building. In what was obviously a brothel, half a dozen unrelated women had been in residence, all described as prostitutes; in another, a laundry, fourteen nameless souls were identified simply as Chinese males. And, in between, sat the residences with large families and the token boarder. One certainly got a feel for what the Barbary Coast must have been like in those days.

Ann's middle brother, Henry Wade, went to Norfolk Island, their mother Kate's birthplace, now reoccupied as a prison outpost. Here he served as a superintendent of agriculture during the period known as the Second Settlement. Later, in Sydney, Henry used his share of the proceeds from his father's land to invest in real estate. His sister Ann was by now married to John Robinson—the great-great-grandfather I had so painstakingly researched. John had become the proprietor of the Boundary Stone Inn, situated on the corner of Bourke and Cleveland streets in Sydney, and there, their fifth child and first daughter, Eliza Robinson, my great-grandmother, was born.

In the course of my investigations into the Wade family, I stumbled upon a quirky fact. Of the four daughters of Kate and John Wade, Ann was the only one who didn't marry a Watson. Her older sister, Catherine, and younger sister, Mary, married two Watson brothers and started families, making their children double first cousins, having all four grandparents in common. After Mary died, the youngest sister, Margaret, moved in to take care of the children and, in the course of time or perhaps for the sake of respectability, married her sister's widower. So, between them, the two Watson boys married three of the Wade girls.

Around the time of this research, I received news in California of Robin Watson, the girl who had been my best friend at Stratherne in Hawthorn. After we left school, Robin had married at age sixteen and started a family while I had gone out on the road with the Folies. Although we had seen each other a couple of times over the years, as so often happens when women divorce, remarry, and take on a new last name, I had lost contact with her. I began writing a letter to Robin to be forwarded on and, as I was telling her about my interest in genealogy, it occurred to me that, with Watson as her maiden name, it was possible that Robin and I could be related.

As my mind shifted gears, the name Catherine came up very strongly and, with my sixth sense, I knew that it had been Robin's name before and that she had been one of the three generations of Catherines in my family tree. But which one? Now I was intrigued. Was it Catherine Clarke-Morgan, Catherine Morgan-Wade, or Catherine Wade-Watson?

My interest in hypnotic regression and reincarnation was ongoing. For years, I had read past-life case histories and session transcripts whenever I could get my hands on them. I now took it as a given that when we have a close connection with someone in this life, either positive or negative, it indicates a previous relationship. I wondered—did Robin and I have a past-life connection?

I knew from my research that we are often drawn to places we have lived before, especially if we have been happy there. Could Robin have had a life in Tasmania? We had holidayed there together and all three Catherines, grandmother, mother, and daughter, had lived there. I also knew of a case of someone reincarnating back into the same family—a woman I'd met who had regressed to being her grandmother's sister who had died as a young girl. Was it possible that there was some genetic link involved with reincarnation?

Robin had always been of a practical, scientific nature and I didn't want to frighten her or make her think I'd "gone Hollywood" with any of this conjecture so I simply inquired about her Watson family tree and at the end of the letter asked, "Do you believe in reincarnation? Does the name Catherine mean anything to you?"

Months passed before I received a warm reply informing me that her father had come from Scotland and had no connection with Tasmania. At the bottom of Robin's letter, she added that while she did not believe in reincarnation, she did believe in ESP and perhaps that was why I had mentioned the name Catherine. She had chosen that name with that exact spelling when expecting her fourth child. However, it had turned out to be a boy, and Wade was now two years old! I nearly fell off my chair; I had not mentioned the name Wade

in my letter to her, and it was not that common a first name. I
decided to consult a psychic.

I have to break the story here and stress that I am not giving
a blanket endorsement of psychics, because so many of them
are charlatans out to make a quick buck. A "gypsy" I met at a
fairground once told me that there was a blond woman who
had designs on my husband but, if I crossed her "gypsy" palm
with ninety-nine dollars, she could say special prayers to make
this mysterious blonde disappear. I told the "gypsy" I'd have to
go home and say some special prayers to see whether or not I
should give her the ninety-nine dollars! Truly genuine psychics
will not use their gift for personal gain but will instead expect
you to contribute either time or money to a charitable cause in
kind. For them to do otherwise is to lose the gift.

The psychic I chose saw clients at her home, which was a
short drive from mine. As I walked in the door she said to me,
"What's this Watson business?" When I made the appointment
I had not mentioned any names or why I wanted a reading.
Taken aback, I asked her what she meant. "Well," she said, "I
was sitting in the bathtub this morning and I knew you were
coming to see me and the name Watson came very strongly
into my head." I began to tell her about Robin and our
correspondence, and she cut me off and said, "Robin was
Catherine Watson and the boy, Wade, was her brother who
drowned." She was referring, of course, to George Wade who
perished in Cook Strait!

In my next letter to Robin, I included a caution that she

should not be concerned if her son, Wade, had a fear of water. She didn't write back, and I wondered if I had overstepped the boundaries.

A few years later, when I was performing at a cabaret room in Melbourne, Robin came to see the show, and I was able to sit with her afterward. Her first words to me were, "How are you at picking racehorses?"

"What do you mean?" I asked.

She said, "My son, Wade, is terrified of water. We can't teach him to swim."

The keystone of reincarnation is karma, the metaphysical law of cause and effect, that states that every action has a reaction. It is neither punishment nor reward but a way of achieving universal balance.

Group karma involves several people—often family members but not necessarily in the same configuration—reincarnating together to resolve unfinished business, so spouses might reincarnate as siblings or vice versa.

Now, here I was with a mother and son who had possibly been brother and sister in a past life and, especially as there was no genetic link between Robin's family and mine, it was more than odd that the same three names, Catherine, Wade, and Watson had recurred. I wasn't aware of any research along these lines. Was it possible that we not only reincarnate back into the same family group, albeit in different configurations, but we are drawn to and replicate the same names?

It was while meditating on these questions that it came to me via my sixth sense that Wallis, Duchess of Windsor, had been King Richard III. It seemed highly implausible, and I pulled out a history book and looked for a picture of him. There is only one existing portrait of Richard III, a three-quarter profile, and although he is wearing a hat the features are quite distinctive. Now I had to find a photo of Wallis at the same angle. I couldn't find a head shot but I did find a full-length photograph where her face was in three-quarter profile. When I placed the two pictures side by side, the resemblance between their faces was uncanny. If you had put a hat on her head and lipstick on him, they would have been identical.

Further illumination would be forthcoming that would answer other questions as well.

# CHAPTER 31

# Royalty and Reincarnation

The British royal family is a clear example of group karma, familial reincarnation, and name replication. Consider the abdication of Edward VIII and why it was a continuance of the Wars of the Roses. I have set it out in a chart on the next page.

*1. Wallis Warfield Simpson, Duchess of Windsor,*
*formerly Richard III.*

Richard III, who died on a field of war, is reborn as Wallis Warfield. Although now in a female body, the newly created ego of Wallis seeks the power that her unconscious remembers. She gravitates toward England, the throne, and the man destined to become King Edward VIII. However, this soul entity has yet to atone for the murder of the two little princes in the tower. Her soul mission, as Wallis, is to ensure that the

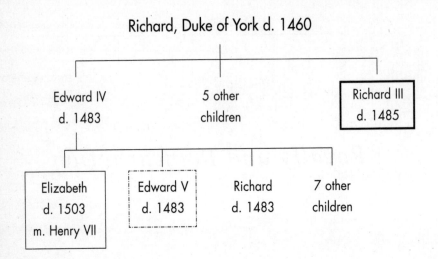

**Richard, Duke of York d. 1460**

- Edward IV
  d. 1483
- 5 other
  children
- Richard III
  d. 1485

(children of Edward IV)
- Elizabeth
  d. 1503
  m. Henry VII
- Edward V
  d. 1483
- Richard
  d. 1483
- 7 other
  children

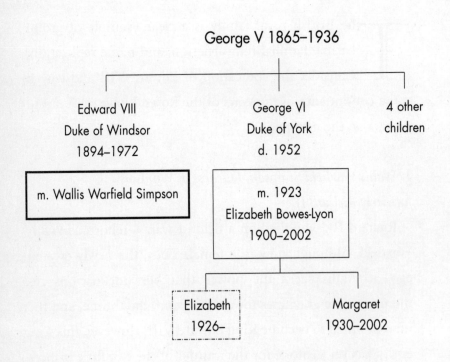

**George V 1865–1936**

- Edward VIII
  Duke of Windsor
  1894–1972
- George VI
  Duke of York
  d. 1952
- 4 other
  children

m. Wallis Warfield Simpson

m. 1923
Elizabeth Bowes-Lyon
1900–2002

- Elizabeth
  1926–
- Margaret
  1930–2002

crown eventually passes to its rightful owner, the one who was deprived of it in the previous existence. To this end, Wallis is also barren so that she can never bear or wield power through a royal child.

*2. Edward VIII, Duke of Windsor, formerly a personal servant to Richard III.*

A life of selfless devotion to his king, Richard III, results in this personal servant being born again as a royal prince. However, on an unconscious level, he feels this role is above his station and he is made uncomfortable by others' obeisance. His life takes on meaning only when his former master, now reincarnated as Wallis, enters the scene and, once again, he can serve his sovereign. As Wallis embodies majesty in his eyes, he is never able to understand why his family will not accept her.

*3. Lady Elizabeth Bowes-Lyon 1900–2002*
   *Duchess of York,*
   *Queen Elizabeth,*
   *The Queen Mother*
   *formerly Princess Elizabeth of York d. 1503,*
   *daughter of Edward IV,*
   *sister of Edward V,*
   *niece of Richard III,*
   *wife of Henry VII,*
   *mother of Henry VIII.*

It is written that the Queen Mother, when she was still a very young Lady Elizabeth Bowes-Lyon, loved to play dress-up games. She used to parade around in finery from the costume box and when asked who she was would reply, "I call myself the Princess Elizabeth."

Not simply Princess Elizabeth but *the* Princess Elizabeth, a title held only by a daughter of the reigning sovereign. And so she had been in a past life. As Princess Elizabeth of York, she had been older sister to the little princes, Edward and Richard, who were murdered in the tower in 1483. And given this Princess Elizabeth's relationship to so many sovereigns, it is not hard to understand why, five hundred years later, reborn as Lady Elizabeth, she should come to be seen as the most royal of her generation.

Elizabeth hates Wallis at first sight as, on an unconscious level, she recognizes her murderous former uncle. Elizabeth sees Wallis as mannish, aggressive, and dangerous, and the enmity is lifelong. After her husband, George VI, dies a premature death, Elizabeth often refers to Wallis as "the woman who killed my husband."

It is interesting to note that had Edward VIII not abdicated, and had his brother therefore remained Duke of York, in widowhood the Queen Mother's title would have been Princess Elizabeth of York.

4. *Queen Elizabeth II, formerly Prince Edward of York, Edward V.*
The two little princes of York would return as the two little

princesses of York, daughters of the Duke and Duchess of York. Their having previously been siblings accounts for the closeness between mother and daughters in this life.

Prince Edward, the elder of the two princes in the tower and legitimate heir to the throne, who was killed so that his uncle could claim the crown, reincarnates in 1926 as Princess Elizabeth. Note that the Queen gave the name Edward to two of her three sons—Andrew Albert Christian Edward and Edward Antony Richard Louis.

### 5. *Princess Margaret, formerly Prince Richard of York.*

The younger brother, nine-year-old Prince Richard, who suffered the same fate in the Tower as his elder brother, comes back in 1930 as Princess Margaret Rose of York.

Princess Margaret also had a life in between as a musical actress who was a royal courtesan. The performing talents and seductive charms she developed with such success in that life would not serve her as well in the next. And being treated with contempt as a mere mistress left her determined to enjoy the full benefits she would be entitled to in her next life, as a princess of the blood royal.

For those who aspire to lead or teach on a grand scale, the lesson of reincarnation is not to be swayed by the adulation of the crowd or corrupted by power. From the perspective of soul growth, the lesson of the use and misuse of power can take many lifetimes to learn. This is why it is not uncommon for famous people to reincarnate as famous people. A king may return as a pop star. Take the example of Elvis Presley.

Elvis was formerly King Tutankhamen. With large numbers of former Egyptians reincarnating in the United States, the timing was perfect for Elvis's arrival on the scene. Consider the following:

He was born and died in Memphis.

He was recognized as "the King."

He received adulation and fanatical devotion out of all proportion to his achievements.

He died the same year that the King Tut exhibition toured American museums. The exhibition, with its artifacts from Tut's funerary procession, was actually on display in Memphis on the day Elvis died. ("They'd come to take him home.")

After much of the above came to me psychically, I noticed others were tuning into similar messages. An illustration I saw in a magazine was an artist's impression of Elvis wearing King Tut headgear; and the report of the birth of Lisa Marie's first child in *People* magazine was headlined KING TOT.

Another example of this theme in reincarnation is that a president may return as a president.

Richard Nixon was formerly Andrew Johnson, who was formerly Thomas Paine.

This entity's soul history is highly connected to the destiny of the United States. Thomas Paine, a founding father who tried to create an ideal system of government, wonders if the impeachment process will work as intended and decides to come back and test it as Andrew Johnson. While the higher self has a pure motive, the brand-new ego of Andrew Johnson is concerned only with its place in history. He avoids the impeachment process by one vote, necessitating yet another rebirth as Richard Nixon. Once again, he reaches the presidency and, for the second time, the newly created ego, which has no memory of its higher destiny, is concerned only with Richard Nixon's place in history and he avoids certain impeachment by resigning. This soul will return as many times as is necessary until the mission undertaken as Thomas Paine is completed. By the way, Johnson's daughter returned as Nixon's daughter Julie.

History will be much kinder to Richard Nixon than his contemporaries have been. Truths will come to light that will reveal him to be a more honorable man than some who have come to that office after him.

# CHAPTER 32

# From London to Sydney

On May 5, 1980, I gave a concert at the Royal Albert Hall in London. Before the show, while I was still at the hotel getting ready to leave for the performance, London's Metropolitan Police commissioner appeared on television, advising anyone going to the Helen Reddy concert that night to stay home. I was rather taken aback to hear this, as I had no plans to cancel the show that evening.

For five days, the Iranian Embassy, which was located next to the Royal Albert Hall in Kensington, had been under siege. Six armed men, members of a dissident Iranian group opposed to the Ayatollah Khomeini, the religious leader who had governed the country since 1979, had taken over the embassy and were holding nineteen hostages. They were demanding the release of ninety-one political prisoners held in Iran, as well as an aircraft to take them and the hostages out of the United

Kingdom. In addition to the Iranians who had been at the embassy when they burst in, they were holding hostage a London police officer acting as embassy guard, a BBC sound man, a BBC news organizer, and some tourists who had been applying for visas. Over the previous days, four of the hostages had been released for medical reasons. When the gunmen shot dead the Iranian press attaché and dumped his body outside the building, threatening to kill the rest of the hostages and blow up the embassy if their demands were not met, the Home Secretary, William Whitelaw, with the approval of the Iranian government, authorized the use of force.

In the event, the SAS launched an attack from the Royal Albert Hall to end the siege during my show. I thought the percussionist was playing really hard that night, but it was machine-gun fire coming from the roof! As I would learn when I read the paper the next morning, more than thirty masked commandos launched their offensive from the basement of the Royal Albert Hall while I was performing onstage. They had stormed the embassy building from the balcony and front and back doors, throwing grenades through the windows. Millions of people had watched the rescue live on television as all three channels had interrupted their regular programming to show the real-life drama unfolding. Screams could be heard from inside the building, and about fifteen minutes later the hostages emerged and were escorted to waiting ambulances by officers from Scotland Yard. Nineteen hostages had been freed but one died and two were injured in the crossfire. Five of the six Iranian gunmen had been killed, and the survivor was under arrest. There were zero casualties, however, inside the Royal Albert Hall, where a lady trained from birth that "the show must go on" and her loyal fans enjoyed an entertaining evening. Who dares, wins? Indeed.

From London I flew to Sydney via Singapore for a command performance at the Sydney Opera House for the Queen and Prince Philip. Sitting in the plane on the tarmac in Singapore, I spotted the large jet of the Queen's Flight parked nearby. We were taking the same route. The command performance on May 27, 1980, was quite a show, featuring an incredible lineup of British and Australian talent. I was very happy to be included.

Bert Newton hosted the evening, and Paul Hogan did his stand-up comedy routine dressed as the day laborer he had once been. He did a funny bit about a lucky number being under someone's seat in the audience—it turned out to be the Queen's seat—which would entitle the winner to spend an evening at home with him and his missus having a barbie and watching the telly. He drew a sustained belly laugh at the idea of that ever happening.

Julie Anthony, an underutilized Aussie talent, sang beautifully, as did Johnny Farnham, and the first half of the show closed with Olivia Newton-John singing a heartfelt "Don't Cry for Me, Argentina."

Peter Allen opened the second half and gave his trademark high-energy performance. He would finally engage the hearts of his countrymen that night with a new song he had written, "I Still Call Australia Home." There were also performances by the Sydney Dance Company and the Australian Ballet.

Before the entire cast assembled onstage to sing "Waltzing Matilda," I would be the closing act, and I felt quite emotional thinking about my great-great-great-great-grandfather having landed in chains near the spot where the Opera House now stood. I felt proud to be representing the six generations who, starting with nothing but the scorn and contempt of their "betters," had built a modern nation. I sang a song written by Barry Manilow that I had never sung before, or since, called "I Am Your Child." I dedicated it to the country I was born and raised in and I meant every word of it.

# CHAPTER 33

# The AIDS Epidemic

In the early eighties the first whisperings surfaced about some new cancer that was affecting gay men. It was only when Rock Hudson's illness became public that many people were aware it had a name. It was called AIDS.

Rock was my first big crush when, at twelve years of age, I pulled a full-page color head shot of him out of a magazine and taped it to the wall alongside my bed. I thought Rock Hudson was more handsome than any other man I had ever seen. Like most adolescent girls, my bedtime fantasy consisted of going to Hollywood, meeting Rock, having him fall madly in love with me, proposing marriage, and then *the kiss*. This moment was always the culmination of passion in films of the era and, consequently, the culmination of mine. My daytime fantasy was choosing names for our five daughters; I recall the first was going to be Rocklyn!

By adulthood I knew what most of show business knew but would never reveal to the general public—Rock was gay. On consideration, having achieved my full adult height, I decided he was way too tall for me, anyway. Still, I think that this twelve-year-old girl would have been thrilled to know that she would grow up, go to Hollywood, meet Rock Hudson, and have dinner with him and his partner. Over the years, I was to often run into him at industry charity events. Rock had a genuine comedic talent and was loved and respected by his peers. That was why it was so shocking to see film footage of him looking gaunt and haggard as this strange new disease ravaged his body.

The medical community seemed mystified by this new malady. Was it an ancient plague that had somehow resurfaced? Was it a man-made virus that had escaped from a laboratory? It was definitely spread through blood or semen. Theories abounded. Meanwhile, some of the most talented members of our artistic community were dying like flies.

It began to hit closer to home. A drag club called La Cage aux Folles had opened in L.A., and I had been told that one of the boys was impersonating me. This sounded like a hoot and something I definitely wanted to see. The performer's name was Kelly Lawrence and he was impersonating Julie Andrews as well as me. As the movie *Victor/Victoria* was a hit at the time, he was in the position of being a man impersonating a woman impersonating a man impersonating a woman. And no, that's not a typo. Despite Kelly visibly trembling with nerves when we met, we hit it off and I invited him to come to Las Vegas and see my show. I also invited him backstage beforehand so that he could see in detail how I did my makeup. He was appreciative of the opportunity, and we had a fun time together. He loved what he was doing and he wanted a career in show business more than anything.

I was surprised one night when I called La Cage to say I was coming in to see him, only to be told that Kelly was in hospital and not expected to return to work. When I visited him the next day, he was in a private room. Although not in isolation, there was a quarantine warning posted on the door cautioning visitors about the possibility of infection. It hit me like a ton of bricks. My poor, dear Kelly.

He was happy to see me and in relatively good spirits. His mother, always supportive of his career, was taking him back home, down south, to recuperate. As he slowly walked me to the elevator, I knew intuitively that he was going home to die and that I would not see him again in this life. We continued to talk via telephone but, with each call, I could hear his voice getting progressively weaker.

Then came the call from his mother telling me that Kelly had passed away. I decided against a wreath and sent instead a dozen long-stemmed red roses in a vase. After all, I was saying farewell to a star.

I was reading a book called *The Women's History of the World* by Dr. Rosalind Miles when I was stunned by a passage about the Kafe people of Papua New Guinea. According to their tribal beliefs, sexual intercourse with a menstruating woman would:

(a) make a man vomit,

(b) turn his blood black,

(c) corrupt his flesh,

(d) addle his wits, and

(e) waste him to death.

These people were describing AIDS! And they knew it was transmitted through blood and/or sexual relations.

In my experience, a question expressed before going into meditation is always answered, so I asked for clarification of what I'd read. This is what came to me: AIDS was one of the biblical plagues and, until recently, had lain dormant for centuries. In ancient times, the temple was the center not only of religious life, but also of healing and lawmaking. The masses were uneducated and relied totally on the priesthood for leadership and guidance. What has come down to us today as sexual taboos, deeply embedded in traditional religious practice, are the remains of old public health laws designed to contain the spread of the disease. Hence, the emphasis on virginity before marriage, sexual relations only within a monogamous union, circumcision for males, and ritual cleansing for postmenstrual women.

# CHAPTER 34

# Capitol Losses, Grosses, and Net

Following a dispute, I ended my long and mutually lucrative relationship with Capitol Records. On the strong recommendation of the head of the company at the time, I had agreed to my next album being produced by a two-man production team who also managed a popular group on the label.

The actual recording went very well, and it was a pleasure to work with great Muscle Shoals musicians—the renowned blues exponents of northwest Alabama—but when I asked for a copy of the tapes and chord charts to take back to California with me so that I could start rehearsing the new songs with my regular road band, the producers gave me a story about how they needed to tweak a few things on the tracks and told me that everything would be sent to me by courier. My alarm bells were clanging—it was standard procedure for the artist to receive a cassette tape at the end of a session. I needed to memorize the songs myself, which was impossible without the charts and backing tapes. Several calls were made to my husband/manager in California on the issue, and only with the personal assurances of the president of Capitol Records did I, against my better judgment, leave Alabama without any evidence that I had recorded an album there. The release of the new album was timed to coincide with my upcoming tour of the UK, and publicity and cross-promotion were all lined up.

What had not been allowed for in the planning was the duplicity and amorality of the production team. Unbeknown to me, they were in the midst of negotiating a new contract with Capitol for the rock group they managed. All copies of my album master recordings, as well as the masters themselves, they held hostage while they negotiated. This was clearly illegal, as the tapes and masters were the property of Capitol Records. Not only that, as the artist, I had paid for the sessions! Given those facts, plus my track record with the company and the rapidly approaching deadline for my new release, I expected the head of Capitol to go to bat for me. He did not. In the end, I had to tour England performing old material and with no new product to promote. Needless to say, that was, for me, the end of my relationship with Capitol Records. I would fold up my tent and go elsewhere while the production team ultimately decided to sign their rock group to a different label. By "not taking sides," the head of the company lost both acts.

My move to MCA Records in the early eighties was a happy one, especially after my former producer, Joe Wissert, came on board in the top slot. Although Joe gave the appearance of being an accountant, and a quiet one at that, he had great musical ears, impeccable musical taste, and had produced some of my best albums as well as those of Boz Scaggs. I was glad to have an artistic ally.

Although my first two albums on the new label had resulted in hit singles in both Asia and Europe, neither had produced a successful hit single for the American pop market. After five straight years of my being on the charts for fifty-two weeks a year, maybe radio listeners needed a break. I know I did.

The recording in Los Angeles of my last album for MCA, called *Imagination,* was to coincide with the end of my second marriage and the dissolution of our business partnership. It was not to be an amicable divorce, and I had to constantly remind myself that I was not dealing with a human being in the normal sense; I was dealing with a human being under the influence of a powerful chemical.

There have been many moments of blinding truth in my life. One was during the dying days of my second marriage. Despite all the denials, it was obvious to me that my husband still had a cocaine problem. He had been treated before for his addiction but his behavior indicated that he was still using—as did his pillow which, by morning, had blood spots, bone fragments and gristle from his nose embedded in it. After he had left the house one morning, I went through the clothes in his wardrobe, something I would never have normally done. Sure enough, I found a vial of cocaine in one of his coat pockets. As I angrily poured the contents into the toilet bowl, I had flashbacks of myself—emptying Mum's hidden brandy bottles down the kitchen sink as a young girl; pouring out my first husband's cheap whiskey the same way; dumping Number Two's diet pills down the toilet; and here I was now with the cocaine doing it again. Obviously what I was doing wasn't working and, as the only common denominator in every scenario was me and my reaction, it would seem that I had a problem. Different city, different person, different substance, but old Helen was still coping in the same way and *it didn't work*. I needed professional help. I called the wife of a colleague I knew to be in a twelve-step program and went to my first Al-Anon meeting the same night.

Al-Anon is a group for friends and family members of alcoholics and addicts. If you are living in this situation, I highly recommend that you try it. Al-Anon is free—donations are optional—and you will be with people who understand your pain and frustration because they have experienced it too. You will learn what you can and cannot do to alleviate the situation. And you will learn, as alcoholics and addicts do in AA, how to recognize and work to eliminate the

character faults common to all of us who grow up in alcoholic families.

I had often been threatened that if I ever left my husband/
manager, he would "bad-mouth me out of the business." An example offered to me of how damaging malicious gossip could be
was that of a popular young actor who became virtually unemployable after allegations spread that he had beaten his dog.
Another example of how heartless and cruel showbiz could be
was the way Peggy Lee was treated by Capitol Records. After years
of making money for them, she received a form letter from their
legal department informing her that she had been dropped from
the label. "The president of the company should have taken her
to lunch and given her the news personally," Number Two would
say. "They didn't treat her like a star." Of course, this was years
before Peggy, by then in a wheelchair, had to take Disney to
court to collect songwriting royalties to which she was entitled.

And speaking of finances, what had been going on with
mine? When I called the pharmacy where I'd had an account
for nine years to request a refill and delivery on my cortisone
prescription, I was told I would have to come down in person
and pay cash as my account was months overdue. To be denied
the one medicine that keeps me alive felt like a direct threat.
When I called our bookkeeper to ask why the bill had not been
paid, she told me to ask my husband and hung up. This conversation was quickly followed by a phone call from him, direct-
ing me not to harass *his* employees. What the hell was going on?

. . .

Many Al-Anon members choose to stay in the relationship, and I gave it my best shot. However, I was dealing with someone who had multiple addictions, was verbally abusive, and had been up on weapons charges twice that year. Although there was newspaper reportage of the charges, neither case made it to court. Because Number Two controlled my career, I had become the cash cow that was enabling his various habits. Clearly, for his sake and mine, I would have to separate our finances.

Despite intensive counseling, the marriage was not salvageable. As he refused to vacate the family home, I would have to leave and take our son with me; Traci was at university by then. A disgustingly ugly custody battle was to ensue, leaving wounds that have still not healed.

Between the time of recording and the time of release of the *Imagination* album there was a major shake-up in the executive offices at MCA Records. Instead of Joe, who would have known how to market and promote the new album to my demographic, I was now dealing with someone of much lower stature in the industry. While whispering in my ear about his big plans for my next album, he had big plans of his own.

During a lunch meeting at the studio, this mister big casually mentioned that my son, Jordan, was staying with his uncle and aunt while his father was in New York. At this news my jaw dropped. I had not been informed that his father had left the state and, if he did, I was supposed to have Jordan returned to me. After a quick phone call from the table to my brother-in-law to confirm the details, I informed him I would be the one to pick Jordan up from school that afternoon.

When I pulled up at the school, the co-principal was standing midpoint up the pathway talking to a student. She saw me and said, loud enough for me to hear, "Here comes trouble," as she turned and walked quickly to her office. As the bell had not yet rung and I was curious to know what "trouble" my arrival could possibly cause, I followed her. I found the principal on the phone to my husband's lawyer, seeking advice. Revelations started coming thick and fast. That shyster had taken my son out of school three times, without my knowledge or consent, for depositions which resulted in a statement, purported to be made by nine-year-old Jordan, saying that he was "fearful of returning to the residence."

This was so patently ridiculous I didn't imagine anyone would take it seriously. Any child who is truly scared to go home would express it in just those simple terms, "I'm scared to go home." I don't even know any adult who would say, "I am fearful of returning to the residence"—other than an unscrupulous attorney putting words into the mouth of a child. However, I was outnumbered and outmaneuvered and had to watch in horror and humiliation as my child, whom the school principal refused to release to me, was placed in the car belonging to his father's housekeeper and driven away. The woman who collected Jordan had been our housekeeper, and I had fired her for dishonesty. As well as padding the grocery bills, I had discovered that she was listening in on the extension whenever my lawyer telephoned, taking notes and passing them on to my estranged husband.

So that was to be the tactic. He planned to accuse me of child abuse, even though I had never in my life raised a hand to my son. It was beyond devastating. He had struck at me where I lived—as a mother.

Other surprises were waiting for me, and I was disturbed to see the extent to which someone's conscience could be destroyed by a drug. A television sitcom pilot that had been in development for me was dropped. Several of my performing contracts were canceled, and one promoter told me he couldn't book me in case a certain someone "came after him with a shotgun." It seemed to me that this person was trying to destroy my livelihood. Why was he doing this, when he was taking away money that his children stood to benefit from? I had hoped that with me no longer acting the role of the enabler financially, it would put brakes on his gambling and drug taking. What I had underestimated was the "old boy" network and the extent to which others were willing to fill the void in his finances.

Evidence of Number Two's bitterness and cold-bloodedness kept coming. At both home and office we had had large double Rolodexes containing all the unlisted phone numbers we used.

Business and personal numbers had been combined because, in Los Angeles, the two are inseparable. My husband/manager commandeered both Rolodexes, leaving me with no way of contacting most of our friends or business associates. I would have to wait for them to call me. In most cases, I'm still waiting.

There was someone who didn't need my number—my next-door neighbor. The wife of a psychiatrist and mother of three boys, we had never exchanged more than a few pleasantries although our sons have remained friends into their thirties. She appeared at my front door and told me that, as their bedroom overlooked our tennis court, she and her husband had unavoidably heard the sounds of our family life over the previous nine years. She said she heard me almost every day out there, throwing a ball to my son or riding bikes around the court with him. She added that she and her husband often heard Jordan's father yelling at his son in an abusive manner. If I needed someone to testify on Jordan's and my behalf at the custody hearing, they would both be happy to oblige.

The day that the *Imagination* album was released I went to Tower Records in Westwood to see what sort of promotion MCA was doing. At the entrance to the store I ran into a young couple who had written one of the songs on the album. They were anxious to buy a copy. It took the three of us, searching independently, fifteen minutes to find one. There were no store displays of any kind. It was not filed under New Releases. It was not to be found under my name in the pop female vocal section or any other category. My new album was finally located in the back of the store in a bin marked Nostalgia and filed under the letter *R*. It had been successfully "buried." And as the new album was never delivered to any radio stations, of course, it received no airplay. Consequently, I was not surprised when I received a form letter from the company's legal department telling me that I'd been dropped from the label. In fact, visions of Peggy Lee danced in my head. Did I mention that the head of MCA named his son after my husband/manager? Or that the housekeeper I'd fired then went to work for him and his wife?

In preparation for the 1982 release of the *Imagination* album, my publicist had arranged for an article in *People* magazine. I had gone to their photographer's studio to have pictures taken to accompany the story. They had also taken pictures of me at home in California and onstage in Atlantic City. My daughter, Traci, was about to graduate from USC Film School—with honors, says proud Mum—and with music videos now the rage, I had asked her if she had any ideas for my new album. She certainly did. With the help of her classmates and a loan from the bank, she made a most imaginative film out of the song *Imagination* for only fifteen thousand dollars. I love film students; their enthusiasm is infectious, and because they live on a budget, they know how to cut corners. I could write a chapter just on the innovative ways they saved money.

To coincide with the album's release, I'd also been booked to appear on *Good Morning America,* and they were flying me from Los Angeles to New York especially for that purpose.

While I was in the air, the latest edition of *People* magazine was hitting the stands. I didn't know it yet but the interview intended as publicity for the *Imagination* album was now a cover story, complete with a smiling picture of me, on "Hollywood's Dirtiest Divorce."

While I was in the limo traveling from JFK Airport into the city, the driver's radiophone rang. We were in heavy traffic and stopped long enough for him to scribble something on a piece of paper. He passed it to me and said that it was important that I call the phone number he'd jotted down as soon as possible. It was a New York number with no name attached. The driver was simply passing on the message. I wondered what on earth could be so important that someone had tracked me down in a moving vehicle and what was so important that it couldn't wait until I arrived at the studio.

Like any parent, my first thoughts were of my kids. Had something happened to either of them? Jordan had been taken to Europe by his father but exactly where they were, I had not been able to ascertain. His father would telephone me but refuse to tell me where they were or allow me to speak to my son. In one conversation I asked, "Where will you be tomorrow so I can call and talk to Jordan?"

He replied, "Either France, Italy, or Switzerland."

I could hear Jordan's voice in the background, "Is that Mommy on the phone? Can I talk to her?"

"Your mother doesn't want to talk to you. She's too busy," I heard him say before he hung up.

My daughter and the young man who later became her husband were also somewhere in Europe, backpacking, and with no itinerary planned in advance, they could be almost anywhere.

At that moment, I had no knowledge of what country either of my children was in. Was it possible that one of them had been hurt or injured in some way? Did they need my consent before the doctors could operate or was it worse than that? The longer we crawled along in the traffic, the more I began to worry. We were stuck on the bridge into Manhattan and not moving when the phone rang again. The driver answered it, hung up and then told me it was urgent that I call the number immediately. I got out of the car, ran across the bridge and found a phone booth. By the time I dialed the number, I could feel the bile rising in my throat. I could not afford to go into Addisonian crisis at that moment and I willed myself not to vomit as the call was answered. It was the talent coordinator from *Good Morning America*!

I had already done the customary pre-interview over the phone from L.A. and had established that I was bringing the video of my new single with me. It would be shown for the first time on their show. I had told her I would be happy to discuss anything except the custody case because a gag order had been placed on those concerned. If I were to discuss the subject in any way, I would be in contempt of court. The matter had been settled, as far as I was concerned.

The talent coordinator informed me that there was no point in my coming on the show if I wasn't going to talk about the custody battle because "our viewers don't care about your music, they just want to hear about your personal life."

Slowly, I walked back to the car to tell the driver to turn around and take me back to the airport. I needed to find another way to earn a living. I couldn't do this any more. I was disgusted by what was happening to show business. My private life was not something to be exploited for the financial benefit of some media mogul. The profession I had been raised in was being reduced to "celebrity chasing," and I wanted no part of it. The problem was that I had no other skills and I was facing a mountain of debts.

One of my nastier surprises around this time was that the home I had insisted on paying cash for had been double-mortgaged. I couldn't understand how this had happened and then I remembered. Because I was in a tax bracket where I had to pay taxes three months in advance of earnings, and as my earnings came in lump sums, I had twice signed what I was told were short-term loans to cover the outlays. Well, not only had the loans not been repaid, the taxes had not been paid, either. They had been accumulating interest and penalties for some time. And there was no point trying to borrow against my life insurance as someone else had thought of that before me. It had a cash value of one cent.

California law is highly explicit when it comes to community property and gifts. For example, if a husband presents his wife with a piece of jewelry on a special occasion, it is regarded as a gift and therefore as her separate property. If, on the other hand, there are pieces which have been purchased as investments, they are considered to be community property.

When I saw that all my jewelry was being listed as community property on a document that my estranged husband was pressuring me to sign, I was deeply hurt. In essence, he was trying to take back all the presents he'd given me over a fifteen-year marriage. I refused to sign anything and wondered how I could prove each piece had been a gift. Then it hit me. We had had an account at Tiffany's for many years. If they still had our records, I could prove by the dates of purchase that different items had been bought for occasions like my birthday, anniversary, Valentine's Day, and Mother's Day. Unfortunately, Tiffany only had records of his last four purchases. Three of them weren't for me! I don't know who received the nine-thousand-dollar bracelet. I do know who ended up paying for it.

Fortunately, I would learn what I needed to know gradually. Had I found out everything all at once, I could not have processed it. I took the advice to "follow the money." A garage full of legal boxes, ceiling to floor, all containing our financial records for the last fifteen years, was delivered to me and, late at night when everyone else was asleep, I would go through the files and "follow the money."

The divorce had been final for months before I worked out the "how" of much of the financial loss I'd been experiencing. A check made out to me personally would be deposited in our joint account; a few days later, the same amount would be transferred to the business account of my ex and, a few days after that, the same amount would be transferred into his personal account. He had taken from me systematically and he had had help. The business managers, accountants, and bookkeepers I had thought were watching over our common interests were instead working for him. When I found a letter he had written to our bank manager, requesting funds to be transferred from our daughter's trust account into his personal account, I was shocked that the bank had not even notified me when both signatures were supposedly required. When I checked the date on the letter and discovered that it had been written on a Monday—his poker night—I was ready to hunt bear. It was one thing to steal from me; it was another to steal from my children.

When I sold my house and closed up my business a few years ago, the legal boxes were moved back into storage. I still go through them from time to time, when I feel up to it. During the writing of this book, while looking for old family photos, my son came across documents showing that the money left to me by my parents, which I had instructed to be paid directly to my sister in Australia, was instead transferred into a bank account in the United States. Guess whose?

During this period, I was seeing a counselor and trying to understand why my son, with whom I had always had a close, loving relationship, was acting in such a surly, hostile manner toward me. If he'd been thirteen I might have considered it normal behavior, but he was barely ten. My counselor warned me that it might be a while before Jordan and I re-established our relationship. I remember asking her, "Can you give me a date?" I desperately needed something hopeful to cling to.

In between his father's drug-fueled rants about what a terrible person his mother was, Jordan was being subjected to viewings of *Kramer vs. Kramer* and *The Champ*, two tear-jerking, emotionally manipulative father-son films.

My experiences of trying to work within the legal system were less than positive. Hoping to expose his father's continuing use of cocaine, I had requested that blood tests be done on both of Jordan's parents before the custody hearing but this was denied. Everything seemed to be slanted in one direction. Justice may be a woman wearing a blindfold, but legality is definitely a man wearing a patch over one eye.

Fortunately, the court did order counseling for Jordan so that he had someone neutral he could talk with, and when I learned that—facing the possibility of having to choose between his parents in court—my son was threatening suicide, I caved in and accepted joint custody.

No one wants to make an unpopular decision, and joint custody appears to offer a judge an equitable solution. In effect, it is a nondecision. It means that two people who are unable to resolve a conflict and have come to the court for help are sent away to work it out themselves. What this means in practical terms is that the bully wins. And for Number Two, it was all about winning, not Jordan's well-being.

For the next few years, I would see my son when his father felt like it.

Had I known how long it would be before Jordan truly became my son again or what he would be subjected to by his cocaine-crazed father, I would have kidnapped him and disappeared.

I can't say that the eighties were my favorite decade by any means. I was drowning in debt not of my own making, and with all the mud that was being slung at me and my ongoing discovery of Number Two's past misdeeds, it's no wonder that I was having nightmares during this period. Two of them stayed with me and required little in the way of analysis. In one, I was at the bottom of a muddy hole. I kept trying to climb out of it, but the mud would come away in my hands and I couldn't get a grip. In the other one, I had been pushed down a staircase, fallen to the bottom, and broken my leg. I was sitting there unable to rise to a standing position and everyone who walked past told me it was my own fault for tripping and kept walking.

One person who helped keep me sane during the divorce period was Graciela Casillas. A kickboxing and martial arts champion I used to work out with, she privately trained lots of celebrities in the L.A. area. Still living at home with her parents and siblings in Ventura County, Graciela sometimes stayed over in the guestroom at my house rather than make the long drive home at night. Through working out together on a daily basis, we had become friends and even did a little piece together in my show. Dressed as a waitress, Graciela would heckle me from the audience, come up onstage, and we would fight a mock battle with sticks for a few minutes. I figured if Elvis could include martial arts in his show, why not? During the divorce she volunteered to move into my house and act as security for me. She also pushed me to keep up my daily workout, and being forced to scream, kick, and punch with full abandon did much to dissipate the anger I was barely able to contain. The amount of stress I was under could have been fatal to someone with Addison's disease. Thank you, Graciela, for being one of my earth angels.

Finally, the divorce was behind me. A frank assessment of my situation? I had lost my home, my husband, my family, my career, and my good name. However, I had no choice but to soldier on as best I could. What I still had was a few really good friends and a bunch of loyal fans who would stick by me through it all. Even so, the emotional toll was devastating, and two years would pass before I was able to get through a day without crying.

It was inevitable, given my vulnerable state and my lack of family support, that I would rebound into the first relationship that came along. My new partner was the opposite of my husband in every way, and I could give you a million reasons why it seemed a good idea at the time. I was under siege; I thought that if I was another man's wife, the persecution—like the eighteen phone calls logged during one night—would end; I wanted to form another relationship quickly before I had a chance to become bitter; I thought I could cover all that pain with an overlay of happiness; I wanted a stable family life for my children, and I needed someone to hold me. Well, it was mistake Number Three. I not only allowed my children no time to adjust to the change, I gave myself no time to heal.

During this time, how I missed Aunty Nell and her wise counsel and guidance. Then again, she'd strongly advised me against marrying Number Two in the first place; she thought he was certifiably insane.

My wedding to Number Three was a happy day in a sea of misery, despite Number Two's efforts to disrupt the occasion. Although he was in Europe at the time, Number Two arranged for me to be served with a subpoena as I was walking down the aisle. Fortunately, my lawyer, who was in attendance as a wedding guest, was able to intercept the server before he reached me. Also among the wedding presents, there was a gift-wrapped box that Number Two had had someone prepare and send me in his absence. Inside was a sweater that I had designed and hand-knitted for him. It had been ripped to shreds, and the card read, "I always hated it." Why on earth would he go to so much bother? And for what? And then I recognized what was going on underneath. A Jewish man rips his clothing when he is overcome with grief. For the first time in a long time, I felt sorry for him. And I understood something of how he felt. Like anyone who has lived with an addict, I mourned the loss of the fun-loving person he had once been and, emotionally, I would swing back and forth between deep shame at having been married to him and missing my best friend and partner of fifteen years.

# CHAPTER 35

# *Back to Basics*

I t would seem that the one who was so determined to make me unemployable had a far reach. Although I had had a multimedia career, I was finding myself blocked at every turn. There was only one area of show business that we had not shared and in which he had no contacts or influence. It now beckoned me home.

In the 1980s I returned to my theatrical roots and performed in my first book musicals in North America, beginning with ith the role of Reno Sweeney in *Anything Goes* at the Sacramento Music Circus. This was followed by a larger production of *Anything Goes* for the Long Beach Civic Light Opera. One of the reviewers was peeved that I did not look or sound like Ethel Merman; as the good lady was already deceased, I was gratefully relieved. I returned to the Sacramento Music Circus to play the title role in *Call Me*

*Madam* and a third time as Edwin Drood in Charles Dickens's *The Mystery of Edwin Drood.*

In theater, I would discover the last bastion of camaraderie and equality in the entertainment world. Unlike film, where actors argue over seconds of camera time and who says what line, the theater retains a vestige of the old trouper mentality. "All for one and one for all" and "the play's the thing" attitudes still exist among performers whose love of their art is larger than their narcissism. It felt good to be back.

At the beginning of every decade, I've noticed that there is a rush to embrace the new and distance oneself from the old. Whatever was fashionable and popular ten years ago will now be denigrated as dated and unattractive. Wait another ten years, however, and what was fashionable and popular two decades ago now becomes retro chic. This phenomenon has been repeating itself every ten years for as long as I've been alive and probably since time immemorial. Believe it or not, during the eighties, I was asked many times if I still believed in feminism! As if it had been a fad like mood rings and pet rocks. I have always felt that if someone truly believes in equal rights for all human beings, it is impossible to change one's mind. However, as the sixties proved, there will always be those who embrace a cause more for the clothing than the concept.

The uniform of the 1980s for women was the power suit, a jacket with gridiron shoulder pads paired with a tight mini-skirt. How's that for a mixed message? Women were entering professions previously not open to them, and law schools and MBA programs were turning out more and more female graduates. Unfortunately, instead of bringing their own uniquely feminine viewpoint to their work, many women were to emulate men as they were forced to compete in a game with rules that favor males. And some, bending over backward to avoid charges of favoritism themselves, imposed higher standards on their sisters.

Yes, the eighties brought many changes, including a backlash against the civil rights gains of minorities and women in the previous decade. Hard-won legislation was overturned and sleaze entered the culture, with the emphasis on celebrity tabloid journalism. It was obvious that those in control of the media—journalists are under editors, who are under publishers—wanted to go back to the old images of women as virgin mother or whore. Lady Diana and Madonna came along and filled the roles perfectly. The latter bothered me, as I did not see going from "I Am Woman" to "Material Girl" as a positive progression. Having spent so much of my life fighting for women to be treated with dignity and respect, I was both dismayed and alarmed by how many pubescent girls I was now seeing dressed in provocative clothing and practicing erotic moves. The sexualization of female children was beginning. I also noticed that as female clothing got skimpier, male clothing became baggier. All you have to do is watch old film footage of a basketball game and see the difference between now and then in uniforms and cheerleading outfits.

I would learn during the eighties how easily gains are lost and how deeply ingrained sexism is in our society. Even now, in the third millennium, I see that the word of a man is still given more credibility than that of a woman, and that the old-boy network is alive and well.

In the eighties the rich would get richer, the poor would get poorer, and the middle class felt the squeeze. This was to transfer to show business as well. Artists who played arenas began to need corporate sponsorship to underwrite their costs and, as competition increased for the shrinking market, production values increased accordingly. Some acts now needed semitrailers for all their special effects and technical equipment. This, in turn, drove up ticket prices, which further increased competition for the ever-diminishing market and continued the cycle. Those who worked the small clubs, and were often paid in cash each night, barely eked out an existence. Artists like myself, who mostly played theaters and concert halls, found their middle-class audience feeling the pinch, and many artists opted to team up for a concert tour so that they could share costs.

I scaled down my show, which had always had a concert format anyway, and looked for multitaskers—like Max Reddy did in Australia years before. The days of traveling with a ten-piece band and three backup singers were over, but I could still achieve a full sound onstage if I hired musicians who could also sing. In order to keep the same vocal harmonics, however, some of the players had to be female. I cut the band down to four members, three of whom could also sing in the required range, which gave me the sound of seven onstage. With a roadie taking care of sound and lights, we were down to a six-member, versatile, and easily transportable company.

A big event for me in 1984 was the wedding of my daughter, Traci, to Lucas Donat, her longtime love. They had first met in fifth grade; perhaps they bonded because they were the two kids in the class with performing parents.

Luke's dad, Peter Donat, is a highly respected actor from a theatrical family. Like his uncle, Robert Donat, Peter is best known for his film roles, particularly in *The Godfather*. Luke's mother, Michael Learned, was playing the mother in *The Waltons*, at the time a hugely popular television series.

Lucas had come to Las Vegas with us on one of our trips there, and I had a feeling there was something special about him. At that age, it was unusual for kids of the opposite sex to be so comfortable with each other.

When they told me, after they reached the age of twenty-one, that they wanted to get married, I gave them both my blessing. What was I going to say, "Wait until you know each other better"? At the time of writing, they have been husband and wife for more than twenty years.

As a courtesy, I had sent a wedding invitation to Aunty Lyle in New Zealand, as she was the only one of my parents' siblings who was still alive. I was delighted when she responded. We started having long chats about the old days, when she and my mother had been *Babes in the Wood,* and her conversation was peppered with constant references to "Mumma and Stella and I."

Like many older folks, Aunty Lyle could take a long time to tell a story; after a while, my attention would sometimes wander and I would simply nod and murmur an occasional acknowledgment. And then, one day, my ears pricked up when I heard her say, ". . . and Mumma would light the candles every Friday night, but *sshh,* don't tell Grandma and Grandpa . . . and Mumma would go miles out of her way to shop at the kosher butcher but *sshh,* don't tell Grandma and Grandpa." Now she had my attention.

I said, "Aunty Lyle, what are you trying to tell me?"

So it was that I would learn, at the age of forty-two, with my daughter about to be married, that my mother's mother had been Jewish. She had married into a Scottish Presbyterian family and did not want her in-laws to know that she still practiced her faith—"Don't tell Grandma and Grandpa"—but her daughters had been aware of it.

There was no room in my budget for holidays, what with the debt load still hanging over my head, but one thing I was able to do during the eighties was use up some of the frequent-flier points I'd been accumulating. I had been all over the world and seen a lot of airports, hotels, and dressing rooms, but there had rarely been time while I was working to do much sightseeing.

I researched where my husband and I could go in Europe to get the most value for my points and came up with Germany, as it was the only country that included hotel rooms in the package. We would also be in Munich for the Oktoberfest. The trip down the Romantic Road, Germany's former medieval trade route, proved to be breathtaking although, by the end of the week, I was tired of eating Wiener schnitzel. It was the only item on the menu that I recognized and, not speaking German, I was afraid of ordering something I might not be able to eat. While in Munich, I was compelled to visit Dachau. Being slightly psychic, I didn't know what kind of energies I might pick up on.

As I walked though the gates, I felt a rush of blood from my womb. It was the only physical reaction I had. Seeing where the camp huts had been before being razed, I felt that the ground had long since been purified. And, even gazing at the one remaining—now freshly painted—oven where humans had been cremated, I felt that the prayers of many people who had come since had cleansed the suffering. I was just thinking that there was no trace left of the evil that had taken place there when I came to the last building, which had housed individual cells for those who were in solitary confinement or who were being tortured. This building was the only one not to have been repainted and it had a grille across the hallway inside, preventing entrance. As I looked through the bars and down the hall, I could hear bloodcurdling screams. At least one poor soul is still trapped in there in purgatory.

. . .

A pattern I have noticed with popular music is that once a genre becomes too complicated, it implodes, and something newer and simpler takes its place. Jazz, for instance, which was enormously popular in the 1950s, started becoming difficult even for other musicians to follow. People like music they can re-create themselves, and folk music, with its simple chords and storyline lyrics, became the big thing on campus in the late fifties and early sixties.

I witnessed something similar happen in the 1980s with rap music. As the drum and the human voice are the only two musical instruments common to every culture on earth, rap is truly global music, although sociologically it tends to deal with local rather than global issues.

My son became greatly enamored of this new form of music and quite expert in his knowledge; his first job out of college, years later, would be at DefJam in New York. In the meantime, I was concerned about his school reports, which showed that he was doing poorly in English. This was hard to understand as he had grown up surrounded by books and had parents who loved to read. For his homework assignments, he was turning in essays that were only half a page long. He'd been classified as gifted, so it wasn't anything to do with a lack of intelligence.

I believe there is a key for each one of us that unlocks the door to knowledge and also creative expression. What was the key for Jordan?

He was a big fan of the original *Blues Brothers* film, and the two of us used to riff together on dialogue from the film. Jordan had even hung out with John Belushi backstage and was shattered when he died. I suggested he approach his next writing assignment as if it were a conversation between Jake and Elwood, the two main characters in the film. I saw the light go on as he grabbed a piece of paper and a pencil and began putting his ideas in dialogue form. For another assignment, my suggestion was that he write it in the form of a rap song. I knew his teacher would read it as verse.

What Jordan had needed was a basic structure to work within. Once he had that, his creativity flowed and his natural talent began to pour out. Today, my son is a writer.

# CHAPTER 36

# Let's Go On with the Show

The early 1990s would find me feeling rather jaded and weary. Singing the same songs over and over had worn out any enthusiasm I had for the road and I longed to do something different. Life was about to throw me a pearl. Velvety-voiced jazz singer Mel Tormé was going out on a concert tour and wanted a female singer to share the bill with him. As well as performing my half of the evening, the show would close with both of us singing a medley of thirty-two songs in counterpoint. Was I interested?

Was I what! The late Mel Tormé was always regarded as the singer's singer; he had a divine instrument, perfect pitch, flawless intonation, and impeccable taste in repertoire. It was a great honor to work with him. He had been writing arrangements for big bands before I was born and yet he had lost none of his enthusiasm. His love of singing was so infectious that I found myself energized by it.

Being exposed to Mel's audience also allowed me to slip a few American songbook standards into my show, and my musicians to slip some jazz chords under the old pop hits. It was a great tour, and the band and I learned a lot from the master.

I had kept up as many contacts as I could on my travels, and with the paucity of work coming in, I began putting together my own world tours. Two years running, I circumnavigated the globe with my band, although it took me months to organize the route. I planned dates so that we would always be traveling westward; it's much easier on the body.

I was living in Santa Monica and I had my office in a separate building on my property. It was convenient being able to call Europe at 4 A.M.—noon their time—while still wearing a bathrobe. I could be showering and eating breakfast as the dawn broke across the Atlantic and back in the office by 6 A.M. to call New York, Atlanta, or Miami—9 A.M. their time. I would follow the sun across North America's time zones and sometimes still be in the office at night, following it across the Pacific if I needed to talk to someone in Hawaii, New Zealand, Australia, or the Far East.

Forty years after my parents had done so, I was to take my own six-member unit to South Korea and Japan to entertain the troops. U.S. forces were still stationed in South Korea, and I did a show right on the 38th parallel for members of the 8th Army, 2nd Infantry Division. As I walked around the table in the border station which straddles North and South Korea, I felt the hostility emanating from the Northern soldiers. One could immediately sense the danger that the guys of 8th 2nd ID face twenty-four hours a day. It must affect the hormones because, standing out onstage, I've never been engulfed by so much testosterone at one time in my life. I can understand why Marilyn Monroe got such a buzz from it.

The band and I also performed a show in an airplane hangar in Japan—which, oddly enough, had the best acoustics I've ever heard outside of the Royal Albert Hall.

The highlight of that Asian tour for me was China. John Denver had been the first male Western star allowed in to perform in the People's Republic; I was to be the first female. I was told by my promoter that securing a visa for me had not been easy, as there was a stigma attached to the "female entertainer" label. This was the job description given by many Western ladies of fortune seeking to sell their wares in an Asian market. Two factors convinced the Chinese government that I was not going there for immoral purposes; one was my age at the time—early fifties; the other was that I had served for three years as a commissioner of parks and recreation for the state of California and, presumably, had already undergone official investigation.

I loved Beijing. I felt very much at home there and found the people to be wonderfully warm and friendly. Everyone seemed happy and, as I was free to wander wherever I wanted, I hardly think they were all smiling for my benefit. I saw only one old man wearing a Mao jacket the whole time I was there. Everyone else was in Western-style clothing. You could tell this was a relatively new concept from the assortment of wildly contrasting shirts and trousers on parade. I don't recall seeing too many coordinated tops and bottoms. However, it felt like I was surrounded by wildflowers wherever I went.

Fascinated with the history of China, I walked the entire area of the Forbidden City, even though I was still on a walking stick, recovering from a compound ankle fracture. I had seen the film *The Last Emperor* and now here I was where the film had been shot and the events depicted had actually taken place. My third husband was with me and, being part Asian himself, he was impressed to see the level of culture his Chinese forebears had achieved while his Anglo ancestors were still running around in animal skins.

What I could foresee was a problem for the Chinese with the consequences of the one-child-only rule. On the streets of Beijing, I saw many more little boys than I did little girls. Where are the brides going to come from in the future? I also wondered, seeing each only child being fussed over by two parents and four grandparents, how the Chinese would go about fostering a belief in their communal system in children who have never had to share anything with a sibling.

Beijing was in the early stages of a building boom, and the contrast between the old and the new was sometimes stunning. It surprised me that the nightclub that I had been booked to play in not only catered to Western diplomats for the most part, but also had a Tex-Mex theme going on, with serapes on the walls and the waitresses wearing holsters. It occurred to me during a show there one night that I had truly achieved my dream of an international career. Here I was, an Australian, singing in French, with an American band, in a Mexican nightclub in China!

The Chinese are thoughtful hosts, and an afternoon tea was arranged for me with some local Chinese performers. They knew my father had been a comedian so I was introduced to two gentlemen who did a comedy double act—they call it "cross-talk." I also met a lady, a former opera star who had been a favorite of Chairman Mao. As well as singing live, she showed us a film clip of herself. I had brought the two female members of my band, Karen and Teresa, who also sang backup with me, and we reciprocated with a performance of "Delta Dawn" sung a cappella but in three-part harmony with hand-clapping, body-slapping, and finger-snapping for rhythm. Our hosts were fascinated, particularly by the harmonies, as their melodic scale is so different from ours. It was an afternoon that I shall never forget. It showed me yet again the bonds that exist between all performers around the world.

Other dates were not so wonderful, and I was becoming alarmed by how much the business was changing. For one engagement, I was offered such low money that it was impossible financially for me to accept the gig. When I heard that the promoter, for whom I had worked previously, was peeved by my refusal, I picked up the phone and called him directly, as I didn't want any bad blood and hoped we would work together again in the future. The promoter couldn't understand why I was turning down his offer, which he thought was more than fair. When I said I couldn't break even on the amount he'd offered me, there was a silence. Then he told me that the offer he had made was double the amount I'd mentioned. Between us, we tracked down four middlemen, all taking a piece out of the pie before it was finally offered to me, by which time the promoter's original offer had been cut in half. And I was dealing with characters I did not want to deal with.

One engagement in Florida was a clear sign from the universe that it was time to change direction. The booking, in an outdoor amphitheater, had come in through a major agency and, as usual, I had built other dates around it so that I could create a minitour and amortize my costs. My contract, like all standard personal appearance contracts, called for 10 percent to be paid on signing, 40 percent to be paid thirty days before the gig, and the remaining 50 percent to be paid before I went onstage. The 10 percent had come in on time, but it was held by the agency—a standard arrangement, which ensured that they got their commission no matter what happened. The 40 percent in advance I relied on to pay for airline tickets, hotel rooms, band meals, and other expenses that I needed to outlay. This amount had not been paid in by the due date and, despite the agent's assurances that everything would be fine, I started to worry. The agency already had its money, what did they care? I was the one who had to lay out thousands of dollars in up-front expenses.

I started ringing the Florida promoter directly. Every time I called his office, he was either in a meeting, on the other line or out of the office; however, his secretary assured me the check was already in the mail. Another week went by with no sign of a check, which his secretary said must have gotten lost. The promoter was still unreachable either at home or at his office.

Finally, two days before the band and I were due to leave for Florida, I phoned yet again and was told by his secretary that the promoter had the 40 percent in cash and he would put it in my hand as I stepped off the plane. I had to explain to her that until the money was in my hand, I would not be stepping on the plane. Unless I received a cashier's check within twenty-four hours, they would have to cancel the gig. I had been stiffed once too often, and you can't repossess a live performance.

Ninety minutes before I was due to leave for the airport, and I was prepared to tell the band to go home and come back tomorrow for the rest of the tour—I would have to pay them anyway—a cashier's check arrived by courier. Now all I had to worry about was collecting the other 50 percent before the show.

It was the secretary, trying very hard to be sincere, who met us at the airport. As the venue was outdoors and our sound-check was in daylight, I could see a man in a suit walking up and down the aisles and talking on a cell phone, but every time I made a move off the stage toward him, he would disappear. I presumed that he was the promoter. I never did meet him or talk with him.

That evening, a local act opened the show while I got made up and dressed. At intermission, the secretary came into my dressing room and proceeded to give me a pep talk about how excited the audience was and how they couldn't wait for me to be out there. Flattery has always left me cold. I told her I would be going out onstage as soon as I received the rest of my money. She disappeared. Then the head of security showed up wearing a Western-style suit and cowboy boots. He opened his coat so that I could see that he was carrying a pistol and he told me I'd better get out there, the audience was getting restless. Was he kidding? What did he plan to do? March me out onstage and hold a gun to my head at the microphone in front of thousands of people? I stood my ground. No money, no show. And I pointed out that he was the one who would have to deal with the disappointed and angry fans. He disappeared, only to reappear about ten minutes later. He had obviously been to the box office to collect the cash because he started pulling fifties and hundreds out of his pockets and cowboy boots. He flung it all on the dressing table, produced a receipt and told me to sign it and get out onstage. I told him I would have to count the money before I signed anything. He was not a happy chap. I counted the money, bundled it into a bag, and had the band take it out onstage with them, as I didn't trust leaving it in the dressing room. I also told them to break down all the equipment as soon as the show ended because I wanted to get out of there as quickly as possible. Once the concert was over, I had no more bargaining chips if the security cowboy tried to take the money back at gunpoint.

We were packed up and ready to go, with the trunks loaded in the car boots and everyone in the limo, when Mr. Security suddenly stuck his head in the car. I shrank back in my seat when he asked me to wait a minute; the promoter wanted something from me. It was an autographed picture! I scribbled my name across an 8-by-10 glossy promo shot and got the hell out of there.

Quite a few of the same major agency's acts played the Florida amphitheater that summer. And the agency collected their commission up front on every one.

I was told that I was the only artist who got paid in full.

CHAPTER 37

# London to New York

Both personally and professionally, I was stuck in a rut
and I did not want to deal with the kinds of people I
was being forced to deal with; something around me
needed to shift. I found myself in a prayer group of people
with strong spiritual energy and I asked the Almighty for a
solution that would be for the good of all concerned.

By then I was already booked for the Christmas/New Year
season at the Café Royal in London. Now closed, the Café
Royal was, in its day, the premier cabaret venue in the city. As
I had not played cabaret in years, I had great fun putting
together a new show and arranging some vocal medleys.

Bill Kenwright, an English producer, called me—not for the
first time—about going into his show *Blood Brothers* in New
York. Years before, I had met Bill and seen the show in London,
starring Kiki Dee. He had approached me to play a role for the

Broadway production, but I had turned him down because I had a home in California and didn't want to move to New York. I also had an obligation to the musicians in my band. In order to keep them together as a band, I had to keep them all working. If I went into a Broadway show for any length of time, I'd lose them. Bill decided on Petula Clark for *Blood Brothers* in New York and covered his bet with the Cassidy brothers playing the twins. I thought it was brilliant casting and made for strong publicity.

Six months later Bill had called again, asking me to take over the role in New York because Petula and the Cassidys were going to tour the States with a new *Blood Brothers* touring company. Once more, I turned him down; same reason as before. Bill then gave Carole King a chance to show New York she could act.

It was shortly before Christmas, another six months on, and Bill was calling a third time. I thought of the story about the man sitting on the roof of his house watching the rising floodwaters. A neighbor comes by rowing a dinghy and tells him to hop in. The man declines, saying, "God will save me." As the water continues to rise, a police launch comes by and the man is told to climb aboard. He waves them away saying, "God will save me." Finally, as the water reaches the eaves of the house, a helicopter hovers overhead and drops a rope ladder down to the man. Once again, he waves the helicopter away saying, "God will save me." Shortly thereafter, the water completely covers the roof of the house and the man drowns.

When he gets to heaven he says to God, "I've always believed in you and prayed to you. Why did you let me drown? Why didn't you save me?," and God replies, "First, I sent a rowboat, then a motorboat, and finally a helicopter. What else could I do?"

Was I resisting the answer to my prayer? I had asked the Holy Spirit for a shift in my situation and yet I had twice refused to move from California when I was offered the opportunity. What I had wanted was for others around me to make the change but it was I who needed to shift. This was the third time I was being offered a way out. There wouldn't be another one.

Of course, the fact that Bill pleaded with me to help him out of a jam—Carole was leaving the show, he couldn't get a replacement, he was appealing to me as a friend, and so on—worked to his advantage. He also mentioned that, as I would be going into the Broadway production only two days after I closed at the Café Royal, I would need to rehearse with the London cast during the day while I was working at night. Was I up to it? Help out a friend? Take up a challenge? He knew me too well.

As it turned out, because of limited rehearsal time in London and because New York has fourteen different unions running its theaters, I made my Broadway debut without ever having fully rehearsed the big closing number. As well as a new company of actors, I was working on a wider stage with a more elaborate set and strange props. The New York cast members were wonderful; they closed ranks around me and helped keep me fully focused on my performance that night.

# CHAPTER 38

# A Weekend in Ireland

During my time playing the mother, Mrs. Johnstone, in Willy Russell's hit stage musical *Blood Brothers*, I was to learn that my genealogical training had unexpected uses.

A good friend from New York—I'll call him Scott—had been working the sound and lights for my cabaret shows each night at the Café Royal in London. Scheduled to step straight into the Broadway production of *Blood Brothers*, I flew back to New York when we finished up at the Café Royal. Scott had decided to stay behind an extra day so that he could have afternoon tea with his English maternal grandmother, a devout Christian Scientist.

Scott's mother had worked as a receptionist at a top hotel in London in her late teens. After a whirlwind courtship she had married a visiting American, also a Christian Scientist, and he had taken her back to the States with him. In less than nine months, Scott was born. Two other children subsequently followed, but the marriage was not destined to last. Although Scott loved his family dearly, he always had the feeling that he was somehow different from the others. His father and brother were both athletic and sports mad; Scott, on the other hand, was passionate about music and theater.

While taking tea with his grandmother, Scott was expressing how comfortable he was in London and that, in fact, he felt more European than American when his grandmother interjected, "Of course you do. You're one hundred percent European. Your father was an Irish bartender!" Scott was still in shock when he came backstage after my Broadway debut the following night and blurted out what he'd been told. It wasn't the time or place to get into a discussion about it so I suggested we meet for coffee the next day.

He was hurt and angry with his mother for not telling him, so I talked for a while about how different things were in those days and the need for forgiveness. Then, I said the fateful words, "If you want to look for your biological father, I'll help you."

It was the beginning of quite an adventure for us both. All we had to go on was the scant information Scott's mother provided after he had called her and demanded the truth. She told Scott that his father was called Paddy O'Riley and that he had worked in the famous American Bar at the Stafford Hotel in London while she was working there as a receptionist. Scott

had been conceived after a staff party one night. This was in
1960. Paddy was from Galway, where his family owned a pub,
and he had either a mother or sister named Mary. Not a great
deal to go on.

I pointed out to Scott that Paddy is a name the English call
any Irishman; it did not necessarily mean that his first name
was Patrick; and half the women in Ireland were called Mary.
Our best lead seemed to be the family pub in Galway. But was
the pub in the town of Galway or the county of Galway? The
Irish diaspora, during the potato famine, left the country with
a diminished population and, in the years following World
War II, few families yet had their own telephone. However, the
local pub is the center of Irish life, and if the O'Riley family
had a pub it would surely have had a telephone. I went to the
New York Public Library and requested all the Irish telephone
books for the 1950s.

It seemed I was in luck. During the whole decade, there was
only one O'Riley's Pub listed in all of Ireland and it was in
County Galway. Of course, the family pub might have been
called the Harp of Erin or the Old Gray Mare, for all I knew,
but I had to start somewhere. O'Riley's Pub was in a village
called Roundstone, which did not appear on my map of
Ireland. I now had a location but, after thirty-five years, was
the family still there?

On my way home from the library I stopped off at a
bookstore hoping to find a larger map of Ireland. While there,
I browsed through the recent Irish travel guides on display.

To my delight, a footnote in the section on Galway in one of the books was a reader's recommendation of the seafood at O'Riley's Pub in Roundstone, followed by a current phone number. The book also had an inset map showing Roundstone's position right on the water at the western end of Galway Bay.

I called Scott with the good news as soon as I got back to my hotel, and we arranged to meet for lunch the following day. What should be our next move? It was decided that I would go back to Scott's office with him after lunch and telephone O'Riley's Pub from there.

Using my married name as a cover, I told the woman who answered the phone that I was researching a travel article on Irish family pubs. O'Riley's had come to my attention because of its highly recommended seafood. Had the pub been in the family long? Indeed it had—three generations' worth. I tried to get as many names as I could from her without being too obvious but couldn't find a piece that fitted. The last person to carry the name O'Riley had been her grandfather, who had sired only girls. She had inherited the property when her mother died, and there wasn't a Patrick to be found among the lot. It seemed like this was the wrong family. Now, what?

Maybe we could pick up Paddy's trail from the American Bar at the Stafford Hotel. Because Europeans don't change jobs as often as Americans do, maybe there was someone still working at the hotel who'd kept in touch with him. Scott determined to return to London as soon as he could find a cheap airfare and get some time off work. In the meantime, he decided to press his mother for more details.

She confided that when Scott was a baby, she had taken a trip back to England to show him off to her parents. While there, she had contacted Paddy, and he had seen his son. She was not happy in her marriage and would have preferred to stay in England but, on learning that she had conceived again before she'd left America, there was no choice except to return to her husband. This revelation didn't give us any more to go on, but at least Scott now knew that Paddy was aware of his existence. Making contact wouldn't be such a shock if we could locate his father.

Several weeks went by before Scott had a chance to get back to London. He headed straight for the American Bar and learned that Charles, the elderly bartender, had worked there for decades. When Scott asked Charles if he had known Paddy, the old man's eyes lit up. Yes, indeed, he and Paddy had worked together side by side on that very spot. Scott couldn't contain himself any longer: "He's my father."

Charles scrutinized Scott's face for a long minute and then said, "You look just like him!" Charles hadn't seen Paddy in many years. Last he'd heard, Paddy was married with a family and living back in Ireland. If Scott should succeed in locating him, would he please give Paddy kindest regards from Charles, who had many happy memories of their times together.

It was a dead end as far as London was concerned but, as Scott flew back to New York, he was beginning to develop a flesh-and-blood image of his father.

With nothing else to go on except that Paddy was probably living in Ireland, it was back to Roundstone and O'Riley's Pub. Perhaps Paddy was a great-uncle or second cousin of the current occupants? While we were debating how and when we could get to Ireland for further research, one of those strange quirks of fate occurred.

Scott had a friend in New Jersey who was a Catholic priest. Out of the blue, he invited Scott to join him for lunch with a visiting priest from Ireland. During the meal, Scott shared his story with the two men and learned, to his astonishment, that the Irish visitor had attended Trinity College in Dublin with the priest presently in the parish at Roundstone. The Irishman was sure his former classmate would be only too happy to check the church registers and inform Scott of the names and dates on any O'Riley tombstones in the parish graveyard. Hope was rekindled.

Several months were to go by before Scott heard anything further. Meanwhile, I was now back in England on tour with *Blood Brothers.*

When Scott eventually received word from the priest, it was to learn that his gravestone investigations and register searches, while painstaking, had turned up nothing new. He could only confirm what I had already been told on the phone when I'd called O'Riley's Pub. We were back to square one.

Our best hope now was to go to Ireland ourselves and see what we could come up with. I had been there before and found the country to be a magical place. I had visited the house in Dublin where my grandfather was born and enjoyed a cup of coffee with the current owner. I had also done research at the Irish Genealogical Society and the Dublin Public Library, so I knew my way around there.

Time was the big problem. All research facilities are closed on Sundays, and Sunday is the only day off in British theater. Performances are given six nights a week. If I were going to meet Scott in Ireland and try to find his father, I would have to do it in a day and a half. It would be like looking for a needle in a haystack, but maybe we'd find something. Scott felt strongly that the answer lay in Roundstone, and we should exhaust any possibilities there first. I had to concur. The O'Rileys there could be distantly related, and we had nothing else to go on. Scott planned to fly from New York to Shannon in southwest Ireland, then rent a car and drive north to Galway. In the meantime, I would fly from Birmingham to Dublin, change planes for Galway and, by the time I landed, Scott would be waiting for me with the rental car. We would then drive west together to Roundstone.

I don't recall whether or not I informed the company manager at the theater that I was leaving the country. Probably not. Not much point, really. I was booked to return the following day, in plenty of time for the evening's performance.

During my brief layover at Dublin Airport, I stopped at a booth and looked through the current phone book. I had a niggling feeling Paddy was in Dublin. There were ten listings under the name Patrick O'Riley. One of the addresses somehow resonated with me and, just in case, I mentally filed it away.

Scott was waiting for me at Galway Airport as planned, and off we went toward the mountains of Connemara. Scott does not own or drive a car in New York. If truth be told, Scott should not drive anywhere, least of all on the opposite side of the road down a country lane in a foreign land. How we managed to stay out of a ditch, I will never know. Livestock scattered in all directions as Scott went speeding along with one eye on the clock. The distance hadn't seemed so far when we'd measured it in miles, but we were used to judging distances via multilane freeways. It took us two hair-raising hours to reach Roundstone.

As we passed O'Riley's Pub, Scott became quite emotional. It was already midafternoon so, after checking into our accommodation, we decided to walk to the pub for a cup of tea. It was hard to know how we could broach the subject of Scott's parentage with people who might not be aware of his existence. If Paddy were married with a family now, things could be awkward. What if they were afraid of scandal? We had no idea what to expect but we had come this far, and the time constraint emboldened us.

We walked into the bar and ordered tea from the young lad behind the counter. Scott is six feet two inches tall, extremely handsome, and very conscious of others' physical appearance. He took one look at the gawky teenager in the full flush of raging acne and said to me *sotto voce,* "I don't think he's a relative."

We sipped our tea but, with no adults in sight and our confidence deflated, we decided to explore the village and come back to the pub later for dinner when, we hoped, there might be someone around we could discreetly question.

Roundstone consisted of one street leading down to a wharf. Not much to explore, but the atmosphere was electric. West Ireland seems to have remained unchanged for centuries, and its beauty is truly indescribable. Scott and I both felt a surge of pride in our Celtic ancestry.

We came back to the pub for dinner and, after some initial awkwardness, began a conversation with the proprietor. It soon became obvious that he was married to the woman I had spoken to on the phone. We were not making much headway in the information department when Scott decided to throw caution to the winds and revealed the purpose of our visit. The publican and his wife were most charming and helpful but, although the pub still had the name O'Riley's out front, there had been no one in their family with the last name O'Riley for three generations, no one who had worked in London, and no one with the name Patrick. It was an absolute and total washout; our trip had been for nothing. Scott and I went back to our accommodation so depressed and disappointed, we couldn't even look at each other as we said goodnight.

The next morning, while downing a hearty Irish breakfast in the hotel dining room, we agreed that we'd been overly optimistic thinking we'd find his father in one weekend. I suggested we get on the road as soon as possible. As we now knew Galway Airport was a two-hour drive from Roundstone, and my flight to Dublin left around lunchtime, I thought we might make the return trip a more leisurely drive. Scott suggested we stop first at the home of the local priest to thank him for his help with our research. I agreed that this was the right thing to do.

The priest was a kind soul. He offered us a cup of tea and empathized with our disappointment. He asked if we'd checked in the current phone book for any other O'Riley's Pubs in Galway. When we said we hadn't, he pulled out his copy and started thumbing through it. Lo and behold, there was another O'Riley's Pub in a place called Castleblakeney. Scott later discovered that this was the only edition of the phone book in twenty years that had listed it. Castleblakeney was an even smaller dot on the map than Roundstone and was directly north of Galway Airport.

Scott was now fired up again. He wanted to drive there immediately, while I was becoming concerned about getting back to Birmingham in time for the show that night. Scott, who had a full week in Ireland before returning to New York, felt no time pressure. I, on the other hand, as a third-generation performer, had "the show must go on" tattooed on my genes and if I missed my plane, would be wracked with guilt. And probably unemployed.

Scott felt we had no choice, having come this far, but to check out Castleblakeney. I agreed but warned that, once we passed Galway Airport and headed north, we would have to time ourselves carefully. However long it took us to reach Castleblakeney from Galway equaled how long it would take us to get back again in time for my flight.

Thirty minutes after passing the airport we arrived at Castleblakeney. No wonder it was barely a dot on the map. The village consisted of a crossroad with a single building on each of the four corners. On one of them stood O'Riley's Pub. It was closed and shuttered and had a large sign on it that said FOR SALE.

The emotional seesaw we'd been riding had left us both in dire need of a nice, hot cup of tea. One of the other corners of Castleblakeney was also occupied by a pub, we went into the bar there in search of refreshment. There were three grizzled old characters standing together at the other end of the counter eyeing us warily. So, as well as the tea, I ordered the three of them a round of whatever they were drinking. As intended, conversation ensued. The Irish are probably the most hospitable people on earth and they love Americans, especially anyone trying to trace their Irish ancestry.

When we told them we were researching the O'Riley family tree and were disappointed to find the other pub locked and empty, they were immediately forthcoming with information as they vied for our attention.

"Well, you see, Pat's been very sick."

"Yes, he had to go to Dublin for an operation."

"It's in the stomach, you know."

"Sean was here runnin' the place for a while, but he's gone back now."

"I don't think old Pat's doin' too well."

"Frank's here, though. He lives just up the road."

Frank, it seemed, was Pat's brother. By now, the hairs on the back of Scott's neck were standing up, while I was estimating how much time we had left on the clock in Castleblakeney. I might as well have been trying to restrain a bloodhound, off the leash, with the scent of the fox in its nostrils. Scott insisted we had to stop at Frank O'Riley's home before leaving for the airport.

The house, a modern brick suburban-style dwelling, seemed out of place with its surroundings—as if only thatched cottages or old stone buildings really belonged in the rustic setting. We walked up to the front door, and Scott knocked on it several times. When it was clear that no one was coming I turned away, reassuring him that at least we had tried our best. Scott grabbed my hand and pulled me along with him as he headed for the rear of the house. I protested that we were trespassing, but you don't argue with a man on a mission, especially when he's twice your size.

In the yard behind the house, there was a teenage girl taking care of a toddler. Scott inquired after Frank, and she said that he'd be back soon, he was down in the field. I started toward the car telling Scott we didn't have time to wait around and we should leave before my job was in jeopardy. He was pleading with me to wait just a few more minutes when the bleating of sheep drew our attention to the road behind us. Like a scene from an old John Ford film, a cloud of cream fluff was moving toward us delineated by black faces and hooves. Behind the flock strode a man with a thick head of wavy white hair, blue eyes that really did seem to twinkle, and a slight resemblance to Scott.

Frank O'Riley greeted us warmly and invited us in for a cup of tea. We were peppering him with questions before we even got to the door.

"Your brother Paddy—did he work as a bartender in London in the early 1960s?"

"Pat? Yes, he did. It would have been around that time."

"Is your mother's name Mary?"

"Well, she was christened Anna May but she's always been called Mary."

Scott and I looked at one other. Maybe we had time for a quick cup of tea.

Frank put the kettle on while chatting away about Pat having been very ill and needing major surgery. He said he hoped his brother was feeling better and, as they hadn't spoken in a few days, maybe he'd call Dublin and see how Pat was doing. As Frank started leafing through his personal index for his brother's number in Dublin, Scott turned green and said he had to go outside for a minute. It was all happening too quickly. His hopes had been frustrated at every turn and now, at the last minute, it seemed the subject of his search might be only a phone call away. He needed to take a deep breath and compose himself.

After inquiring about Pat's health, Frank proceeded to chat with his brother about other family matters for a while until

Scott walked back in the room. Then he said, "Pat—there's a feller and his missus here from America asking after you. What was the name of that hotel you were working at in London? Oh, it was the Stafford, was it? Well, I'll let you talk to them yourself—I'm glad you're feeling better. I'll be calling you again later in the week."

With that, Frank handed the phone to Scott and started back towards the kitchen. He had noticed Scott's pallor. As he walked past me, he asked, "Is your husband all right?"

"Oh, he's not my husband," I said, and then, "He's Paddy's son."

Frank's eyes opened wide, then he quickly closed the door as he said with a nod, "I'll leave you alone, then."

And so it was that on the twenty-eighth day of August in the year of Our Lord nineteen hundred and ninety-five, Scott found Patrick O'Riley.

Scott seemed calm and confident as he took the phone. He began by asking Pat if he remembered a very pretty girl who had worked as a receptionist at the Stafford Hotel when he was there. Pat was at first evasive and mumbled something about it being a long time ago. In retrospect, we realized that Frank having referred to us as "a feller and his missus from America" probably caused Pat to think we were Scott's mother and her husband. Scott pressed on asking, "Do you remember her having a baby she brought back to London and showed you?"

"Oh, that's water under the bridge," he quickly replied.

"I am that baby," said Scott.

There was a pause and then Pat said, "Well, you're not a baby anymore, are you?"

With the ice broken, Scott began telling Pat about himself. He told him that he'd had a happy childhood and that his American father was a good, kind man who had always treated him well. Scott also told Pat that he had only learned the truth of his parentage eight months previously and he had been looking for Pat ever since. He didn't want anything from him, Scott simply wanted to meet his father and shake his hand. At that, Pat's attitude seemed to change and he began telling Scott about himself, his family, and his recent health problems.

By now I was verging on panic with regard to the time and, catching Scott's eye, began pointing at my watch. He looked at me with outrage and said, "I'm talking to my father!"

Scott told Pat he would be in Dublin in four days' time, and they agreed to meet at a pub near Pat's home. Frank, meanwhile, had not only prepared the tea but also pulled out some family photo albums for us to look at. After hanging up the phone, Scott decided to drop me off at Galway Airport and then return to spend some more leisurely time with his uncle.

Our adrenaline was really pumping on that half-hour drive back to Galway. We were both higher than kites with the elation of having accomplished our mission. I made my plane with only minutes to spare, while Scott promised to call me in four days' time after meeting his father in person.

Back at the theater, standing in the wings waiting to go on that night, I wondered if anyone else in the cast had had a weekend as action packed as mine.

For the next four days, I was on tenterhooks waiting and hoping for Scott's sake that his meeting with Pat would go well. They recognized each other from across the street and waved shyly at one another. As they shared a pot of tea in the pub, Scott was amazed at the characteristics he and Pat had in common. They were both nondrinkers, and Scott noticed that he and his father had the same wrists and hands. Pat was delighted that Scott had inherited his love of music and theater and revealed that he, too, had wanted to be an actor/singer. Pat was still weak from his surgery and confided that he had had cancer of the stomach.

In discussing his illness with Scott, Pat mentioned that he'd been given a book to read that he was finding particularly interesting. On learning the title, Scott went out to the car to fetch his copy so that his father could see they were both reading the same book, *You Can Heal Your Life* by Louise L. Hay. When we were both still in New York, I had presented Scott with the book, as it had changed my life, and we had both brought our copies to Ireland with us. Mine was so well worn that it could no longer be held together with sticky tape and rubber bands but had to be carried in a plastic ziplock bag.

Scott had brought with him some old family photos so that Pat could see what Scott had looked like at different stages of his life, as well as a more recent photo of his mother. He referred to the time when she had brought her infant son back to London and asked Pat:

"Did you ever think about me?"

"Every day of my life," his father replied.

By the end of their meeting Pat was giving serious consideration to telling his family about Scott. After all, Scott had been conceived well before Pat had married; it wasn't as if he had been unfaithful. Father and son resolved that they would keep in touch.

After the initial shock had worn off, Pat's wife was accepting, and his adult children were eager to meet their American half brother. After exchanging letters and several transatlantic phone calls, Scott returned to Ireland. He was met at Dublin Airport by his Irish sister and her husband and stayed with them in their home. He also met Sean, his brother. It turned out that Pat and his wife, Mary, lived at the address that had resonated with me when I'd read it in the Dublin phone book! Scott also met his ninety-six-year-old grandmother, as well as a host of uncles, aunts, and cousins, who welcomed him into the bosom of the O'Riley family. Sadly, Pat seemed to have not fully recovered from his cancer surgery.

Less than a year after finding his father, Scott called Dublin from his New York apartment, and Mary told him that Pat was going downhill fast. "He's asking for you," she said.

Scott was able to get a few days off work and flew immediately to Ireland. This time he stayed with Pat and Mary under their roof. Pat was now frail but could sit downstairs with the family for dinner. Scott played the piano and sang for his father for the first and only time. Afterward, Scott and Sean helped their father upstairs and into bed.

It was painfully obvious that death would be coming soon, but Pat felt he had now had closure. Lying there, holding hands with Scott and Sean on either side of him he said, "I have both my sons with me now."

Today, Scott keeps in regular contact with his Irish family. His brother and sister have visited him in New York, and he has made several trips to Dublin to stay with Mary. Most recently, he served as godfather at the christening of his Irish nephew, one of the grandsons Pat did not live to see.

# CHAPTER 39

# On Tour with Willy Russell

During the rehearsal period in London for the UK *Blood Brothers* tour, I was able to spend some time with one of the greatest old people I have ever met, the mother of one of my dearest friends. Fanny Janes lived in London her whole life, and what a life she lived. A pioneer in business at a time when women didn't do such things, she deserves an entire book to herself, and I hope someone writes it. Even if I were in London for only the day, I always went to visit her. Time with her was so precious. Only six weeks before she died, I invited her to afternoon tea at the Ritz on Piccadilly. My Broadway hair and wig man from New York, Robert-Charles, was with me, and I wanted him to meet her.

Fanny arrived in a taxi, dressed in a smart cherry red wool suit. Although in her early nineties, her hair and nails had just been done and she flirted overtly but charmingly with the driver and the doorman. The waiter, however, was a rather dour type, and when Fanny sweetly inquired as to whether it was possible to purchase one of the little pink napkins with "The Ritz" embroidered in blue thread at one corner, he became snooty and dismissive.

Afterward, we took Fanny home and, as we were helping her up the stairs into her building, I told her that I thought the waiter had been extremely rude in response to her request. Then I said, "So here, darling, you can have mine," as I pulled the little napkin I'd nicked for her out of my pocket. She laughed so hard I thought she'd fall over.

Then Robert-Charles said to me, "I'm glad you gave her your napkin because, if you hadn't, I was going to give her mine," as he pulled one out of his pocket, too.

We'd both been so bothered by the waiter's rude refusal to the guest of honor that we'd each nicked a napkin for Fanny, something we would normally never have done. Furthermore, despite our lack of experience in such matters, neither of us had seen the other one do the nicking. Needless to say, Fanny was utterly delighted—or should I say captivated?—by our caper.

The highlight of the UK tour of *Blood Brothers* for me was, undoubtedly, playing the Empire Theatre in Liverpool with Willy Russell in the audience. Despite fatigue and an oncoming cold, I was in good voice on the night and managed to give one of my better performances. Willy was the first person to come backstage afterward, modestly introducing himself. Like I didn't know who he was! I was thrilled that he felt I had done justice to the wonderful role he had written.

Mrs. Johnstone is referred to throughout the show as either Mrs. Johnstone or simply Mrs. J. She is never called by her first name—the only clue is when the postman announces that he has mail for Mrs. G. Johnstone. There had been speculation among the cast as to what the *G* might stand for. Some thought her husband's name could have been George, while others believed that it was her own name that started with the letter *G*. I had the playwright in my dressing room so I couldn't resist asking him, "What's Mrs. Johnstone's first name? I've got my money on Gloria."

"She's never had one, but Gloria it is," Willy replied.

If I hadn't loved him before, I certainly loved him after that.

Over a period of three years I was to perform in three productions of Willy Russell's *Blood Brothers* and four productions of his brilliant one-woman play, *Shirley Valentine*.

If you saw the film, you know the story of *Shirley Valentine*, but unless you've seen the original play you won't know that one actor plays all the parts. It is a *tour de force* indeed and a joy to perform. It is also a two-hour monologue that took me two months to memorize.

I was scheduled to go into *Shirley* immediately following *Blood Brothers*, which meant having to rehearse one role during the day while playing another at night. Two factors worked to my advantage: One was having an audiotape of Willy himself reading the play in his Liverpool accent; I would listen to it every night as I walked to and from my hotel on West 58th Street and the Music Box Theatre. The other advantage was that as both plays required a Liverpool accent—Shirley's a bit more upmarket than Mrs. J.'s—I was able to immerse myself in Liverpudlian argot. I was even dreaming in that accent!

One interviewer asked me if I was worried about forgetting my words on opening night. I replied that I was more concerned I might set fire to the set. Shirley actually cooks eggs onstage during Act One, and anyone who knows me will tell you I am a disaster in the kitchen. I am prone to burning myself, cutting myself, and breaking things. There were many nights onstage when I poured the eggs from the pan onto the plate, grateful that only those sitting in the balcony could witness my humiliation.

There was one performance of *Shirley* I will never forget. It was on a one-nighter tour, and we were traveling with the bare minimum—two backdrop cloths and a few basic props. Each theater had to provide the other requirements—a table and chairs, fridge, stove, and so on for the kitchen set in Act One and a beach chair and umbrella table for Act Two, which is set in Greece. As these items would usually be on loan from a local furniture store in exchange for advertising in the program, things worked out well all around. Except that I had to work with different props and a different set on a different stage every night; only the backdrop was the same and, as this was behind me, there was little comfort to be drawn from its familiarity. However, adaptability is the key to survival.

On this particular night I had a problem because, instead of a sturdy wineglass, I had been provided with a very fine piece of crystal. Shirley likes to sip a glass of wine while she's peeling the potatoes and talking to the wall. As I picked up the glass it broke in my hand and shattered all over the table and kitchen floor/stage. The first thing that went through my head was that the stage crew would be coming on in the dark for a quick scene change and someone might be injured. What would Shirley do? Well, it was her mess and her kitchen so she'd clean it up, wouldn't she? I'd kept the monologue going on autopilot while I was thinking. Fortunately, I had a wet dishrag and a large plastic bowl onstage with me as props, so I was able to pick up every sliver of glass. As I did this, I realized that my timing was now off as I had always paced my delivery according to the size of the potatoes I was supposed to be preparing. I was going to have to slow the speed of my speaking way down because, after I cleaned up the mess, I still had to peel and slice the potatoes and drop them in the oil before I ran out of words. Fortunately, we had fake French fries as regular props for the finished product.

I was peeling and chopping away at those spuds with such speed I began to feel believable as someone who can really cook. I was just congratulating myself on having jumped that hurdle when my mind, working a paragraph ahead, saw a line coming where I had to take a sip from the glass and make a reference to the wine. I looked into the wings and saw my stage manager, Norman, standing there, holding a fresh glass of wine—in actual fact, it was a special tea for the throat. I stood up, made a circle of the stage and managed to retrieve the new glass without missing a beat and in perfect time for the sip of wine and the line.

There are nights when years of experience allow you to keep going and rise to the occasion. I love those nights. It's like every performance that you've ever given is a stitch in a security blanket which now covers you with the reassuring wisdom of experience.

# CHAPTER 40

# Mothers and Daughters

t happened when I was about to leave for Toronto and a nine-week run there in *Shirley Valentine;* after that it would be back to London and a three-month run as Mrs. Johnstone in the West End production of *Blood Brothers.* My daughter broke the news to me that after twelve years of marriage, she and her husband were expecting a baby. I had given up hope, and they almost had, too. Sometimes you have to let go of what you most want to allow it to come to you. I was going to be a grandmother. I started seeing life in a different way.

Most trained actors use "sense memory" in their work. This involves the actor recalling a personal life experience which will produce the same emotions being experienced by the character the actor is playing. While this can give a performance gut- wrenching reality on screen, there is a serious downside for stage actors, who have to immerse themselves in negative emotions eight times a week for months on end; mental and emotional imbalances can easily occur. I had to face this problem when I was playing Mrs. Johnstone in *Blood Brothers*. Even though it is a musical, the climax of the show is highly dramatic. Mrs. Johnstone has to run through the audience and onto the stage with tears of anguish streaming down her face. I reasoned that as tears can also be the result of extreme happiness, I would be better off thinking about something joyous to produce them. I can't watch childbirth on television without bawling, so I decided I would focus on thinking about the coming birth of my grandchild, and the resultant joy it would bring, to produce the tears every night. It worked.

I was in London when the results of Traci's ultrasound came through. I was overjoyed to learn that all was well, and the baby was a girl, to be named Lily. My son-in-law, Lucas, would later inform me that she had appeared to him in a dream and asked to be called by that name. That night, when I returned from the theater and walked through the revolving door into the hotel, I was overwhelmed by the scent of lilies. Right inside the entrance was a new floral arrangement, the largest one I have ever seen, floor to ceiling and all varieties of lilies. As I inhaled deeply, a wonderful sense of calm came over me. My granddaughter was saying hello, and letting me know that she would arrive safely.

As I wanted more than anything to be there for my daughter when her first child was born, I planned my schedule so that I would be in Los Angeles and off work for a four-month period. I intended to be with Traci for the last month of her pregnancy and available for the first three months of Lily's life, if I was needed.

I was on the road in my fourth production of *Shirley Valentine*, and it was the last night of the tour. We were in Ashland, Oregon, and I was about to leave the hotel for the show when Lucas called to say that Traci's water had broken and he was taking her to the hospital. Lily was going to be a Scorpio instead of a Sagittarius.

I was scheduled to leave for L.A. the next day on the first available commercial flight, which would not arrive until 3:30 P.M. Although I certainly did not wish for my daughter to have that long a labor, I was overwhelmed with disappointment and guilt. I had tried so hard to be there for my kids when they needed me and now I would be letting my daughter down and missing out on one of the most important events in life. There were no other flights I could take unless . . . my mind started ticking over. The show venue was a half-hour drive from the hotel, and the hotel was only fifteen minutes away from the airport. I asked Norman, my stage manager, to make inquiries as soon as we got to the theater about hiring a private plane. Maybe, just maybe, there was a chance I could get there in time. I was sitting at my dressing table, putting on my Act One makeup, when Norman came back and told me that he'd located a pilot and a single-engine plane that could take me down to Los Angeles. However, we would need to stop and refuel on the way, and the earliest we could land in L.A. would be around 6 A.M. As much as I wanted to be there for the birth, I was hoping for Traci's sake that Lily would be born well before then. Nevertheless, the little plane would get me there nine hours ahead of the commercial flight, so it was worth doing. I asked Norman to go ahead and book the plane; I'd use my credit card to pay for it. Then I gave the whole thing up to God. I simply released the desire and prayed that if it was Divine Will that I should be there in time for the birth, the angels would pave my way.

Norm came back at intermission and told me that he had now located a twin-engine plane which could fly direct to Los Angeles, plus two pilots. If we took off right after the show, I could arrive in L.A. around 1 A.M. Then I realized that if we landed at Santa Monica Airport instead of LAX, I would be twenty minutes closer to the hospital. Every minute now counted, so the flight plan was changed. An added bonus was that my home in Santa Monica was between the airport and the hospital. I would be able to drop off my bags en route instead of arriving at the hospital with suitcases in hand.

Act Two of the play was a whirlwind. I did not delete one word from the script but delivered my lines so quickly that, between the two acts, I cut ten minutes off the length of the show. Willy was not thrilled when I told him. As this was the last night of the tour, it was breakdown night. This meant sorting through the props and wardrobe so that everything could be returned to its rightful owner. Although I had contributed some of my own clothing, I didn't care to hang around afterward to retrieve it. I was on a mission. I was blessed to have the help of two wonderful people. Amber Rose, my dresser, and Norman Dutweiller, my stage manager, could not have been more helpful in speeding me on my way, and I will be forever grateful to them.

I hopped on board the plane still wearing Shirley's Act Two hair and makeup. My thoughts and prayers were with Traci the whole trip. I knew how much this baby meant to her and I hoped her labor was going smoothly. As we neared Santa Monica, the pilots radioed ahead to have a taxi waiting for me. I just had time to quickly relieve myself while the pilots transferred my bags into the cab, and it was off to the hospital.

I once read a statistical time study on how many years of our lives we spend on various activities. When I read that, over the course of a lifetime, sitting at red lights added up to several years, I decided I was not going to waste any of my precious time doing that. I've always loved maps, so I had charted routes to and from my house that avoided most of the red lights. I was the bane of taxi drivers with my constant backseat directions but I didn't care. I knew the quickest route and I was the one paying the fare. It was knowledge that stood me in good stead that night. We made it to my house in less than ten minutes. I told the driver to keep the engine running, tore up the front path, opened the door, threw the bags into the vestibule and ran back to the cab.

Cedars-Sinai Hospital is a vast complex of buildings, and I had no idea which one Traci was in, but my angels were guiding us and the cabdriver dropped me off at exactly the right door. It was almost 1 A.M.

The first person I saw was Michael Learned, Luke's mother and Lily's other grandmother. She had been sitting there in the waiting room for hours and was as anxious for news as I was. She took one look at me and said, "You stopped to put all that makeup on?"

"No," I replied, "I didn't stop to take it off."

I went immediately to the nurses' station and saw Peter, my former brother-in-law, who was in attendance as Lily's pediatrician. Traci was still in labor, and he ushered me into the delivery room. My daughter took one look at me and said, "Oh, Mom, I'm so glad you made it."

Twenty minutes later, with her husband holding one of her hands while I held the other, my daughter was safely delivered of a daughter. A perfect, beautiful, healthy baby girl. I was surprised by my reaction. I didn't cry! What I did feel was overwhelming love and pride in my own baby girl. She had chosen to have a drug-free labor and delivery, and I knew she was going to be a wonderful mother.

Seeing Lucas hold his daughter for the first time, I remembered that Michael was still sitting in the waiting room. I ran out to tell her that our grandchild had arrived and brought her into the delivery room to share the joy.

# CHAPTER 41

# *Diana*

As a feminist, I had at first been less than enchanted with Prince Charles's choice of a bride. Lady Diana seemed much too young for him and to have been chosen mainly for her virginity. Her paternal ancestry was frequently referred to, but I had been curious to check out her matrilineal ancestry. The mother/daughter bond is a primal one, and if the mother has been the one to raise the child, she will have infused the child with an unconscious awareness of what is expected of her. Over successive generations, those expectations can expand exponentially. Sure enough, as I suspected, Diana had been born and bred to "marry up" as far back as her foremothers could be traced (see chart opposite).

I never knew Diana, Princess of Wales, but I do know that I'm a better person because she lived. I would come to admire the courage of the young girl who grew so magnificently into

# Matrilineal Ancestry of Diana, Princess of Wales

Eliza KEWARK
(An Armenian)
d. after Sep.1820

never married;
(mother and daughter
mentioned in Forbes's
will)

Theodore FORBES
Indian merchant
bap. Forgue,
    Aberdeenshire,
    Aug. 3,1788
d. at sea on board the
    Blenden Hall,
    Sep. 24,1820

Katherine Scott FORBES
b. Bombay, India,
    Dec. 1,1812
d. 16 Bon Accord
    Square, Aberdeen,
    Apr.10, 1893

m.

James CROMBIE
of Goval Bank, New
    Machar, Aberdeenshire,
b. Jan. 13,1810
d. Jan. 31,1878

Jane CROMBIE
b. Goval 1843
d. 9 Rubislaw Terrace,
    Aberdeen,
    Sep.19,1917

m.
Goval, New Machar,
Aberdeenshire
Aug. 29, 1872

David LITTLEJOHN LLD, DL
b. 19 Union St.,Aberdeen,
    Apr. 3, 1841
m. (2) Jane Crombie
d. 9 Rubislaw Terrace,
    Aberdeen,
    May 11, 1924

Ruth LITTLEJOHN
b. Cotton Lodge,
    Woodside,
    nr. Aberdeen,
    Dec. 4,1879
d. Dalhebity, Bieldside,
    Aberdeenshire,
    Aug. 24,1964

m.
Queen's Cross Free
Church, Aberdeen,
Jun. 30, 1898

Col. William Smith GILL
    CB, VD, DL
b. 5 Rosemont Terrace,
    Aberdeen,
    Feb. 16, 1865
d. Dalhebity, Bieldside,
    Aberdeenshire,
    Dec. 25, 1957

Ruth Sylvia GILL
    Baroness Fermoy
    DCVO, OBE
b. Dalhebity, Bieldside,
    Aberdeenshire,
    Oct. 2, 1908
d. Eaton Square, London,
    Jul. 6, 1993

m.
St Devenick's Bieldside,
Aberdeenshire,
Sep. 17, 1931

Edmund Maurice Blake
    ROCHE
4th Baron Fermoy
b. Chelsea,
    May 15, 1885
d. King's Lynn,
    Jul. 8, 1955

Hon. Frances Ruth Burke
    ROCHE
b. Park House,
    Sandringham,
    Jan. 20, 1936
d. Scotland,
    Jun. 3, 2004

m.
Westminster Abbey,
Jun. 1,1954

Edward John SPENCER
8th Earl Spencer MVO
b. 24 Sussex Square,
    London,
    Jan. 24, 1924
d. London,
    Mar. 29, 1992

Lady Diana Frances
    SPENCER
b. Park House,
    Sandringham, Norfolk,
    Jul. 1,1961
d. Paris, France,
    Aug. 31, 1997

m.
St Paul's Cathedral,
July 29, 1981

Prince CHARLES
The Prince of Wales
b. Nov. 14, 1948

the role she had undertaken and, to a royal family still living a nineteenth-century lifestyle, she brought the promise of change. Her ability to treat all people equally humanized her and made her everyone's daughter, sister, or friend. She understood pain, and by the end of a life she had to fight hard to gain control over, she had become an advocate for humanity and a feminist icon. I happened to be living and working in the heart of London when Diana died. It was a time and place that had to be experienced to be understood.

Charles and Diana had been divorced for almost a year. Every newspaper carried a daily story about Diana with lots of pictures. The loss of her royal status had done nothing to diminish her popularity with the public. The palace had hired public relations "spin doctors" to promote Charles and denigrate Diana, but some of the newspaper bias was transparent. There was public resentment that Diana had been stripped of a title many believed she had earned. In the issue that marked the first anniversary of their divorce, a pictorial weekly with regular royal features had displayed on its cover individual full-length pictures of Charles and Diana side by side. The accompanying story alleged that Diana was floundering since the divorce while Charles had it all together and was forging ahead. It was obvious that the opposite was the case. Charles was the one who seemed to be unsure of himself and deeply unhappy. Diana, on the other hand, had come into her own, with a confident manner and a brave commitment to controversial causes.

Some friends were staying with me in my hotel apartment overlooking Piccadilly when the news came on the television that Sunday morning. Princess Diana was dead. It seemed unbelievable. There was numbness at first, as if we were trying to hold the loss at bay. When I went down to breakfast, I noticed that the flags were not flying at half-mast. I asked the manager why not, and he said that no instructions had come down from the top to do so. It was the same throughout London. Not one flag lowered. No official response whatsoever. What on earth was going on? The TV news later that Sunday morning showed Diana's boys being taken to a regular church service in Scotland. Charles sat between his sons in the backseat of the car with his hands on his knees. Why wasn't he holding hands with the two motherless boys on either side of him? There was further outrage when it was revealed that there had been no acknowledgment in the church service of the tragedy or even of Diana's existence. The Windsors had never been known for their warmth, but this went beyond coldness. I don't think there was a woman in England who didn't long to hold those two boys and comfort them.

I had made prior arrangements to spend that Sunday at Cambridge. One of my guests was a Trinity College alumnus, who planned to show me around the College, take me punting on the river, followed by dinner with the masters at High Table. The irony of spending the day at Prince Charles's old university was not lost on me. I found it odd that not once during the whole day did anyone I met mention Diana or what had happened. Nor was there any conversation about the accident at the dinner table. Had they not heard? Did they not care? Was this silence born of loyalty to Prince Charles? There were times that day when I felt as if I was in a time warp, and the accident in Paris had not really happened.

Back in London that night, it was again all too real. The city was strangely quiet for a Sunday evening. Most people were glued to the television and the unfolding drama. Anger was beginning to stir. Charles had gone to Paris to claim the body of the woman he had abandoned in life. Why him? She should have been brought home by someone who had loved her and cared for her.

The next morning, I felt compelled to walk to Buckingham Palace, although I had no idea why. I was not the only one. As I walked through Green Park, I saw a woman in front of me, dressed like a secretary but all in black and carrying flowers. She was hurrying as if she was late for work. I looked around and saw people coming from all directions across the park and all speedily heading for the palace. The same thing was happening at Diana's home, Kensington Palace. There was a sense of quiet urgency.

As it was now Monday, it was back to work for me that night, a prospect I did not relish. I was appearing in the West End in *Blood Brothers*. I loved doing the show and playing a dramatic part I could really sink my teeth into, but the performance that evening was going to be different.

*Blood Brothers* opens and closes with my character, Mrs Johnstone, singing:

"Tell me it's not true,
say it's just a story,
something on the news . . ."

How on earth was I going to get through the show without breaking down?

Unlike film, where songs are prerecorded and the actors just move their lips, stagework demands physical control as well as emotional truth. Producing real tears and singing full voice, while maintaining tonal quality, is a challenge to the best of us. I wouldn't need to draw on "sense memory" tonight; the tears would flow freely. I just hoped that I could turn them off. If I didn't control my emotions, nasal congestion would make the lyrics unintelligible. Everything I had ever learned about "the show must go on" would have to come into play. I had been taught that even if there was a death in the family, it was my duty to go out and give the best performance I possibly could. I had been trained to put my personal feelings on hold when onstage. I could and would get through it.

Each day, throughout London, crowds would increase as the people were drawn like magnets to the palaces. As the bouquets of flowers began to spread across Kensington Gardens, there was growing anger at the royal family, bunkered down at Balmoral. They had disrespected Diana in life and now they were disrespecting her in death. And where were the boys? That was every mother's concern. They had not been seen since church on Sunday. Were they safe? Was anyone holding them and comforting them?

Charles finally emerged with his sons to inspect the messages and flowers left at the gates of Balmoral. As Harry kneeled down to read one of the notes, he spontaneously reached up for his father's hand. That picture of father and son holding hands appeared on television and newspaper covers. A collective sigh of relief swept across Britain.

Still there had been no word from the Queen, no acknowledgment of the loss that her people were clearly feeling. Everyone knew something big was going on up in Scotland but no one knew exactly what. Rumors of rows and royal rifts were circulating. The inaction and indecision seemed to suggest a crisis in leadership.

London was eerily silent, and an atmosphere of cold anger was beginning to build. Walking down the street and absorbing the zeitgeist triggered a past-life memory flash in me. I remember thinking to myself, "This is how it feels to be in a revolution." Had the Queen waited one more day before returning to her capital, I think the growing crowds might have turned ugly. No doubt the royal family feared the same thing. With no one running the show, the British people were taking matters into their own hands. They demanded that flags be flown at half-mast all over London, including at Buckingham Palace. The royal family returned from Scotland. I was with the crowd outside the palace that day and witnessed the hissing and boos as the Queen and Prince Philip arrived, dressed in black, smiling and waving at the crowds from their car.

A coworker of mine from the theater had gone to Buckingham Palace to take pictures of the Union Jack being raised and then lowered to half-mast over the palace, as it was a historic event. The Queen's official flagpole normally flew only the Queen's personal standard and then, only when she was in residence. The republican symbolism in the flag of Great Britain replacing her own above the palace was not lost on the Queen. My coworker had a new camera with a zoom lens and was focusing on the flagpole when she noticed sunlight reflecting on lines along the roof. As she adjusted the zoom lens, she could see that there were snipers on the palace roof, and their weapons were pointed at the crowd.

More than a million people came into London for the funeral, but there was no sign of rowdiness. They had come in sorrow, and the mood was somber. In order to survive World War II the British people had needed to keep a stiff upper lip, detach from their emotions, and soldier on. While this philosophy had saved them at the height of the bombardment, it had become so ingrained in the national character that it was effectively closing off Britain's collective heart chakra. Diana was the catalyst for change. She made it acceptable to be in touch with and express feelings. Her funeral, and the collective outpouring of emotions which it induced, caused a profound change in the British consciousness. Like everyone else that day, I wept when I saw the card with "Mummy" written in little Harry's childish hand atop the coffin; and I applauded Earl Spencer's chivalrous and long overdue defense of his sister in his eloquent eulogy. Indeed, it may be said that through the power of television, the whole world was connected by grief at the same time, causing a planetary opening of the heart chakra and an evolutionary leap in consciousness. We are all here to learn how to love.

History is full of what-ifs? I used to wonder what could have evolved if Diana had been treated like the Queen Mother. What if the Queen Mother had been treated like Diana? Both women came into the royal family as the daughters of earls.

What if Lady Diana Spencer had been welcomed into the royal family as warmly as Lady Elizabeth Bowes-Lyon had been some fifty years earlier? What if the senior royals had been proud of her popularity instead of threatened by it? What if they had welcomed her sensitivity and empathy with others as ideal attributes for the position she now held? What if they had recognized that change is the only constant in the universe and allowed her youthful energy and fresh viewpoint to help re-vitalize the monarchy?

And what if Lady Elizabeth Bowes-Lyon had been dismissed by the Windsors as coldly as Lady Diana would be more than fifty years later? There would be no royal walkabout today. There would probably be no royal family in Britain today. It is doubtful whether the English would have made it through World War II without the courage and common touch of the Lady who became their Queen. It was she who initiated many changes at court, moving the monarchy away from the stiff formality of her in-laws—Queen Mary always dressed for dinner in full evening gown, jewels, and tiara, even when dining alone—and concentrating attention, both public and private, on her own family unit. What if?

And what if Australia had accepted Prince Charles as Governor-General after his marriage? Away from the machinations of the palace cabal, Charles might have had the freedom to become his own man. Away from the influence of his mistress, Charles might have gotten to know his wife. Away from his own country, and without his customary sycophantic social network, he might have gotten to know himself.

I have come to the conclusion that Diana's life unfolded exactly the way it was supposed to. She needed to experience the rejection she suffered as a child, and as a young bride, to sensitize her to the feelings of others. It's been said by many that Diana could walk into a room and go immediately to the person who had suffered the most. She expressed the belief many times that her personal life experience had fine-tuned her instincts.

As many do, I believe that Diana's death was not an accident. By proving how much influence she had to bring about peaceful change, Diana became a target of those forces that profit from death and destruction. She was destined to die young as her death was to be a lesson for the planet in many ways, some of which have not yet been entirely revealed.

The historical revisionists continue to deride or attempt to discredit Diana. They simply never "got" what she was about and they never will. She understood how loveless life can be for so many of us, especially the aged, who receive so little in the way of physical affection or human touch. To see Diana's ungloved hand gently stroke the cheek of an elderly person and the resultant joy on that person's face was to see love in action. There had never been a princess like her before; I doubt that there will be again.

# CHAPTER 42

# Toward the Millennium

I remember as a little girl sitting on the verandah at 51 Gipps Street, East Melbourne, looking at the trees in the park opposite, wondering how old they were and wondering how much taller they'd be when I was old. I thought about how my grandmother was able to remember the turn of the century. It sounded really exciting, and then I realized that I possibly might still be alive at the turn of the next century. I would be, let's see, fifty-eight years old, probably a grandmother myself. I was delighted at the thought but, at that age, I had no sense of a new millennium.

Like most people, when the time came around, I needed to celebrate the arrival of the year 2000 with a loved one. I was in Sydney with my sister, and we chose to have a quiet, sober New Year's Eve. Toni cooked a delicious dinner, and the two of us watched the fireworks from her apartment, which directly faced Sydney Harbour Bridge. Later on, after she'd gone to bed, I sat up watching the twenty-four-hour television coverage as the new century made its way around the globe. I was fascinated to see how different countries celebrated, how they saw themselves and how they wanted others to see them. I hoped the new century would be good for us all.

My health had been slowly deteriorating for several years, largely because my miracle worker, Dr. Giorgi, was no longer around. I missed old Elsie in more ways than one. She had succumbed to Alzheimer's and, while at times she was her old self, at others, she would ask me my name and symptoms as if I were a new patient. When I visited her in the hospital, she told me that she'd rung down to the nurse in Records for my chart and asked how I was feeling. Medicine had been her entire life and once she was no longer able to practice, I think she lost her reason for being. None of us had any idea exactly how old she was but she lived to a great age.

Elsie had been a change-of-life baby, born when her mother was fifty-one, so, by the time Elsie grew old, all her siblings were long gone. She had never married or had a child, and her patients had been her family. Some referred to her as Dr. Dearie, the name she was in the habit of calling everyone. I called her Mama Mia. I think we'd all had her over at least once for Thanksgiving dinner.

Florence Henderson of *The Brady Bunch* fame, one of earth's angels, took responsibility for Elsie at the end of her life. They

*Left:* With Traci aged three weeks. *(From the personal collection of Helen Reddy)*

*Below:* With Traci and Jordan, born ten years apart. *(From the personal collection of Helen Reddy)*

Coming to America, 1966. *(From the personal collection of Helen Reddy)*

With Jordan aged two. *(From the personal collection of Helen Reddy)*

*Above*: With Jordan at a charity fundraiser. *(From the personal collection of Helen Reddy)*

*Above*: With Traci at Jordan's wedding. *(From the personal collection of Helen Reddy)*

*Above*: With Lily aged 10 minutes. *(From the personal collection of Helen Reddy)*

*Above*: A weary mother and two delighted grandmothers.
*(Photo courtesy of Michael Learned, from the personal collection of Helen Reddy)*

*Above*: Our first kiss – Lily had just sucked my cheek and I'm in heaven! *(From the personal collection of Helen Reddy)*

*Above*: Cuddles and giggles with 'Nanna Bananna'. *(From the personal collection of Helen Reddy)*

*Above*: 'Gotcha' – *This is Your Life*, September 2002. *(Reprinted courtesy of Photofest)*

*Above*: A star in the Hollywood Walk of Fame. *(Reprinted courtesy of Photofest)*

had been close friends for many years—both came from families of ten children—and it was Florence who arranged the memorial celebration. I thought she planned it perfectly. At the door there was a stack of photocopies of Dr. Giorgi's obituary from the *Los Angeles Times*. I had saved the original but took one of the copies anyway. Italian music was played, and some of us whose lives the good doctor had saved stood up and spoke, including Quincy Jones, Anjelica Huston, Kate Jackson, and yours truly.

Although we had all known that Elsie had quite a few celebrity patients, none of us really knew who the others were. And as we talked about her with each other, we discovered that every one of us had believed we were her favorite. Such was her capacity for love. Someone remarked that when you were lying in the emergency room and you heard the distinctive click of Elsie's heels coming down the hallway, you knew that you were going to be all right. That summed it up. She had been my security blanket.

Florence brought the service to an end with a song in Elsie's honor, in that glorious voice Elsie had so loved to hear.

I was really happy to see Florence again after so long. We had played tennis together during our Las Vegas years but had lost touch with each other since then. We had both divorced and remarried in the intervening years, and grandchildren had been born. We had a lot of catching up to do. I asked her for her phone number and jotted it down on the back of the obituary photocopy sheet.

.  .  .

I had been spending time in the Southern Hemisphere at a remote island location in the hope that the pure air, water, and stress-free environment would improve my health. Instead I found it was worsening. My need of a good diagnostician was becoming more urgent. I'd seen two different specialists in Los Angeles and been told by one that he couldn't find anything wrong with me, and by the other, that it would be a good idea to put my affairs in order. Oh, and I'd received the inevitable prescription for tranquilizers, which made me glassy-eyed and listless, so I threw them away.

I was at a difficult time in life for women. Both my children were now married and no longer needed me. Financially speaking, although still saddled with debt, I could see the light at the end of the tunnel; I was well set up for retirement but, with the arrogance of youth, I had not planned on any interim source of cash flow other than my regular personal appearance work. The work I was now being offered, once I'd calculated production costs, wasn't worth leaving home for most of the time. Transportation, accommodation, and salaries had trebled and quadrupled, and my budget had already been cut to the bone. Also, the physical strain of years of one-nighter gigs had obviously taken its toll on my body. For decades, I'd been out there crisscrossing the country and circling the globe. For the sake of my health, I needed to get out of show business but I was still eighteen months away from being able to access my pension fund.

And there was another little problem. Every time I'd tried to leave the business before, something would pull me back in. I had always been the breadwinner and obliged to earn a living with the only skills I had. Those skills had served me well, but now that I was finally free of financial dependents for the first time since the age of twenty-one, what did I want to do? And how much life did I have left in which to do it?

There is a lovely spot on Norfolk Island where one can sit undisturbed and watch the waves crashing against the cliffs, with the blue Pacific stretching endlessly into the distance. During an extended stay there, it became a favorite place for me to go each day for my prayers and meditation. Some days I would limp all the way there, the pain was so bad in my hips and legs. I was obviously at a crossroads in life.

A psychic friend of my sister had advised me to meditate on certain colors and geometric shapes that, she believed, would allow doctors from "the other side" to examine me while I slept. If one of those doctors was going to be Elsie Giorgi, then I would be in good hands. As I stared out at the infinite horizon, I wondered if Elsie was watching over her old patients. Just in case she was, I asked her if she could help me out with a diagnosis. I was also asking Holy Spirit for guidance.

If I was being kept alive for some purpose, then I was willing to submit to Divine Will and give the rest of my life up to that service, whatever it might mean.

# CHAPTER 43

# Diagnosis Coming Up

A few days later I received a phone call from my daughter. Dick Van Dyke was trying to locate me, Traci said. He and his wife, Michelle, thought I would be perfect for a role coming up in an episode of Dick's television series, *Diagnosis Murder*. The character was a singer/songwriter of a mature age, in the early stages of Alzheimer's disease. Here we go again. As usual, I was being lured back into show business with an offer I couldn't refuse.

I flew to Los Angeles within the week. Dick was a delight to work with, as I knew he would be. The script gave me a chance to sing and dance with him, as well as offering a big dramatic scene between us that was pure meat for me as an actor. I thoroughly enjoyed the whole experience, except for the physical pain and discomfort I had to constantly hide.

The week after filming ended, I was sitting in Malibu having a cup of coffee with Michelle Van Dyke when she brought up the subject of Dr. Giorgi. I said, "You knew Elsie Giorgi?"

"*Diagnosis Murder* was based on Elsie," she said. "We changed the character from female to male so that Dick could play the role."

I was astounded. Elsie was definitely still around.

My conscious mind put it all together later, when I was in the shower—it must have something to do with those negative ions. Elsie was watching over the show as well as over me and she'd put us together because she wanted me to get out the word about Alzheimer's. So that was to be my mission. Just then I sensed Elsie saying, "Listen, dearie, the TV show was just a ploy. I wanted you back here with doctors I know and can work through."

With that message came the awareness that I had to locate a female gastroenterologist whom Elsie had sent me to several years before. She had been a young woman just starting out in her own practice then. I couldn't recall her name but I remembered what she looked like and that her office was in Santa Monica. My GP recognized the description and gave me her name as well as ordering a whole new range of tests for me.

Addison's disease is so rare, and the cortisone used to control it so recent (1950s), that long-term effects are still unknown. Those of us who have lived with the disease for decades now are in the dark as to what the future holds. And because of Addison's wide-ranging symptoms, we tend to look at those symptoms first when there is a problem. However, Elsie had diagnosed me and placed me in good hands. She could see that my problem had nothing to do with Addison's disease. That's why she didn't send me to an endocrinologist, she sent me to a gastroenterologist.

The young doctor found that I had picked up a rare bacteria somewhere on my travels and it had been eating its way around my insides for some time. This accounted for the pain and the internal bleeding. The problem with my hips and legs was simply osteoarthritis and the wear and tear from years of acrobatic dancing and working out. After some minor surgery and a few "wonder drugs," I felt better than I had in years.

# CHAPTER 44

# Nancy

Having helped others find their previously un-acknowledged biological relations, I was surprised to learn that a similar situation existed in my own family. As my genealogical interests were mostly confined to Australian history and maternal lines, I had long since stopped researching the Reddy branch of my family tree.

As a young boy, my grandfather, Norman Reddy, had come to Australia from Ireland with his parents. Little Norman and his sister, Kathleen, had been the only two Reddy offspring to survive to adulthood, and Kathleen had died divorced and childless. That left my father and his siblings as the only members of the family in Australia, or so I thought.

My great-aunt, Kathleen Reddy, had died of kidney problems in 1927 in her fortieth year. According to Aunty Nell, who remembered her well, her Aunt Kathleen had been an elegant dresser, an accomplished horsewoman, and very much a lady. In 1908, at the age of twenty-one, she had made a favorable marriage to a cattleman by the name of Adrian VanRenen who had a large property in Victoria.

Who can ever say what went wrong in someone else's marriage? It must have been a major problem as the union did not last long, and they were divorced, a highly irregular event at the time and certainly within those social circles. Kathleen also converted to Catholicism, a move probably not favored by her fiercely Orange brother.

It seems Kathleen fell in love with another man, a Catholic, but they could never marry because she was divorced. My Aunty Nell always used adjectives like "poor," "sad," and "tragic" when referring to her Aunt Kathleen and told me that she had supposedly died of a broken heart. I had included her vital statistics in the family tree and thought that was that.

Around the turn of the millennium, I received an e-mail from a woman in Melbourne named Julie who was tracing her family tree. Julie's mother, Nancy, born in 1912, had been adopted as a baby, and with the original birth records now open, Julie was most keen to trace her mother's biological family. Nancy had been baptized four days after her birth at Women's Hospital by a priest from St. Patrick's Cathedral in Melbourne. On the relevant documents, her parents were named Kathleen and Thomas Daley, but Julie had been unable to find a record of any marriage between them.

Although now in her late eighties, Nancy could still remember being visited regularly when she was a little girl by a smartly dressed lady she called Mrs. Van Ran. On one visit, the lady had talked about going to South Africa and taking little Nancy with her. Nancy's foster parents had then moved rather suddenly to a new house, and Nancy never saw Mrs. Van Ran again.

Many years later, after Nancy's foster-mother died, she found a photo of the lady she remembered as Mrs. Van Ran among her mother's things. Nancy wondered if the elegant and expensively dressed woman in the photograph had been her real mother.

Nancy's daughter, Julie, at a dead end and with only her mother's hunch to go on, had researched all marriages in the state of Victoria between a Kathleen and anyone with a last name resembling "Van Ran." The only match she had come up with was a Kathleen Reddy who had married an Adrian Van-Renen. She knew that I was a genealogical researcher. Could this possibly be anyone in my family?

At first I was a bit skeptical, as I had donated my research to the archives years before. Anyone could have accessed those records and claimed to be a long-lost relative. However, Julie had included in the email a photo of her mother taken when Nancy was a young woman. As the image on the screen began to scan down, I was taken by the familiarity of Nancy's face. We had never met; why did I feel as if I knew her?

After I had printed out a copy of the e-mail, I pulled out some old photos of the Reddy family and found one of my father when he was around the same age as Nancy in her photo and taken at the same angle. When I placed them side by side, I was astonished.

The hair, hairline, forehead, eyebrows, eyes, nose, cheek-bones, lips, teeth, chin, and jawline were all identical. Only the ears were different. She looked more like my father than any of his three sisters. It was obvious that they were closely related. I e-mailed Julie back and told her that, on the basis of physical resemblance alone, I recognized her mother as my father's first cousin.

On my next visit to Melbourne, I was able to meet Nancy and Julie and spend time with their family. Now, between us, we could put some of the pieces together.

Aunty Nell had described her aunt, Kathleen, as a tragic figure who died of a broken heart. I don't know if Aunty Nell ever knew that her aunt had borne a child or whether she would have told me had she known. Such things were not discussed. Having a child out of wedlock was the worst sin a woman could commit in those days. But bear a child Kathleen undoubtedly did, with hope in her heart that she and the love of her life would marry and raise their family together. To this end, she had kept her baby daughter, Nancy, but placed her in care with a couple until that time came. Kathleen had the means to provide for her child and visited her regularly. Finally, when she believed that they could start a new life together as a family in South Africa—whether it was true or still just a cherished dream—she gave voice to it.

This must have struck terror into the heart of little Nancy's foster mother, who had cared for the child for several years and regarded her as her own. Desperate not to have Nancy taken away from her, the foster mother had moved immediately to another location, leaving no forwarding address. Poor Kathleen would have had to abandon any plans for South Africa and a new life there. Being able to have Nancy with her would have been the whole point of it all. And how would she have gone about searching for a child whose very existence she had been forced to deny? Kathleen probably scanned the face of every young girl she saw for the next ten years but she would go to her grave without ever seeing her daughter again.

I feel sad that Nancy grew up as an only child and never knew that she had five Reddy first cousins living right there in Melbourne. How many times must she have heard my father on the radio or seen him on television, never knowing the connection?

Learning that she had not been abandoned by her birth mother, but spirited away by a foster mother who feared losing her and was willing to take on the financial responsibility for her upbringing, has given Nancy a sense of closure. She was loved and wanted by two mothers. She now feels deep compassion for Kathleen and how she must have suffered losing her only child in this way. I was gratified to learn that Nancy and Julie visited Kathleen's grave together. I hope her spirit is at rest now.

I was a surprise guest at Nancy's ninetieth birthday party, and she and I continue to correspond as this is being written. She tells me that, after a lifetime with no biological relations, I'm worth the wait!

# CHAPTER 45

# Christmas Angels

I was back in Los Angeles as New Year's Eve 2000/2001 came around. I had just spent a delightful Christmas with my daughter and her family. Three-year-old Lily had slept in the big guest bed with me on Christmas Eve, and we had talked and listened for Santa's sleigh bells until she fell asleep. My heart was very full and I had decided that I wanted to spend the true millennium eve alone in prayer and meditation.

As I was selling my house in Santa Monica and moving on, most of the furniture had already been disposed of. I had kept back the basic essentials—bed, desk, TV, etc.—until moving day, and a lot of my office papers were in boxes waiting to go into storage. I was relishing having the house to myself and being able to give free rein to the emotions that were surging through me.

During the week between Christmas and New Year, I had received a visit from Mercy Valdez. I was first introduced to

Mercy in 1973 by Aunty Nell, who had been visiting from Melbourne and spied her, waiting in the corridor at NBC, hoping to meet me. Mercy became head of my West Coast fan club and, over the course of more than thirty years, a cherished friend. She had stopped by with a belated Christmas gift and brought one of her many nephews with her. He informed me that he had just been learning about me in school. I was taken aback. He looked too young to be at university, and I was presuming he meant an elective course on female songwriters or some such thing. No, he was in high school and, in his assigned *Modern American History* textbook, in a section on the rise of feminism in the seventies, I was mentioned along with the printed lyrics to "I Am Woman." I was flabbergasted. I didn't know how to process it. Even in a profession that rewards some of us very well, I had never in my wildest dreams imagined becoming part of American history. I realized that Lily, a first-generation American, would one day learn about her grandmother in high school. I was overwhelmed with humility and gratitude and for the next three days I would cry uncontrollably.

I was also ready to review my life. And what a life it had been. I had always been so focused on finding the next job that I had never paused and taken stock of a career that had spanned more than fifty years. Could I walk away from a business I had spent my entire life in? I certainly didn't need the applause. If I did a good show, I was the first one to know it; and if I thought I did a bad one, all the applause in the world couldn't convince me otherwise.

Did I have an emotional attachment to something I thought I had left undone? I had wanted an international multimedia career as a solo performer. Had I actually achieved it?

I had certainly traveled the world. Two particular weeks in the mid-nineties stood out in my mind. One December, I had gone from a performance for the King and Queen of Sweden in Stockholm, to a huge charity fund-raiser in Salt Lake City, to a corporate engagement in Hong Kong; three continents in eight days and, with all the holiday decorations everywhere I went, it felt as if I had spent Christmas in all three places. It was magical.

Another favorite week was one in which I sang two nights with a jazz combo, two nights with a symphony orchestra, and spent two nights acting in *Shirley Valentine*. It had been a lot of memorizing to keep on the front burner of one's mind, but ah! the variety.

And twice in my life, thanks to the Concorde, I had had breakfast in Paris, lunch in London, and dinner in New York, all on the same day.

I had dined on my birthday with the Prince of Wales and danced in the White House with the President of the United States. I had had a life and a career richer and more varied than anything I could ever have imagined as a girl in Melbourne.

In broadcasting, I had won the Peabody Award, America's highest honor. As a recording artist, I had had more than a dozen Top 40 hits in the United States and had become the first Australian to win a Grammy award. In television, I had been the first Australian to host my own one-hour prime-time weekly variety show on an American network, as well as several specials that were seen in more than forty countries. In theater, I had starred in London's West End and on Broadway in New York. As a solo concert artist, I had played at Carnegie Hall and Lincoln Center in New York and the Royal Albert Hall and the Palladium in London.

It was true that I had never achieved anything approaching that level of success in my own country but it was hardly my fault if Australian radio chose not to play a lot of my hits and that no Australian network opted to buy my TV series. For that matter, who knew that I had composed the theme music for *The Don Lane Show*? I had achieved success where it mattered most in terms of global exposure, the United States of America.

The one area where I felt a twinge of disappointment was in film. I just hadn't found being a film actor as pleasurable as I thought I would. I much preferred stagework, where you could build a character and play it in sequence. And I resented the wasted time, which I could have spent with my children. Surely, it wasn't that disappointing an experience?

Well, there had been two moments of joy during filming, and I'm talking about the kind that starts way down and emerges through the top of your head. Both moments had occurred while filming the big musical number, "There's Room for Everyone," with a group of children for the film *Pete's Dragon*. The first moment happened when I was running up the hill with the children behind me, and the second when I was on the swing being pushed by the dragon.

Hold that thought! At the same moment, I heard some of my neighbors wishing each other a Happy New Year. I turned on the television expecting to see fireworks and found instead *Pete's Dragon* playing, right at the start of that musical number. So I was able to re-experience those two joyous moments.

Yes, the career was complete, and that particular film scene airing at that particular moment was serendipitous rather than coincidental.

I knew I wanted to move out of show business and do something else but I wasn't sure what that something was. I knew it had to be something that benefited others and also satisfied my thirst for knowledge. I had always been drawn to metaphysical research and something in this area would be wonderful. But where to begin?

In the house I had lived in for seventeen years, the place in Santa Monica that I was selling, there was a staircase from the living room to the upstairs landing. Identical light fixtures were embedded in the ceiling above both the top and bottom staircase landings. Each fixture contained two sixty-watt light-bulbs and at this particular time, in both fixtures, one bulb had burned out, leaving the other one still burning. I had delayed getting the ladder to climb up and change the bulbs as I thought I'd wait until both lights had burned out in one of the fixtures and then I'd change them all at the same time.

Well, I was watching television in the living room, with only the stair lights on in the house, when I noticed a sudden brightness as if someone had switched on a light. I got up and saw that both light fixtures above the stairs, top and bottom, each had two bulbs now glowing at 150 watts each, at least. I wondered if there had been a power surge, but the TV had not been affected, and the lights continued to burn that brightly until I switched them off when I went to bed.

The next morning, I turned the lights on to check them, and they were both back to having only one sixty-watt bulb each. However, that night, again the lights suddenly went from two sixty-watt bulbs to four 150-watt bulbs. And they continued to burn that brightly until I turned them off on retiring. Again, they were back to normal the following morning. What did this mean? My name, Helen, means light. Someone was trying to get my attention. Bright lights on an ascending staircase? I was beginning to get the message.

Something beyond words took place. I felt myself surrounded by love far greater than anything I have ever experienced on earth. It was as if the happiest moment of my life had been magnified a thousand times, almost more than my heart could contain. I have never felt such deep emotions, never been less lonely, and I have never felt so loved, so humble, so grateful, so blessed. I now truly and totally understood the meaning of divine grace and bliss.

And it became clear that life was not finished with me yet.

There were assignments still ahead of me, and my work on earth was far from over. I was given a revelation of the role of feminism at this point in the history of our planet. At this time I can say little, except that I believe that it will be Third World women who will save the earth from destruction.

I still didn't understand why I had been given this information. Out of billions of souls in the universe, why choose me? What was I supposed to be doing? And could they let me know fairly soon because I was moving house?

When the pupil is ready, the teacher will appear. I walked into my office and found a message from Dr. Elsie Giorgi on my desk. I don't know how the piece of paper found its way there, but it was the photocopy of her newspaper obituary and it was facedown so that Florence Henderson's phone number was faceup. I remembered that Florence was now married to a hypnotherapist. I called her first thing after New Year, and we arranged to meet in the next few days for brunch at their yacht club at the marina. Dr. John Kappas, Florence's husband, was waiting on the steps for me when I arrived. He recognized me and introduced himself. Florence was sitting at the table inside, and the three of us had an enjoyable time together.

Dr. Kappas, I would quickly learn, had founded the only accredited institute for the study and practice of clinical hypnotherapy in the United States. The new school year was beginning on January 8, just days away, and I would be able to transfer my credits in psychology and parapsychology from

UCLA. The institute was located over the hill in the San Fernando Valley and, as it had its own clinic attached, the requisite six-month residency could be fulfilled in-house. If I enrolled to study full-time, I could take on a double course load and graduate sooner.

I was thrilled to be back studying again and loved meeting such an interesting cross section of new people.

My house in Santa Monica sold, and after signing the papers, I spent the afternoon sobbing in sheer relief. I had done it. I was finally out of debt after seventeen years. Not only that, I'd been putting money into my pension plan all that time and would soon be old enough to start accessing it. I moved into a one-bedroom self-contained unit in a residential motel less than a kilometer from the clinic and focused all my energies on my studies.

# CHAPTER 46

# *Hypnotherapy*

It is now fifty years since I had the out-of-body experience as an eleven-year-old schoolgirl. My curiosity has led me to explore the whys and wherefores of human existence. I have studied transcripts and tapes of hundreds of past-life regressions, not to mention those I have witnessed and also conducted in my capacity as a clinical hypnotherapist. I have come to believe that human life begins when a soul enters a physical body. That entry can take place before or after birth; the soul decides. Some wait for the beginning of earthly life and enter with the first breath; others may enter beforehand to accustom themselves to the new vehicle they'll be operating—much like getting a new car, in a way; some of us want to sit behind the wheel and get the feel of it before we drive out of the showroom. Each new personality brings with it a brand-new ego and the awareness of its own mortality, but no conscious memory of its divine purpose.

One of the most amazing regression sessions I've ever conducted was during my clinical residency in West Los Angeles. The client was a woman in her thirties; her parents had been at Woodstock, and she was obviously a child of that generation. After taking down her history, I asked why she wanted to be regressed and what she was hoping to get out of it. She said there were two questions she wanted answered. The first was, Why did she have a fear of loud noises? I told her it is believed that every infant is born with two fears: one is of falling, and the other is of loud noises. She felt, however, that her fear was abnormally strong, and the noises seemed louder in her left ear. The second question also related to the left side of her head; she has a birthmark on her scalp in the left crown area. She had read that a birthmark may be a sign of a past-life injury in the same area. Was it true? I replied that there were many case sessions on file suggesting this possibility. Current research in this field is showing that around 90 percent of subjects with birthmarks can regress to a past life where there was an entry wound in that spot.

The woman had been hypnotized before, was a willing subject, and went very quickly into deep hypnosis. Here are some edited excerpts from the session notes:

"Where are you?"
"Poland."

"What year is it?"

"Nineteen forty-six."

Showing signs of pain, the subject begins muttering,
"The bastards, the bastards."

"Who are the bastards?"

"The soldiers."

She refers throughout simply to soldiers and the army. When asked if they were Germans or Nazis, she answered in the affirmative. As World War II ended in 1945, could they have been Russian soldiers? Did she have the date wrong? Am I leading her? Subjects often want to please the hypnotist by agreeing.

The session continues, and the subject is now an older male working with others in a labor gang. Under armed guard, they are being forced to break rocks with large hammers.

"Are you a Jew?"

"Yes. If we don't break one with the first blow, we get a blow."

The subject is showing extreme fear; she knows she is being forced to dig her own grave. "I can't believe they're going to kill us." She looks at the soldier executing her as she receives a gunshot to the head in the left crown area.

"It's over; I didn't suffer," she says as she pulls back into spirit, "but the soldier who killed me is suffering terribly."

She views the rest of his life: "He suffers his whole life from this terrible guilt." As the soldier passes over, her face undergoes a profound change. It registers, at first, astonishment. "We agreed on this beforehand!" She gives a beatific smile.

"He's my best friend." She stands up, radiating joy; her eyes, which were extremely glazed, have remained open the whole time.

"We're riding together at the base of the mountains. I can feel the wind in my hair and the flesh of the horse against the inside of my thigh."

"Are you riding bareback?"

"Of course!"

"Are you Native American?"

"Yes."

She has now gone back further, to a scene from a life as a young Native American male, son of the tribe's shaman and destined to inherit that position. She described that life in some detail, then her peaceful death of old age. Her best friend, who had died before her, was a member of her soul group, and they were joyfully reunited.

In between lives, when choosing human assignments for their next learning period in earthly form, the friend, in order to develop more compassion, needed to experience guilt. He chose the role of soldier in wartime. Because of the deep love between them, my client volunteered to live the role of victim. Thus can love sometimes be expressed, but only in this context; there is a big difference between someone who kills under orders and someone who kills out of malice. We are judged by what is in our hearts.

I asked the subject if the friend was anyone she knew in her present life. She gave another look of astonishment. "He's my brother—and he's still carrying all that guilt. I'm going to have to tell him about this."

Over three lifetimes these two had been together as best friends, as victim and executioner, and as siblings.

These sort of cases illustrate the power of love, its expression in reincarnation, and the part that hypnotherapy can play in spiritual healing. (I later found out that she went back to study clinical hypnotherapy.)

Something unusual came up while I was still in my residency. A client who had come for a past-life regression, under deep hypnosis, met up with her deceased mother instead. Since then, I have had the same experience with other clients. I am able to guide them to a place where they can meet up with their deceased loved ones. These sessions are highly emotional and seem to hasten the healing process. There is no doubt in my mind that at times I feel myself being guided in this work and I always remain aware that I am merely a channel for healing energies.

A client in Los Angeles had hepatitis C, and as I was guiding her in visualizing light in her favorite aqua color washing over her internal organs, I heard myself say, "and the purple light shining on your liver."

Later on, before meditating, I was wondering what had made me substitute purple for aqua. I was told that for visualization healing technique using color therapy, the opposite color on the color wheel can neutralize a disorder, based on the color of the illness. For example, diseases of the liver such as hepatitis or jaundice cause the skin and whites of the eyes to turn yellow. By having the sufferer, under hypnosis, visualize a purple light shining internally on their liver, a lot of repair work can take place.

Another client I saw in a different location, a young man, was referred to me by a doctor who had done as much as he could for him. Married with several small children, this gentle soul had been working in a toxic environment which had destroyed 75 percent of his liver. I saw this client achieve a miracle in organ regeneration within weeks of one treatment. However, the effectiveness of this method seems to depend upon the depth of hypnosis to which the client is suggestible and, ultimately, on the client's trust in the facilitator.

I am of the opinion that a good therapist will have studied the rituals and beliefs of many different religions. I find that working within other people's belief systems can fast-track healing in many cases.

Many women seem addicted to bad relationships. One client had allergies so disabling that she rarely left the house. It soon became obvious that what she was allergic to was the domineering man she'd been married to for twenty-five years. He was so in-her-face, she was having trouble breathing. He was literally "taking her breath away." Yet, her fear of being alone and her resistance to change meant that therapy was not an option for her. I have seen that mind-set many times in clients of either gender; as soon as they sense that you know what the problem is and that the solution will involve change and effort on their part, they run a mile. They would rather put up with a lifetime of unhappiness and keep up the façade than make any changes in themselves. They don't trust their ability to create their own future. They see themselves as having failed when, in reality, there are no failures, only learning experiences.

A lot of the aches and pains of old age are past emotional hurts deeply lodged in the body. I once had a client in my chair, almost eighty years of age, who sobbed with indignation at every session over an unkind remark her mother had made to her when she was only ten. Seventy years had passed, her mother was long gone and unable to hurt her ever again, yet this woman persisted in keeping the pain alive and nurturing it. She was strongly resistant to letting go of the hurt and unable or unwilling to grasp the concept of release through forgiveness. She was determined to hang on to the bitterness and resentment that was twisting her mouth and making her ill. I believe that some people are so emotionally deadened that they hold on to anger in order to feel alive. How can we help older people experience joy instead?

The brain is a computer that operates on the data we feed into it. How we choose to think determines how we live our lives. Acquiring new information fires up new brain cells and can delay the aging process. I believe mental exercise is just as important as physical exercise and something like doing a crossword puzzle every day helps to keep your wits sharp. No matter how old you may be, learning a new skill, such as another language, is never a waste of time, and no knowledge is ever truly lost. You will take it into your next life with you as it becomes part of your natural talent.

Hobbies like knitting or woodwork that involve using the hands seem to help delay the onset of dementia in some older people as the hand/brain connection is continually reactivated.

Music therapy can also be beneficial for some patients. My sister, Toni Lamond, works with the elderly in nursing homes and has recorded several CDs of songs from previous eras. Patients who have not spoken or responded in years may suddenly react to an old song from their youth and start to sing along. This activates the brain/speech connection and has led to patients speaking again.

I believe forgiveness is the best weapon of all against encroaching senility. Every day we're alive we have more to remember. The mind can store only so much information on the front burner, and letting go of old hurtful memories frees up storage room.

Many years ago, I unwittingly made an enemy of someone working at the William Morris talent agency, someone who would go on to become a major operator in the music industry. Having been around homosexual men who were comfortably out of the closet all my life, and not yet being familiar with the deeply puritanical attitude North Americans have toward anything sexual, I had not spotted that this poor soul was not only deep in the closet, he was hiding under a blanket. Unknowingly, I outed him, and his enmity would last for years and hurt me both personally and professionally.

I look back now and see what a wonderful opportunity he gave me for spiritual growth. When nothing else worked, I would finally learn that sending loving, positive energy to someone can deflect negative energy, and our paths would no longer cross.

It was to be another two decades before he would publicly declare his orientation. By then, I had advanced enough spiritually to appreciate just how much courage it had taken for him to do that.

They say you should be careful what you condemn because that is what you will become. I did a past-life reading on him and was taken back to Ancient Egypt at a time when Jews were held in slavery and homosexuals were put to death. He was a high priest. In his present life, he is both Jewish and homosexual and, on an unconscious level, coming out for him equaled a death sentence. With this understanding, I was able to see that his hatred for me was based on a deep-seated fear which I had nothing to do with, and I could forgive him his trespasses against me.

# CHAPTER 47

# Past, Present, and Future

I f you've read this far you've probably noticed that throughout my life I have experienced, at various times, what I refer to as flashes or visions.

A flash can be triggered by a smell, a combination of colors or one particular hue, a pattern or a symbol; in other words, the same things that trigger a flash of present-life memory can also trigger a flash of past-life memory.

Although in physical time it is momentary, a flash can leave you with sudden knowledge and understanding that it might take you thirty to forty minutes to impart to someone else. In a past-life flash you are aware of being in a different body at a different time in a different place. Over my present lifetime, as I have found myself recognizing different flashes as being from particular lives, so I have gotten deeper insight into some of my former personalities.

Once I was trying to open an old warped door by inserting a knife between the cracks when I had a flash of holding a very thin wedge-shaped tool. I knew that I was Egyptian and male and that I worked as a foreman during the building of one of the pyramids. It was my job to check that the building blocks were positioned together so tightly that I could not get my instrument between them.

In another flash at a different time, I saw myself in the same life but at home with my wife and twelve children. Home was an adobe house, and all these brown-skinned children in short white tunics were climbing in and out of low, open windows and noisily chasing each other around. My attitude was very much, "Can't a man get some peace and quiet in his own home after a hard day's work?"

Many years ago I was told by a psychic that I had been an Austrian banker but I did not relate to this information and could not conjure up any images of myself sitting behind a grille in a bank. I didn't think about it again until dozens of years later when I was visiting Austria and a memory was triggered in Salzburg. I was lying in bed, in that in-between stage of wakefulness, staring at the curtains which, backlit by the morning sun, had taken on a vivid rosy hue. I could hear the clip-clop of horses going by over the cobblestones outside my window.

I suddenly found myself sitting inside a horse-drawn carriage staring at the seat cushion opposite me. It was covered in material the same color as the curtains and on the seat were two very large ledgers. I knew that I carried them from town to town with me and I saw myself writing columns of figures in these ledgers. I was intent on collecting monies owed. I was a large, unpleasant man dressed in a black suit with a large hat. I had big feet encased in white hose and black shoes with gold buckles.

I realized that I had previously had a vision of my home life as this man when I recognized my wife. She was also large, with greasy hair plaited in thick braids and, at night, she wore a voluminous white nightgown and a cap on her head that tied under her chin.

In a vision of myself as a Persian merchant/trader on caravan across the desert, I note that there are rugs underfoot. Others are with me. It is very windy, and the sides of the tent are flapping. I hear horses coming and feel tremendous fear. They enter, and I see a curved sword. End of vision.

A psychic told me that I had been traveling with my wives and concubines when I was killed by Bedouin tribesmen. Meditation took me back to my crossing over at the end of that life. I experienced deep guilt that I had not protected my women. They had been my responsibility and, after my death, they had been carried away and enslaved by the horsemen. Is this part of my feminism today, wanting to set women free?

I can sometimes look at someone and "see" them in a past life. I have seen a Latino drummer morph into a Japanese geisha and an English classical musician morph into an eighteen-year-old Luftwaffe pilot, shot down over Britain in the last days of World War II.

Unfortunately, I have no control over when the flashes or visions occur. They can't be produced on command. Visions tend to be longer and more complex than flashes and are usually experienced just before falling asleep or before waking, when one is in a natural state of hypnosis. They can also be induced through self-hypnosis.

When I took Shirley MacLaine's first seminar many years ago, one of the exercises we were given was to pair up with a total stranger and, using a psychic-enhancing technique, try to "read" each other. I was finding the woman I had been partnered with difficult to read because I seemed to be getting conflicting messages. I was seeing, symbolically, babies being born one after the other in rapid succession. However, my gut was telling me that not only had this woman never borne a child, she was a lesbian. I was confused, so I asked her if she had a lot of children. She replied that she had one adopted son, so, no, she had never given birth. Still, these images of childbirth continued to come. When I finally told her what I was seeing she informed me that she was a midwife! This was a good lesson for me in learning how to interpret symbols. I had been witnessing the births but not experiencing them from the mother's point of view. I had been seeing the babies emerge through the eyes of a midwife/observer.

The problem with much information that is channeled psychically is that it is being filtered through an impure, that is to say human, conscious mind, which attaches its own opinions and prejudices to the interpretation. This is why three different astrologers can read the same chart and come up with three different interpretations.

I have found that questions asked before meditating are usually answered in simple and logical terms. For example, I asked why there is such a noticeable increase in the number of interracial children being born.

I was told that this is evolution at work. All life is programmed to reproduce itself and, with the growing destruction of the ozone layer in our atmosphere and the rise of skin cancer, the human species will need darker skin in order to survive. On the level of the collective unconscious, we know this and are breeding accordingly.

When it comes to the future, any question has a multiple-choice answer. It is we who will determine the eventual outcome. Through our God-given gifts of free will and the power of thought, we have the ability to create our own future.

Instead of "stinking thinking," a steadily downward spiral of negative thoughts, we should instead concentrate our mental energies on visualizing a perfect world. What we focus our attention on grows. When the number of humans willing to take on this form of mental discipline reaches a critical mass, profound and positive changes will take place on the planet.

Will there be peace between Israel and the Palestinians? Peace will come only when those who are committed to peace are in charge of making decisions on both sides.

I visited Israel in 1994 and found its people deeply divided. While many yearned for a negotiated peace, others were against any agreement and highly militaristic in their attitudes. I was also aware of strong antifemale bias emanating from men in traditional orthodox garb when I visited the Wailing Wall, even though I was praying on the female side of the wall.

I was being driven between Jerusalem and Tel Aviv when the driver/guide casually waved up toward the hills and said, "There's a village up there where Arabs and Jews live together in peace."

I was intrigued and insisted we drive there immediately.

Neve Shalom/Wahat Al Salaam, or Oasis of Peace, was founded in the early 1970s by a Catholic priest against the wishes of the Israeli government. Backed by the courage and support of many families committed to peaceful coexistence, the village was designed as an experiment in integrated living in a bilingual society. All housing is allotted alternately so that every Jewish family has an Arab family living on either side and every Arab family has a Jewish family living on either side. All education is bilingual, starting at kindergarten. Every classroom has both an Arabic- and a Hebrew-speaking teacher. The village also has a School of Peace which welcomes students from all over the world to be trained in the art of making peace, as opposed to diplomatic and political skills.

My driver had never visited the village before and was as fascinated as I was. He explained that many Palestinians already speak Hebrew because they work in Israeli homes and businesses, but that few Israelis speak Arabic or have any desire to learn. However, he felt that the future belonged to those who were fluent in both languages. He was so impressed by the peaceful and positive atmosphere he experienced in the village that day, he wondered if he might be able to enroll his sons in the school there.

A few years after my visit to Israel, I found myself on a domestic U.S. flight, seated next to a man who was friendly with the Clintons, at that time occupying the White House. I talked to him during the trip about Neve Shalom/Wahat Al Salaam, and despite being a major fund-raiser for Jewish charities and a frequent visitor to Israel, he had never heard of the place. On the Clintons' subsequent trip to Israel, I was pleased to see in the press a photo of Hillary visiting the village and its people.

Despite opposition from the Israeli government, Neve Shalom/Wahat Al Salaam has now been functioning for more than thirty years. It could hardly be called an experiment any longer, and a new generation has already grown up under this system. This new generation of young people, who regard each other as Semitic siblings, is now spreading the seeds of peace outside their village, promoting bilingual education and peacemaking skills.

After the wall presently being built is torn down, these are the people best suited to occupy the borderlands between Israel and Palestine.

.   .   .

What about Armageddon? Gloom-and-doom extremists, hell-bent on bringing about a biblical Armageddon scenario, should remember that for those writing the Bible, the whole world at that time was confined to what we now call the Middle East. This area has certainly suffered turmoil and destruction in the last dozen years, but the profound earth changes which have been predicted by many prophets relate as much to changes in consciousness, as humans learn that the power of love will always be stronger than the power of fear. We are evolving from five-sensory beings into multisensory beings as our higher chakras are activated. We are consciousness, and as consciousness is energy, we can never cease to exist in one form or another.

Many truths will be revealed in the next few years as light is shone into the planet's darkest corners. Secrets and lies will be exposed, and every human being empowered.

As for the planet, Mother Earth is always in the process of healing herself, and upheavals will naturally occur in different places at different times. Earth changes that began in the fifties are accelerating, and global warming is making us all more aware of how shamefully we have treated our planet home. Areas of the earth that have been rendered uninhabitable by contamination will need to be covered over for millennia, and new virgin land will appear where ice has melted.

It is important to understand that thought-power produces energy. Constant worrying produces negative energy. What-ever we focus our attention on grows accordingly. If you are spending your time thinking about death, destruction, and the forces of evil, then that is what you will help bring into being.

If, on the other hand, you decide to concentrate your mental energy on positive images, then you will find the world around you corresponding accordingly. When you join together with others of like mind, the concentration of thought-power can accomplish miracles. And we all have the power to choose what thoughts to think. For example, while certain earth changes are inevitable because our planet is a living entity, the power of concentrated positive thought can deflect these changes by time and place so that there is mimimal loss of life. We see examples of this in the violent eruption of Washington State's Mount St. Helens in an uninhabited wilderness—a volcanic eruption of such magnitude in a more populated area might have caused deaths in the hundreds of thousands. Also, the last big earthquake in Los Angeles occurred at the one hour out of twenty-four when there is the least amount of traffic on the freeways. The night shift had gone home, the day shift had yet to rise, an overwhelming majority of Angelenos—I was one of them—were asleep in their beds when the first tremor hit. The total number of deaths was around forty; astonishing in a city with a population in the multimillions.

As we all are when disaster strikes, I was gratified to see how my local neighborhood pulled together. I had returned to L.A. only the day before from a symphony orchestra date in Canada and had not had a chance to shop at a supermarket, all of which were now closed. One of my neighbors gave me a loaf of bread and some peanut butter; another invited me over for dinner. Sometimes it takes a disaster to turn strangers into friends and maybe that's the divine point.

For people who fear passing over, what happens on Judgment Day? With the help of a guide or guides we review our lives and pass judgment on ourselves. The catch is that we must use, as our yardstick, the same measure which we used to judge others in life. "Judge not, lest ye be judged."

When in human form, we tend to project our faults onto others. Mirrored back to us, we are then able to see the fault objectively, without owning it. How easy it then becomes to pass judgment on others who are merely reflecting us back to ourselves. The more kindly we are able to see others now, the kinder we will be in viewing our own faults later. There is no hypocrisy on the "other side."

Each lifetime is but a day in a lifetime of lives, and as long as we continue to take on human form, our souls will be overseeing egos determined to have their own way.

In the early eighties, while in an alpha state, I had the following vision: I'm lying in a hospital bed; I don't know what country I'm in, how old I am, or what is wrong with me. I'm in a four-bed ward, two beds on either side as you enter. Mine is farthest from the door on the right-hand side; this is the same placement and configuration as the ward in which I almost died in 1959 when my kidney ruptured.

My father comes in. He is wearing a white doctor's coat.

Immediately, I know what he's up to. He is impersonating a doctor so that he can see me after visiting hours. Although, in life, my father had the coarse, mottled complexion of an alcoholic, his skin is now translucent, and I can see that there are no toxins in his system. I go along with the game by introducing him to the three other patients in the room as "my father, Dr. Reddy." He gives me a conspiratorial smile. It's a familiar expression. He says to me, "Come on. I've come to take you home. Mum's there, waiting for you. Everyone's there."

I notice that the wall to my right has glass French doors which open out. I don't remember them being there before. I can't see what is beyond them as they are covered by white filmy curtains. The curtains are billowing softly, and I feel a warm, gentle breeze. I know we will exit the hospital through these doors. I am sublimely happy and looking forward to seeing Mum and my family and friends as I get up and go with my father.

I have no doubt that this is a precognitive vision of my death.

Reincarnation, the life cycle, and our relationship to our creator may be better understood if we think of the source of our creation as an ocean. Now, imagine all of us as drops of water originating in this ocean. As long as each droplet is part of the larger body of water, it is one with it. It is only when the droplet vaporizes and separates from the whole that it can experience its individuality and take on different forms.

Each snowflake is as individual as we are in human form.

No two are ever the same. They are as unique as we are with our fingerprints and our DNA. Does ice remember when it was liquid or is it experiencing itself "in the moment" as ice?

There may be varying degrees of time and travail involved before that drop returns to the ocean. Highly polluted water would certainly need a longer cleansing period for the purification process. However, each single drop of water must eventually return to the ocean, its true home, as it can never cease to exist. When that drop reunites with the ocean, it becomes one with itself, once again.

# CHAPTER 48

# *Life Lines*

I have often told my children that their experiences are their only true wealth. You can lose your job, your house, your car, and anything else you care to name, but no one can rob you of your life experience. In a material sense, I have been rich, I have been poor, and I have been middle-class and, if you asked me what was best, I would say having the chance to experience all three in one lifetime.

After all, what does wealth really mean?

Brazil is a country where extremes of wealth and poverty sit cheek by jowl. But the beach is everyone's backyard and it is the great equalizer. There's no room for designer labels on a string bikini. I remember sitting on Ipanema beach in Rio watching a spectacular sunset, the kind you want to gaze at until the last ray of light has disappeared from the sky. As the glorious sunset spread across the vast sky, reflected in the Atlantic

Ocean, I realized that every single person sitting on the beach with me was truly wealthy, and that not even the world's most avaricious profiteer could lock up that view and charge admission to see it.

I believe that every season of life is special and should be enjoyed for what it is. Getting old is unavoidable; I've yet to meet anyone getting younger, have you? Growing older is a choice.

When I think of cosmetic surgery in an effort to look younger, I think of a girl in a bathing suit pretending it's still summer, even though the sun is lower in the sky and there is a chill in the air. Her friends are calling to her to come with them to New England to see the changing of the leaves and appreciate autumn at the height of its loveliness. She ignores them. She's convinced that if she can just find the right bathing suit, it will be summer forever.

Personally, I'm finding my autumn years to be the happiest ones so far, and given my lifestyle of constant traveling and meeting new people, it's comforting to know that I can always look in the mirror and see the familiar face of an old friend.

Mother Nature is truly ingenious in the way she provides for our needs throughout our lives. Think of babies getting ready to crawl. At a time when they are going to be at risk of bumps and falls, a stage when their little bones need extra protection, Mother Nature gives them extra padding in the form of fat. Every baby goes through a multi-chins period if it's a healthy baby.

And so it is for menopausal women. Elderly ladies don't break their hips because they fall; they fall because their hips break. At a time in our lives when we are going to be at risk of falling because of fragile bones, Mother Nature provides us with extra padding in the form of fat, especially around the hips, our most vulnerable area. We are not meant to maintain exactly the same weight and shape every day of our lives. The multibillion-dollar diet industry knows this and is making a killing by convincing us otherwise. In their own way, they are as insidious as the tobacco industry in their marketing tactics.

Each one of us is born to be a winner. Our brains are hard-wired to succeed and cannot follow through on a command to "lose"; the conflicting orders will cancel each other out. That's why you cannot lose weight on something like a weight-loss program. The diet industry knows this, that's why they chose the word. Are you old enough to remember when it was called weight reduction, not weight loss? They also know that every time you go on a crash diet, you cause a permanent change in your metabolism, which will make you a customer for life.

If you're uncomfortable with how heavy you feel, start thinking in terms of "becoming lighter." Begin to pay attention to what you say about your body, especially to yourself. If you hear yourself using the words, "lose" or "loss," cancel them out and say to yourself, "I am becoming lighter." Remember that the words we continually say to ourselves program our mental computer and create our reality. You may find yourself becoming lighter in more ways than one.

George Burns once told me—and he lived to be one hundred years old—"As you get older, cultivate younger friends so that when the older ones die, you won't be the only one left."

I took his words to heart and continue to cultivate friends of different ages. I think it also helps keep one mentally fresh and in tune with what's going on.

Once upon a time, when my family and I were holidaying in Hawaii, and George was staying at the same hotel, we had dinner together. As we were walking back to our rooms George, then eighty-three, was walking ahead holding the hand of my then three-year-old son. He looked back over his shoulder and said to me, "These are the two ages you can get away with anything."

Actually, George dispensed a lot of sage advice about aging. He used to say that it was important to bathe twice a day after a certain age because old people tend to get lazy about bathing and don't realize that they smell. Personally, I find I spend longer in the shower these days because I have trouble remembering which parts I've already washed!

As an older woman living on her own, one thing I am now trying to make a regular part of my life is taking myself out on a date once a week. Women of my era were raised to always put others first. Consequently, we have spent a lot of our lives either doing what others wanted to do and not having a very good time or occasionally doing what we wanted to do and not having a very good time because we were worried that others might not be enjoying themselves as well.

So now I have my special "spoil Helen" days when I take myself out to things I can enjoy without guilt or interruption. This past month I've lingered as long as I wanted at two different museum exhibitions that interested me, seen a small independent film as well as a French comedy, and ridden on every type of public transportation Sydney has to offer in one day. Why sit at home when you could be showing yourself a good time?

One Saturday night, I took myself out for an early dinner to a nearby tourist resort where they had a buffet. It was off-season, and as I looked around, I could see that there were only three other occupied tables in the whole dining room.

While being single and dining alone took some getting used to at first, I find I now enjoy the chance to observe other people and their interactions. I will admit to an occasional twinge of loneliness and, that night, I was questioning the wisdom of my decision not to remarry. At the table nearest to me was a couple in their late thirties. During the entire meal, I did not hear them exchange one word nor did I see them make eye contact with each other. I wondered why they were still together when it was obvious the love was long gone. What could be lonelier than that?

At the next table over from them was an older married couple. He was a very large man, disinclined to leave his chair to peruse the buffet table, and barking orders at his wife as she waited on him. I looked at her pinched, unhappy face and felt sad for her. What kind of life did she have?

The last table was against the wall and two little old ladies were dining together. They were both well over seventy and presumably widows. They talked nonstop throughout their meal, accompanied by frequent laughter. It was a pleasure to be in the same room as two people having such a good time in each other's company.

I decided I wanted to be one of them when I grew up.

.    .    .

The first recording artist in the family was my mother, Stella Lamond. As a child I remember Mum's old 78 "The Girl at the Ironing Board" with the Jim Gussey Orchestra. It sat in the cabinet, and we were not allowed to play it as it was considered to be too fragile. When Mum died in 1973, my sister donated it to a museum.

In January 2003, my cousin Ken from Melbourne came to visit me, bringing with him a tape that he had recorded off the radio. We were running late for our lunch reservation but he insisted on playing it for me before we left for the restaurant. It was Mum singing the comedy song, "The Girl at the Ironing Board." Despite the appalling sound quality and the uneven vocal track, I found it quite moving, almost thirty years after her death, to hear the voice of my mother as a young girl.

Afterward, when we entered the restaurant, Ken pointed out to me that there was a girl just inside the front door standing at an ironing board. It seems one of the waitresses had injured her foot and couldn't wait on tables. The boss had put her to work ironing table linen. Was it coincidence or was Mum saying shello?

Six months later, I was with my sister at her home in Sydney when she showed me a new CD she'd just obtained. Someone had taken all the old Jim Gussey recordings and, with modern studio techniques, had been able to remix the tracks and bring the vocals forward. My sister played "The Girl at the Ironing Board" for me, and Stella's voice rang out loud and clear with the song about a girl who works in a laundry and falls in love with a man whose shirts and shorts she's ironing. Toni said, "It's the only recording we have of our mother singing. What a pity she's playing a comedy character and not singing in her own lovely voice."

"Yes," I replied, "but have you noticed that when you and I are together, it's much easier for Mum to come through?"

I had found over the years that when Toni and I combined our energy, our mother's presence could sometimes be felt. My sister then proceeded to play *Center Stage,* my album of Broadway show tunes.

Remarkably, my sister and I have only once appeared in a book musical together. It was in California at the Sacramento Music Circus in a production of *The Mystery of Edwin Drood.* Toni played Princess Puffer, the part originated by Cleo Laine, while I was Edwin Drood, the role played on Broadway by Betty Buckley.

I subsequently worked with Betty several times on Andrew Lloyd Webber productions and admired her both personally and professionally. I thought her performance on Broadway in *Sunset Boulevard* was electrifying, and I loved seeing her afterward in her dressing room, surrounded by old friends from Texas who still called her Betty Lynn.

Later on, I read a piece about her that I found touching in one of the American weekly magazines. It seems that Betty's father had never wanted her to go into show business and had done his best to talk her out of it. He didn't think she had what it takes; he didn't want to see her get hurt, and so on. He never came to hear her sing and never saw her in any of the shows in which she had starred. Finally, when she was appearing solo in concert at Carnegie Hall, Betty's father came to New York for the performance. Afterward, he went backstage to see his daughter and, as he walked into the dressing room, he looked at her and said, "World-class, Betty Lynn, world-class."

When I read the story, I had been moved to tears and I envied Betty for having had the experience. I would never be able to hear those words from my father.

I knew that Toni had not seen the magazine and I began to tell her the story. The big closing number from *Edwin Drood* that I recorded was playing in the background. I got as far as telling her that Betty's father had gone to New York when I choked. I was too emotional to finish the story. I would have to tell Toni what Betty's father had said some other time. As we sat there listening to the end of the song, with its big finish, I felt a twinge of nostalgia for the career I had walked away from with no regrets. I said to my sister, "I was pretty good, wasn't I?" She looked at me and said, "World-class, Helen, world-class."

Dad had been dead for thirty years already. Was it possible that he was still around watching over me? Sometimes, I had felt as if he was helping me, when I was planning a tour or pacing a show. Now, I really needed to know if he was the one who had put those words in my sister's mouth. I put the question out into the ether and asked my father to send me a tangible sign that would be distinctly him. I was curious as to how he would find a way to respond.

A few weeks later, I was in London and in session with an English client who had issues with her father. Regression therapy gave her valuable insight into the situation, and the groundwork was laid for forgiveness. A day or so later, I received a thank-you note from her, written inside a vintage card which she thought I might enjoy. She had bought the card in Melbourne years before while there on a working holiday and kept it on her wall. Her glance had fallen on it when she thought about writing to me, and she remembered I was from Melbourne. On the cover was an old color photo of the entrance to Luna Park in St. Kilda.

"Loo-nah Pahk—jes' fo' fun—ha ha!"

Hello, Dad.

## I Am Woman

*I am Woman, hear me roar*
*In numbers too big to ignore*
*And I know too much to go back and pretend.*
*'Cause I've heard it all before*
*And I've been down there on the floor*
*And no one's ever gonna keep me down again.*

Chorus
*Oh yes I am wise*
*But it's wisdom born of pain.*
*Yes, I've paid the price*
*But look how much I gained.*
*If I have to, I can do anything.*
*I am strong.*
*I am invincible.*
*I am Woman.*

*You can bend but never break me*
*'Cause it only serves to make me*
*More determined to achieve my final goal.*
*And I come back even stronger*
*Not a novice any longer*
*'Cause you've deepened the conviction in my soul.*

Chorus
*I am Woman, watch me grow*
*See me standing toe to toe*
*As I spread my lovin' arms across the land.*
*But I'm still an embryo*
*With a long, long way to go*
*Until I make my brother understand.*
*Oh yes I am wise*
*But it's wisdom born of pain.*
*Yes, I've paid the price*
*But look how much I gained.*
*If I have to, I can face anything.*
*I am strong.*
*I am invincible.*
*I am Woman.*

# Epilogue

Between the completion of this book and its publication, my family suffered a tragic loss. My beloved daughter-in-law, while on a conference call at her office, collapsed and died of a pulmonary embolism. She was thirty-six.

*Maria Eugenia*
*Like everyone else*
*I called her*
*Maru*
*Like no one else*
*She called me*
*Mamacita*

When my son, Jordan, first told me that he'd met someone special—"She's perfect, Mom. I can't find anything wrong with her!"—I thought to myself, Oh boy, my son must really be in love to be exaggerating like that. And then I met Maru. And there was no exaggeration.

Her beauty was the first thing you noticed about her. A former Miss Panama finalist, Maru was a glorious mixture of Panamanian, Colombian, Chinese, and Philippine ancestry. I was impressed that she wore hardly any makeup and had a natural loveliness and sweetness about her. She was also savvy. Maru had started her own business in Panama while still in her teens. She had sold the business and moved to Miami in her twenties and now worked as a producer of television commercials for the Latin American market. Poise, grace, intelligence—she had it all. My son seemed to have found the perfect woman. I wondered how she would fit in with my crazy family. I needn't have worried.

It was in New York that I first met Maru. She and Jordan were in the early days of their relationship, taking it slowly, both knowing that this time it was special. Although they had met in Los Angeles, Maru was still firmly based in Miami, where most Hispanic television commercials originate, and where she also owned a condominium. At first, it was a bi-coastal relationship and they would occasionally meet mid-point at other locations. New York would be a trifecta.

My hotel was only one block from Central Park, and it was one of those crisp, clear days when it feels good to be alive. The three of us had been walking in the park and stopped by a large rock to admire the view. The music from the skating rink nearby was playing and Maru started to dance and Jordan started to dance and I started to dance. And, as the three of us held hands, dancing around together on that rock, laughing our heads off, I thought to myself, Oh, she'll fit into our family just fine. The more I saw of her, the more I liked her. My only concern was the age difference. She was four years older than Jordan, more mature emotionally, and further along in her career goals. Was he ready to be a husband?

When Jordan called from Panama the following New Year's Eve to tell me that Maru had accepted his proposal, I burst into tears of joy. He had presented her with a ruby engagement ring, but my son had found a woman whose price was far above rubies.

Envisioning myself as the wise mother-in-law dispensing sage advice to my new daughter-in-law, I would learn instead how much Maru had to teach me. She was neater than I was, she was more organized than I was, and she was infinitely more gracious. I still treasure every note and card she sent me—most of all the letter in which she expressed how grateful she was that I had raised such a wonderful son. She would always sign off with *besitos*—Spanish for "little kisses."

*Maru*
*I forgive you*
*for taking my boy away from me*
*And I thank you*
*and bless you*
*for leaving me with a man.*

I was in Sydney when Traci telephoned to tell me that Maru had died. I was on the next available flight to Los Angeles. Overnight, my son seemed to have aged ten years.

The last time I had seen Maru had been three months earlier, on my most recent trip to L.A. Although they were still in daily contact, she and Jordan had been living apart for months, and I was beginning to give up hope that they would reconcile. Stubbornness seemed to be the order of the day, and neither would bend. I was equally determined that I was not going to lose Maru from my life. I told her over tea that day that even if she and my son divorced, I would still always regard her as my daughter and, if she remarried and had children, they would still be my grandchildren as far as I was concerned.

Congratulations were also in order that day. Maru had been made a partner at the company where she worked, and she was constantly jetting off somewhere—Barcelona one week, Buenos Aires the next. Unfortunately, it may have been on one of those long flights that she developed the blood clot that caused her death. My daughter-in-law had become quite spiritual in the last year of her life, and she confided in me that afternoon a sense that she did not have long to live. This was not a thought I wanted to put energy into, and I dismissed it with, "Nonsense, you'll probably live longer than any of us." Maybe on an unconscious level we both knew what was to come. When we said good-bye, we held each other for longer than usual.

Death visits daily in Los Angeles County, and an autopsy is mandatory if that visit is a sudden one. However, the county no longer has the staff and facilities to cope with the growing number of cases, and there is a backlog. With Jordan's blessing, Maru's parents wanted to take their daughter's ashes back to Panama, to be interred in the family crypt following a High Mass in the cathedral. As events played out, we had to wait almost a week for the autopsy to be performed and a death certificate issued before we could even order the cremation. Then it was another wait of several days before it could be performed and the ashes delivered. All this time, I had to watch the agony of a mother and father who had lost their youngest child, caught in limbo, not knowing when they could go home.

Jordan wanted to give Maru a memorial service in L.A. that would celebrate her life. We booked the ballroom at her favorite hotel, and Traci ordered it filled with roses, Maru's favorite flowers. Lucas, my son-in-law, and his partner, using still photographs and home-movie footage, put together three short films for the service. The first was of Maru's early years in Panama, the second of her career, and the third of her seven years in California. Jordan wanted the films to have music playing underneath. He had taken Maru's CD case out of her car so he could choose some of her favorite tracks, and as we drove together to Forest Lawn in Glendale to make arrangements for the cremation, we were listening to Maru's music. That girl had sure loved to dance. One track after another seemed to have a driving Latin beat. It was a happy reminder of the time we'd all taken a salsa class together, but it was not appropriate music for a memorial service.

We were walking up the path to Forest Lawn's office when I noticed a perfect long-stemmed red rosebud lying on the walkway. I picked it up and said to my son, "Jordan, I think this is meant for you and it's from Maru." He shrugged as he answered, "Oh, Mom, you see signs in everything." Later, as we were driving back, listening again to her music, a more suitable ballad began playing. My Spanish is far from fluent, but I recognized the words *una rosa*. As I turned to my son to ask, "Jordan, what are the words of this song saying?" I saw that his face had drained of color and he replied, "I found a rose lying on the ground, it was a gift."

*Dance with the angels,*
*my darling.*
*Besitos.*